THE SECRET
MUSEUM

ACKNOWLEDGMENTS

I ACCEPT FULL RESPONSIBILITY for the shortcomings of this book, though several people have contributed to whatever virtues it may possess. I especially wish to thank David Berry, Robin Berry, Mark Caldwell, Robert Cornfield, Giovanni D. Favretti, Eliot Fremont-Smith, Christopher Graham, Rosalind Krauss, M. Mark, Perry Meisel, Tom Schmidt, Tonice Sgrignoli, Polly Shulman, Jennifer Stone, Dinny Taylor, Mark Taylor, Michael Timko, and Amanda Vaill.

Thanks are also due to Fordham University and the staffs of the New York Public and New York University libraries.

My greatest debt is to Dan Applebaum, who tried (not always successfully) to keep me sane.

THE SECRET MUSEUM

PORNOGRAPHY
IN MODERN CULTURE

WALTER KENDRICK

UNIVERSITY OF CALIFORNIA PRESS
BERKELEY · LOS ANGELES · LONDON

University of California Press
Berkeley and Los Angeles, California

University of California Press, Ltd.
London, England

First California Paperback Printing 1996

Grateful acknowledgment is made for permission to reprint excerpts from the following copyrighted material:

"Art of Poetry," from *The Satires and Epistles of Horace: A Modern English Verse Translation*, translated by Smith Palmer Bovie, published by The University of Chicago Press. Copyright © 1959 University of Chicago.

"Carmen 16," by Catullus, from *The Garden of Priapus: Sexuality and Aggression in Roman Humor*, by Amy Richlin, published by Yale University Press.

Library of Congress Cataloging-in-Publication Data

Kendrick, Walter M.
      The secret museum : pornography in modern culture / Walter
Kendrick.
          p.   cm.
      Originally published: New York : Viking, 1987. With new afterword.
      Includes bibliographical references and index.
      ISBN 0-520-20729-7 (alk. paper)
      1. Pornography—History.   I. Title.
[HQ471.K45   1996]
363.4'7'09—dc20   96-8107
                                                                       CIP

Printed in the United States of America

1   2   3   4   5   6   7   8   9

The paper used in this publication meets the minimum requirements of American National Standard for Information Sciences—Permanence of Paper for Printed Library Materials, ANSI Z39.48-1984. ∞

FOR DAN,
WHO PUT UP WITH IT

CONTENTS

Preface to the Paperback Edition

In part iii of *Gulliver's Travels*, Gulliver visits the kingdom of Balnibarbi, whose citizens have fallen under the spell of the ridiculous schemes cooked up in the Academy of Lagado, the capital city. The result is universal misery. As an unhappy local nobleman tells Gulliver,

> The professors contrive new methods of agriculture and building, and new instruments and tools for all trades and manufactures, whereby, as they undertake, one man shall do the work of ten; a palace may be built in a week, of materials so durable as to last for ever without repairing. All the fruits of the earth shall come to maturity at whatever season we think fit to choose, and increase an hundredfold more than they do at present, with innumerable other happy proposals. The only inconvenience is, that none of these projects are yet brought to perfection, and in the meantime the whole country lies miserably waste, the houses in ruins, and the people without food or clothes.[1]

Eager to see the source of the blight, Gulliver is given a tour of the pernicious Academy, where, in the school of languages, he encounters the silliest scheme of all:

> Since words are only names for *things*, it would be more convenient for all men to carry about them such *things* as were necessary to express the particular business they are to discourse on. . . . [M]any of the most learned and wise adhere to the new scheme of expressing themselves by *things*, which hath only this inconvenience attending it, that if a man's business be very great, and of various kinds, he must be obliged in proportion to carry a greater bundle of *things* upon his back,

unless he can afford one or two strong servants to attend him. I have often beheld two of those sages almost sinking under the weight of their packs, like pedlars among us . . .²

Swift's satire was aimed at the Royal Society, established in 1660, which had debated even farther-fetched plans than this one. Fortunately for the welfare of England, the dreams of its "sages" generally went unheeded; otherwise, the nation might soon have been plunged into the wretchedness of the imaginary Balnibarbi.

Some silly ideas, however, have long, stubborn lives; among the stubbornest (and silliest) is the notion that "words are only names for *things*." Swift mocked it two-and-a-half centuries ago, but it still survives—much to our detriment and confusion. If the proposition were literally true, we would of course be unable to talk about such abstractions as "freedom" and "justice"; the fact that we do go on talking about them, even laying down our lives in their service, suggests that we know how complex the relation between words and things can be. There are certain words, however, that habitually cause trouble because their unstable, shifting connection to things gets either ignored or denied. "Love" ranks at the top of this list, but "pornography" comes in a close second.

If a modern-day Balnibarbian sage wished to chat about "pornography," he would have to tote a formidable bundle of *things* on his back. First, he would need a few frescoes from Pompeii, along with a selection of statues, necklaces, amulets, and the like. Buried by Vesuvius in 79 A.D., exhumed by a project begun in the early eighteenth century and continuing today, these relics inspired curators and cataloguers to coin the term "pornography"—quarrying the word from Greek, though the ancient Greeks (who, it seems, painted explicit sex scenes at every opportunity) would have had no idea what "pornography" was supposed to mean. The works of Catullus, Juvenal, Martial, Suetonius, and several other Roman authors would also have to be loaded on, because though the Romans saw nothing objectionable in them, a later age called them "pornography."

The Middle Ages would contribute sparse pickings, but much of

Chaucer would join the pile, along with Boccaccio and Margaret of Navarre. Most of Renaissance literature deserves packing in, including (as the Bowdler clan discovered) great chunks of Shakespeare. As we move toward our own time, the sage's bundle comes to resemble a universal anthology. Just about every Jacobean and Restoration play would be found "pornographic," and though the Earl of Rochester knew nothing of the word, his name would become virtually synonymous with it. As for the ephemera of those days, Pepys acted presciently when he burned his copy of *L'Ecole des Filles*, "that it might not be among my books to my shame."

The eighteenth century provides, along with the first Pompeiian relics, a book so quintessentially "pornographic" that it would not be legally sold in the United States until 1966, more than two hundred years after its initial publication—John Cleland's *Memoirs of a Woman of Pleasure*, better known as *Fanny Hill*. Not to be outdone, France furnishes the legendary Donatien-Alphonse-François, Marquis de Sade, whose voluminous complete works belong in the collection, if not also his very name. But in addition to these notorious cases, much of eighteenth-century fiction and a good deal of its pictorial art would get bundled up. Fielding, Sterne, Smollett, Rowlandson, and Hogarth in England; Prévost, Rousseau, Fragonard, and nearly everything French—all were described as "pornographic" at some later time. Swift, too, of course: it would surprise later generations to learn that Gulliver made three voyages, not one, and that he doused a Lilliputian conflagration by pissing on it.

When we reach the nineteenth century and the first half of the twentieth, we can leave off enumerating the works our bent-backed sage will need by him. Everything written, drawn, or otherwise portrayed that was not of a strictly informative or instructional nature (and even a good deal of that) must come aboard. For we have entered the great age of "pornography," when the word was invented and the past was scoured to locate those books and pictures that had been "pornographic" all along without anyone knowing it. Now the burden gets multiplied by the parallel invention of new media, each of which contributes its "pornographic" share. Indeed, as time goes on, books—the definitive "pornographic" medium since the Renaissance—slip gradually into irrelevance, until by the late twentieth century, the bundle will be taking on practically nothing but photographs, films, videotapes, and even telephone messages. As far as bulk is concerned, however, the poor Balnibarbian will obtain small relief from the dropping of books. According to the 1986 Attorney General's Commission on Pornography, the output of pornography had boomed fearfully in only the last sixteen years, reaching an annual volume of nine billion dollars in the United States alone. All this, too, must join the bundle if the sage wishes to express himself on "pornography"—and the discussion hasn't even begun yet.

In *The Secret Museum*, I might have taken on the silliest of Balnibarbian tasks—to trot out everything that has ever been called "pornography" and attempt to discuss the word by displaying those *things*. If I had done this, I'd still have been a step ahead of most commentators on the subject, who evidently believe that the *things* they see before them are "pornography" as it is now and must always be. But I've attempted yet another step—to recognize that "pornography" has named so many things during the century and a half of its existence that any statement of what it means now must degenerate into nonsense within a very short time. In the mid-nineteenth century, Pompeiian frescoes were deemed "pornographic" and locked away in secret chambers safe from virginal minds; not long thereafter, *Madame Bovary* was put on trial for harboring the same danger. A century-long parade of court cases ensued, deliberating the perniciousness of *Ulysses*, *Lady Chatterley's Lover*, *Tropic of Cancer*, and scores of other fictions, many of which now appear routinely on the syllabi of college literature courses. All these *things* were "pornographic" once and have ceased to be so; now the stigma goes to sexually explicit pictures, films, and videotapes. It would be laughably egotistical to suppose that our parents and grandparents called the wrong things "pornographic" out of blindness or stupidity. It would be equally stupid to think that we, at long last, have found in our X-rated images the *real* pornography. Given the history of the word, it seems likely that future generations, if they use the term at all, will mean by it something quite different—something as unimaginable today as *Debbie Does Dallas* was fifty years ago.

In the chapters that follow, "pornography" appears most often within quotation marks, as a sign that what is being talked about is not a thing but a concept, a thought structure that has changed remarkably little since the name was first applied to it a century and a half ago. "Pornography" names an imaginary scenario of danger and rescue, a perennial little melodrama in which, though new players have replaced old, the parts remain much as they were first written. By taking this approach, I have sought to escape the fate of the Balnibarbian sage, crushed under a monstrous bundle of things that have little in common except that they were once, or are now, called "pornographic." In *The Secret Museum*, I have talked a good deal about the paintings, books, and pictures that have instigated battles over "pornography," but I have devoted less attention to the things themselves than to what was thought and felt about them—the threat they posed, the victims they claimed, the usually self-appointed rescuers they galvanized. *The Secret Museum* is not a history of pornography; it is a history of "pornography." There is a considerable difference.

With surprising uniformity, arguments about "pornography" for the past hundred and fifty years have boiled down to a pair of assertions: "This is pornographic" and "No, it isn't." "This" may be a book, a photograph, a film, or virtually anything else, from *Ulysses* to a decorated deck of cards; it hardly matters. Both sides in such arguments have agreed that there is something in the world properly called "pornographic"; they differ only on the merits of whatever is up for debate at the moment. As a result, despite hundreds of books, pamphlets, picketing campaigns, and court trials, confusion is endemic. Legal history teaches that *Ulysses* is not pornographic, *The Well of Loneliness* is not, even *Fanny Hill* and *Secret Museum of Anthropology* are not, but it fails to provide any guidance as to what this elusive thing really is. Attempts at definition have not been wanting; they pile one on top of the other, each tinkering with the last and leaving flaws for the next to tinker with, but none has come closer to pinning down the thing than Supreme Court Justice Potter Stewart's unjudicial bleat: "I know it when I see it." If no one could define a skunk more closely than that, campers would be in trouble.

The real existence of any *thing* ought to be thrown in doubt by the failure of several generations' efforts to define it. That this has not happened with "pornography," that indeed the struggle gets fiercer as reality resists, indicates clearly enough that desire, not logic, is at work—a desire so imperious that no default of logic can slow it down. This desire is also called "pornography," and *The Secret Museum* tells its story.

CHAPTER ONE

ORIGINS

WHAT DOES "pornography" mean? The *American Heritage Dictionary* (1975) gives a single, apparently decisive definition: "Written, graphic, or other forms of communication intended to excite lascivious feelings." Etymology suggests that the word is as old as Western culture: "From Greek *pornographos*, writing about prostitutes." There is something strange about this, though it need not be troublesome. Most modern writing about prostitutes seems intended to excite feelings of indignation or compassion, not lasciviousness. Prostitutes still endeavor to excite their clients' lust, but—nowadays, at least—writing about prostitutes seldom tries for that effect. Yet it is not hard to imagine a past time, a more primitive one, when whore writing sought to do exactly what whores did. As an ancient word, "pornography" would naturally show traces of its oldest meaning, an identity that time has split apart.

If we go back a few decades, however, we find that the opposite is true. The fifty-year project of the *Oxford English Dictionary* reached "P" in 1909; its definition of "pornography" is, oddly, more complex than any later one. The first meaning, surprising to a modern reader, comes from an 1857 medical dictionary: "a description of prostitutes or of prostitution, as a matter of public hygiene." Modern readers are familiar with this kind of whore-writing, but the last thing we would call it today is "pornography." The OED's second definition is somewhat more up to date: "Description of the life, manners, etc., of prostitutes and their patrons: hence, the

1

expression or suggestion of obscene or unchaste subjects in literature or art." It seems strange that this, a close approximation of what we now mean by "pornography," ranked second in 1909 behind a definition that now is completely outmoded. The vocabulary is outmoded, too: we seldom use the word "obscene" nowadays, and "unchaste" never. And though we may still have some recollection of a time when literature and art were called "pornographic," that time is far behind us. Instead of starting out simple and turning complex with the passage of time, "pornography" seems to have moved in reverse, growing perversely from multiplicity to oneness.

If we go back further, an even stranger thing happens: "pornography" disappears. Samuel Johnson's *Dictionary* of 1755 jumps from "porkling" to "porosity" with nothing in between, an unaccountable leap if the Greeks already had a word for it: *pornographos*. In 1857, "pornography" meant something very different from what it now means; in 1755, "pornography" meant nothing at all. The inescapable conclusion is that, sometime in the century between 1755 and 1857, "pornography" was born. But it must have been already ancient at birth, rising from the grave instead of coming new into the world. Vampires are said to do this; so did "pornography."

Around 1710 an Italian peasant was digging a well in Resina, a small town south of Naples. He unearthed a mass of marble and alabaster, including fragments of *gallo antico*, the yellow marble prized by ancient Roman architects. Antiquarianism was not yet the rage it would later become, but Giovanni Battista Nocerino was well aware that this was no ordinary mud. Rich foreigners often paid high prices for *gallo antico* and alabaster; Nocerino sold his fragments to a local dealer who specialized in this taste. It was an especially profitable line around 1710, because southern Italy was at that time in the hands of the Austrians, represented by figures like Supreme Officer of the Guard Maurice de Lorraine, Prince d'Elboeuf. D'Elboeuf was building a villa at nearby Portici and was on the lookout for relics from the history of the country he had appropriated. Happening to visit the same dealer to whom Nocerino had sold his discoveries, the prince bought them. His first purpose was to decorate his newly built walls, but soon he became interested in the archaeological value of Nocerino's find. He pensioned the peasant and bought his land, ordering the well dug down to a depth of sixty feet, where horizontal shafts were sent out in random directions. A few Roman artifacts were discovered, including a marble Hercules; they were restored in Rome and shipped back to Vienna, for the delectation of Prince Eugene of Savoy. But the depth of the excavation, and the solid rock that had to be cut through, made progress laboriously slow. When, after a couple of years, the trove seemed to peter out, d'Elboeuf's project was abandoned.

Not until 1738, when the Spanish had retaken Naples, was work resumed, at the direction of King Charles of the Two Sicilies. Other impressive objects were unearthed, and it was determined that Nocerino's well had plunged directly into the amphitheatre of Herculaneum, one of the three ancient cities buried by the eruption of Mount Vesuvius in 79 A.D. For a while, discoveries came so thick and fast that a museum was set up to house them—the Museo Borbonico ("Bourbon Museum"), named for the current ruling family of that unstable area. Again, however, the well ran dry. By 1745, Herculaneum having apparently failed, the excavators turned their attention a few miles to the southeast, where under a hill provocatively named *Civitâ* ("City"), Pompeii had to lie waiting. Digging at the new site proved much easier, since Pompeii had been engulfed in ashes and small stones—not, like Herculaneum, in a sea of mud that later petrified. Pompeii soon eclipsed Herculaneum as a source of excitement and treasure. In April 1748, the first intact fresco was discovered, in what proved to be an ancient dining room; later the same month a skeleton emerged, still clutching coins stamped with images of Nero and Vespasian.

For its first century and more, the excavation of Pompeii more nearly resembled a circus than a modern archaeological dig. On many occasions, when a notable find was made, it was buried again in order to be refound before the eyes of some visiting noble personage. In the earliest days, thievery was common; even when objects were carefully transported to the Museum, so little was known about how to preserve them—delicate frescoes in particular—that very often they were damaged beyond repair. Systematic excavation did not begin until the appointment of Giuseppe Fiorelli as head of the project in 1860. It was Fiorelli who first rationally mapped the city—so that the original location of an artifact would not be forgotten as soon as it had been removed—and who established the practice, still in use today, of preserving most finds in place, "instead of ripping out the more spectacular and leaving the rest to disintegrate."[1] Despite haphazardness and rapacity, however, the gradual unveiling of the Vesuvian cities made a profound impression on the imagination of Western culture. It was de rigueur, of course, for tourists to visit the Museum and take a day trip to the excavations. Meanwhile, those unfortunates who had to stay at home could find in a thickening swarm of guidebooks and catalogues, often with lavish illustrations, a convenient substitute for firsthand experience.

Among the stay-at-homes was eighteen-year-old Thomas Babington Macaulay, who nevertheless, in 1819, won the chancellor's gold medal at Trinity College, Cambridge, with his poem "Pompeii." After a strained description of the ancient catastrophe, Macaulay exhorted a modern visitor:

> Advance, and wander on through crumbling halls,
> Through prostrate gates and ivied pedestals,
> Arches, whose echoes now no chariots rouse,
> Tombs, on whose summits goats undaunted browse,
> See where yon ruined wall on earth reclines,
> Through weeds and moss the half-seen painting shines,
> Still vivid midst the dewy cowslip grows,
> Or blends its colours with the blushing rose.[2]

This prizewinner offers no glimpse of the future historian's genius (the goats are especially embarrassing), but it does sum up current clichés about Pompeii, jumbling together observable facts and fanciful Gothic views of Roman ruins. Most typical is the young Macaulay's labored juxtaposition of the ancient and the new, the dilapidated and the fresh: amid scenes of neglect, the "half-seen painting," eighteen centuries old, is as vivid as this season's rose. For Pompeii's early enthusiasts, the fascination of the place came from its eerie immediacy, the sense that ancient and modern worlds had met face to face.

An 1830 guidebook put it this way:

But the most astonishing thing is that this city, which was surprised by an unprecedented eruption and disappeared from the face of the Campania, as if by magic, in a few hours, still preserves all the identifying marks of recent human activity and existence. Palmyra, Babylon, Rome, Athens, Canopus—all have nothing to show us but ruins that bear witness to the slow progress of years and the traces of pillage by barbarians who, like violent storms, have left on them the signs of their passage. Pompeii, on the other hand, looks like a city deserted a few moments ago. It is as if the citizens had all flocked to one of those religious festivals that used to draw whole nations, and that were so characteristic of paganism.[3]

To an age deeply versed in classical literature, Pompeii offered the compelling spectacle of an unmediated vision. Here was no cold collection of white marble, no venerable hoard of texts encrusted with centuries of commentary. At Pompeii, tradition had been short-circuited; the actual color and texture of ancient life were on display, complete with all the trivial accoutrements that literature disdained to mention.

Of course there were lessons to be drawn. In his immensely popular novel *The Last Days of Pompeii* (1834), Edward Bulwer-Lytton made an obvious point:

Pompeii was the miniature of the civilisation of that age. Within the narrow compass of its walls was contained, as it were, a specimen of every gift which luxury offered to power. In its minute but glittering shops, its tiny palaces, its baths, its forum, its theatre, its circus,—in the energy yet corruption, in the refinement yet the vice, of its people, you beheld a model of the whole empire. It was a toy, a plaything, a showbox, in which the gods seemed pleased to keep the representation of the great monarchy of earth, and which they afterwards hid from time to the wonder of posterity,—the moral of the maxim, that under the sun there is nothing new.[4]

Despite its frivolous tone, Bulwer's conclusion had ominous implications. It was widely believed (the belief is with us still) that the Roman Empire had fallen on account of internal depravity; monitory analogies with modern corruption had been commonplace since Edward Gibbon's *Decline and Fall of the Roman Empire* (1776–88). Pompeii was buried three centuries before Rome "fell," at a time when the Empire had in fact been at the peak of its vigor; but among its relics was an embarrassingly large number that seemed to document a moral laxity far more extreme than even the bitterest satires of Juvenal had suggested. If modern civilization resembled its Pompeiian predecessor in any way, it was in a perilous state indeed.

From very early in the excavations, objects were being unearthed that presented a special problem to the authorities. Already in 1758, for example, rumors circulated that "lascivious" frescoes had been found; not long thereafter, a particularly outrageous artifact turned up—a small marble statue, highly naturalistic in style, representing a satyr in sexual congress with an apparently undaunted goat. This distressing artwork, under special orders from King Charles, was entrusted to the royal sculptor, Joseph Canart, with the "strict injunction that no one should be allowed access to it."[5] Evidently, the order was not strictly obeyed, because in 1786, in his *Discourse on the Worship of Priapus*, Richard Payne Knight referred to the statue, "kept concealed in the Royal Museum of Portici," as "well known."[6] No doubt the procedure was already in operation, as it remained two centuries later, that a gentleman with appropriate demeanor (and ready cash for the custodian) would be admitted to the locked chamber where controversial items lurked; women, children, and the poor of both sexes and all ages were excluded. Makeshift in origin, this method of segregation worked well enough to be extended to the *lupanaria* (brothels) that were uncovered from time to time as the digging went on.

The plan was less practicable, however, for the authors of guidebooks and catalogues. They were faced with the awkward choice of omitting such objects and places from their accounts—thereby rendering them incomplete—or of somehow mentioning the unmentionable. The former course was taken by Sir William Gell, whose *Pompeiana* (1824), a supposedly comprehensive guide to the city, claimed to be the first work of its kind in English.[7] Gell managed to get through two thick, heavily illustrated volumes without once letting on that anything untoward was to be found either among the excavations or in the Museo Borbonico. His foremost English successor, Thomas H. Dyer, performed the same feat in his anonymous contribution to the *Library of Entertaining Knowledge* in 1836.[8] Forty years later, however, perhaps because *lupanaria* had gone on being discovered with some regularity, Dyer felt obliged to cast a brief glance at one of them. "We cannot venture," he snippily remarked, "upon a description of this resort of Pagan immorality. It is kept locked up, but the guide will procure the key for those who may wish to see it."[9] As one might expect, Continental guides were less reticent, though only slightly so. Writing in 1830, three years after the first Pompeiian *lupanar* had been unearthed, Charles Bonucci laconically summed up its aura: "The neighboring chamber was devoted to licentious scenes; its paintings indicate this only too clearly."[10] In 1870, commenting on the same unwholesome room, Ernest Breton made a similar observation: "The coarse paintings which decorate this place evidently indicate that it was intended for the most shameful debaucheries."[11]

Popular guidebooks could afford their reticence; suitable tourists (gentlemen) would be able to fill in the gaps without much trouble. This was less true, however, for catalogues of Pompeiian artifacts, since comprehensiveness is among the main reasons for issuing a catalogue in the first place. Following the lead of the Museo Borbonico, which began publishing official catalogues in 1755, a number of similar compilations appeared, in all European languages, during the subsequent century. These ranged from grandiose picture books in elephant folio, full of color plates and short on text, to multivolumed works packed with allusions to the classics.[12] The official catalogues came out in limited editions intended for an erudite, specialized readership. All other versions were based on them and often merely translated their commentaries. Unofficial catalogues, however, were intended for an audience which, though far from general by twentieth-century standards, nevertheless comprised readers who were able neither to visit Naples nor to read Italian. Such books therefore encountered a problem that could not be solved by the easy expedient of locking a gate.

Pierre Sylvain Maréchal's nine-volume catalogue of 1780, though it is not absolutely complete (the well-known satyr and goat are missing), contains enough eyebrow-raising plates to call for special comment by the author. The questionable objects were mostly representations of Priapus, god of generation and protector of gardens, whose worship was widespread in the ancient world and continued, under a thin Christian veneer, well into the eighteenth century in regions of Sicily and the Campania. Priapus can be identified by his gigantic erect phallus, often out of all human scale, which he brandishes because it is his essence. Maréchal did not segregate his Priapean engravings; he scattered them here and there throughout the work. But each time he came to one, he apologized for it: "Antiquated religious notions, just as much as libertinism, multiplied these images, symbols of generation and also of the universal cause of life. So extremes meet—or rather, in their customs, men change and differ! The simplicity and innocence of our ancestors found nothing indecent in objects which today make modesty blush."[13]

Most of the time, like a faithful disciple of Rousseau, Maréchal was inclined to criticize his own age for having fallen away from an imaginary state of primal innocence to which the Romans were much closer:

Ancient relics . . . are full of objects so indecent, if we compare them to modern compositions, that the brush or needle of our

Artists hardly dares to reproduce them for us. Nevertheless, we should not take this as an opportunity to slander the customs of the people who left us such relics. One blushes, perhaps, only to the degree that one has strayed from nature; and a virgin's eye can linger with impunity on objects which arouse vicious ideas in a woman who has lost her innocence.[14]

Now and then, however, this rose-tinted view of the ancient past failed to account for the evidence. So Maréchal shifted his stance:

I know of no way to justify the Ancients in this cynical habit. Their imagination, inflamed by the lure of pleasure, desired that all objects, even the most indifferent and alien to this purpose, should remind them of what seems to have been the sole focus of their existence. Vases, lamps, everyday utensils, and the most necessary articles of furniture became, as it were, accomplices of their libertinism, by showing them its crude simulacrum. We must believe that articles shaped like this were intended only for bawdyhouses.[15]

Despite all appearances to the contrary, and despite his own predilection for the more "natural" ancient world, Maréchal could not bring himself to believe that the Romans spent their days amid a forest of phalluses. Such things were too highly charged to be dispersed throughout the environment. They had to be set apart, and the best place for them was a brothel.

This was the largest problem for early cataloguers of Pompeii. As the city gradually came into the light, it grew more and more obvious that images which a modern sensibility would secure behind locked doors had been indiscriminately on display there. Paintings of nude bodies, even in the act of sex, had been placed side by side with landscapes and still lifes, forming a jumble that mystified modern observers. Maréchal's first way out—that the Romans were childlike enough to gaze upon anything safely—hardly sufficed; it also failed to tally with the scarifying accounts of Roman debauchery supplied by Juvenal, Petronius, Suetonius, and others.

Maréchal's second escape route was taken fifty years after him by
Bonucci, and by Breton forty years later still: any room where
obscene paintings were displayed must have been devoted to obscene activities. This explanation worked well in some cases—
lupanaria, for example, and nuptial chambers—but it would have
become rather frightening if it had been extended to account for
the erect phalluses found at many Pompeiian streetcorners, or the
statues and paintings of Priapus that adorned the foyers of private
homes. Confronting these unappealing alternatives, some commentators threw up their hands: "the inhabitants of Pompeii," sighed
a cataloguer of 1842, "placed these subjects, repulsed by modesty,
in the most conspicuous places, so widely did their ideas of morals
differ from ours."[16] In the twentieth century, it has been generally
accepted that, for the most part, such images had a mystical function, free from incitement to lust. At the entrance to a home, for
instance, Priapus served "to bring good luck and to ward off evil
spirits."[17] This solution was available to early cataloguers and sometimes invoked by them. Yet it, too, was inadequate to the real
problem that underlay these confused haggles about Roman morality. The problem was purely modern: however the Romans might
have responded to such representations, what was one to do with
them *now?*

Of course, they could not be destroyed. Had they been of recent
manufacture, this would have been the obvious expedient; but any
relic of the ancient world possessed, merely thanks to its survival,
a value that overrode the nature of the relic itself. Besides, it was
essential to the charm of Pompeii that many of the objects found
there had equivalents nowhere else. Perversely, this added value
accrued principally to two classes of relics, the trivial and the obscene. Though both kinds had presumably been distributed
throughout the Roman Empire, trivial things had mostly vanished
in centuries of neglect, while obscene ones had succumbed to the
zealous progress of Christianity. When it came to obscene objects,
an unsettling inverse ratio applied: the more obscene an object was,
the more liable it had been to destruction anywhere but at Pompeii,
and the more necessary its Pompeiian preservation therefore became.

The matter was further complicated by the fact that mere preservation was not enough. Pompeiian artifacts were valuable because they formed a source of knowledge, and knowledge requires dissemination; somebody besides diggers and custodians had to view these things if their value was to be realized. While Pompeii was alive, anyone and everyone had had access to them, but from the moment the first obscene artifact was unearthed, it was apparent that the ancient and modern worlds differed drastically in this regard. Depending on their inclinations, early commentators condemned the one as debauched or the other as prudish, sometimes both by turns; but all agreed that the ancient system of organizing images—which amounted, it seemed, to no system at all—would never do in a later age. What was required was a new taxonomy: if Pompeii's priceless obscenities were to be properly managed, they would have to be systematically named and placed. The name chosen for them was "pornography," and they were housed in the Secret Museum.

It was in this context that a form of the word "pornography" first appeared in English print, in a translation of German art historian C. O. Müller's *Handbuch der Archäologie der Kunst* (1850). Late in the volume, Müller briefly alluded to "the great number of obscene representations . . . to which also mythology gave frequent occasion"; he dubbed the producers of such representations "pornographers" *(Pornographen)*.[18] The source of Müller's coinage was a unique instance in classical Greek of the word *pornographoi* ("whore-painters"), tucked away deep in the *Deipnosophistai* ("Learned Banquet") by the second-century compiler Athenaeus. Like the Pompeiian artifacts themselves, Athenaeus' influence had had to wait a millennium and a half to exert its full effect, though in a very different way from any he could have intended or foreseen. At about the same time Müller was digging him up to name a new category of art, others were drawing on him for an apparently remote purpose—the history of prostitution.

Among the many, mostly dry topics covered in the *Deipnosophistai* were the prostitutes of Athenaeus' day, on many of whom he is the unique surviving authority. He therefore earned special gratitude from the new scholars of prostitution, like the bibliophile Paul

Lacroix (1806–84), whose six-volume *History of Prostitution among All the Peoples of the World from the Remotest Antiquity to Our Own Time* (1851–53), published under the pen name "Pierre Dufour," is certainly the longest, if not the most reliable, early work of its kind. For his discussion of Greek prostitution, Lacroix relied heavily on Athenaeus:

> Athenaeus, who draws by handfuls from a heap of books we no longer possess, identifies by their surnames a great number of courtesans whose entire history is confined to these sometimes amphibolous sobriquets. He enumerates, with all the stolidity of a scholar unafraid to squeeze his subject dry, the names provided by his authorities Timocles, Menander, Polemon, and all the other Greek pornographers. . . .[19]

In this context, Lacroix employed "pornographers" *(pornographes)* in a more or less neutral sense: they were writers who had described prostitutes. A few pages later, however, freely paraphrasing his source, he explained the word's ancient meaning:

> We therefore believe that the artists who were called painters of courtesans (πορνογράφοι), like the Pausanias Aristides and Niophanes mentioned by Athenaeus, did not restrict themselves to making portraits of *hetairai* and to representing their erotic academies. When the occasion arose, they did not disdain to paint a courtesan's face, just as they painted the statues of gods and goddesses in the temples.[20]

By retaining Athenaeus' Greek, Lacroix sought to obscure any link between his own *History of Prostitution* and that other, disreputable form of "pornography." His book was intended to join the *Deipnosophistai* among the "pornographic compilations,"[21] but it did not at all resemble, said Lacroix, the works of those obliging artists who painted the whore herself as willingly as her portrait.

Instead of merely representing prostitutes, ancient pornographers had decorated them, thereby abetting the trade and allying themselves with it. The term "pornography"—"whore-painter" or "whore-writer"—is an ambiguous one, since it fails to specify on which end of the brush or pen the whore is to be found. Modern pornographers in the fields of artistic and social history struggled to tame a wanton word by insisting with wearisome frequency that they had remained untainted, and that readers who imitated them could do the same. In the long run, as we know, they failed: the whore in twentieth-century pornography is the maker or witness of the representation, not the person or scene represented. Perhaps there is something whorish about the very act of representing, since its product—a book or picture—is promiscuously available to all eyes, unless some outside authority restricts access to it. Any book or picture will give itself equally to all comers, and the author or painter, no matter how loudly he protests his good intentions, has no control over his work once he has made it public.

The 1864 edition of Webster's Dictionary defined pornography as "licentious painting employed to decorate the walls of rooms sacred to bacchanalian orgies, examples of which exist in Pompeii." Here, as is often the case with attempts to pin down this unruly word, Webster's made its definition both too precise and too general. By no means all of the "pornographic" representations unearthed at Pompeii were intended to spur imitation in the flesh; not every ancient "pornographer" moved with the ease of Niophanes from painting images of licentious scenes to daubing the actors in them. Early commentators expended a great deal of effort—without much success—distinguishing what we may call "innocent" pornography, with its primarily religious or mystical import, from a less common, "guilty" variety, which may indeed have had the aim of inciting lewd behavior by representing it.

This rather profound difference, however, did not prevent the two kinds from being lumped together as "pornographic." The old locked room at the Museo Borbonico (by then transformed into the National Museum of Naples) obtained its first systematic catalogue in 1866, under the title "Pornographic Collection,"[22] but this gross designation, which sufficed for the museum's custodians, only aggravated the difficulties of other commentators. M. L. Barré's French compilation of 1875–77, for example, reserved the "pornographic collection" for the eighth and last volume as the *Musée Secret;*[23] his introduction cited so many sources of value for these prohibited objects that an uninformed reader might have wondered why they were not the showpieces of the whole establishment. First of all, according to Barré, they gave unique evidence of the "regular or irregular, legitimate or illegitimate relations between the sexes." Interesting in themselves, these relations held "the meaning and as it were the key of the most important and poorly understood events; they are, so to speak, the secret articles of a treaty, in which alone we often find its whole spirit."[24]

In addition, relics of this kind—"which one might call 'pornographic Relics' "—helped to validate the claims made by ancient satirists. They established the impartiality of historians like Tacitus, whose accounts of imperial debauchery had often seemed purely malicious; they provided priceless information on "licentious poems or treatises" which had been handed down only in fragments or in secondhand summaries by the likes of Athenaeus. Even those relics for which no such excuse could be made would be rendered innocent if everyone involved, writer and readers alike, underwent a bizarre transformation:

> Besides, the majority of the relics we are concerned with are truly chaste even in their obscenity, thanks to the artist's strict intention and style, along with the sanctity of the ideas they are supposed to arouse. . . . Let us see these coarse representations through the eyes of those who dwelt upon the plains of Latium—ignorant and rustic people who consequently remained pure and virtuous even during the most elegant and depraved days of the Empire. . . .[25]

Barré's romanticized vision of ancient history was identical to Maréchal's a century before him; but he pushed the myth to the breaking point. It is inconceivable that sophisticated French readers of 1877 could make themselves over into illiterate Roman peasants; it is equally inconceivable that Barré seriously expected them to do so. Yet the fiction of such a conjuring trick was necessary, if these precious, poisonous objects were to be rendered safe.

Evidently mistrustful of his readers' mental agility, and perhaps uncertain of his own, Barré concluded his introduction to the Secret Museum with the assurance that a battery of safeguards had been installed:

> Even so, we have taken all the prudential measures applicable to such a collection of engravings and text. We have endeavored to make its reading inaccessible, so to speak, to poorly educated persons, as well as to those whose sex and age forbid any exception to the laws of decency and modesty. With this end in mind, we have done our best to regard each of the objects we have had to describe from an exclusively archaeological and scientific point of view. It has been our intention to remain calm and serious throughout. In the exercise of his holy office, the man of science must neither blush nor smile. We have looked upon our statues as an anatomist contemplates his cadavers.

Just as at the real Secret Museum, Barré's printed version excluded women, children, and men lacking the price of admission. Without further aid, the high-priced sumptuousness of his eight volumes would have discouraged the last of these classes; but, books being sluttish as they are, Barré could not duplicate the case-by-case surveillance exercised by Neapolitan gatekeepers. Instead of money, therefore, he stretched out his palm for erudition—a less tangible currency, but one that had the virtue of scarcity among all three of the groups who ought not to see what the Secret Museum put on display.

Barré never let his own text stand alone; the pornographic cadavers were always "surrounded by a venerable retinue of ancient authors who explicate for us the profane debris of antiquity." Their words had not been translated, for an obvious reason:

> If we were treating another subject, we might be criticized for this extravagance of erudition; here, however, we will no doubt

be commended, just as sculptors are forgiven the overgrowth of foliage that sometimes screens the nudity of their human figures.[26]

Of course the poor would be ignorant of Latin and Greek, as would all but the most exceptional women and children. Barré's volume, however, also contained engravings plain to even the least lettered mind. Disdaining fig leaves—which earlier illustrators had applied[27]—his engravers had chosen a much stranger device:

> Our draftsmen have obeyed an analogous rule; but instead of tacking on draperies or other accessories to their designs—which might have spoiled the spirit of the composition or distorted the thought of the ancient artist—they have restricted themselves to miniaturizing a few things. The truly erotic nudity of these rare subjects has thereby been stripped of the excessively crude and impertinent features that marked the originals. They have lost their importance; sometimes, without detriment, they have utterly vanished.[28]

The result of this odd policy is that phalluses, naturalistic in the originals, taper off like uptilted icicles in Barré's engravings; while the actors in sex scenes have a plaintive look, since instead of genitals they are endowed only with patches of fog.

Barré's rather comical anxiety arose from a pair of dilemmas that haunted all those who wished to set up secret museums, especially in print. It is impossible to display things—as museums do—and keep them hidden at the same time; internal safeguards, no matter how ingenious, can hardly take the place of living gatekeepers. A second problem was even more troublesome. Any museum (or catalogue) gives publicity to its exhibits; if those exhibits promote lewdness, no amount of self-justification by the curator can dispel the impression that he is playing the role of pander. This is what Athenaeus' *pornographoi* did, earning centuries of scorn; later, scholarly pornographers could not rid themselves of the fear that to display pictures of whores was to encourage whorish behavior. The word "pornography" contains this slippery ambivalence, and even the most restrained cataloguer of ancient obscenity was made anxious by it.

That whoredom, however, was metaphoric. During the same period when museum cataloguers were struggling in vain with these problems, another group of scholars was encountering them in literal form. In its characteristically fractious way, "pornography" was not content with a single origin; it insisted upon having two, which only gradually combined to produce our modern definition. The OED's first meaning is medical: "a description of prostitutes or of prostitution, as a matter of public hygiene." In this, the OED agrees with Littré's French dictionary of 1866, which defines *pornographe* ("pornographer") as "one who writes on prostitution" and *pornographie* as "(1) a treatise on prostitution, (2) a description of prostitutes in connection with public hygiene." Already in 1842, however, the Académie Française had certified *pornographe* in only a single sense: "one who treats of obscene subjects"; *pornographie* followed as "the production of obscene things." These rival definitions, which have become the basis of our modern ones, place second and third in Littré: a *pornographe* is also "a painter who treats of obscene subjects," and the last definition of *pornographie* is "obscene painting." In its second definition of "pornography" the OED attempts to make a connection between these two divergent lines: "Description of the life, manners, etc., of prostitutes and their patrons; hence, the expression or suggestion of obscene or unchaste subjects in literature or art."

A large step is taken in that "hence"—exactly the step the cataloguers of the Secret Museum tried their best to forestall. The connection would have been even more dismaying to the earnest researchers who gave both Littré and the OED their first definitions of "pornography." These pornographers were mostly doctors and public-health officials, who saw prostitution as not only a historical phenomenon but also a present menace. They wrote books on the unsavory subject with the aim of stimulating public awareness; they hoped to alleviate an evil that, if it continued to be ignored, might turn lethal. They fell, of course, into the same quandary that ensnared Pompeiian curators: to shine light on dark corners makes those corners known and possibly seductive. If that were not enough, they also faced the disturbing fact that their own brand of "pornography" had a dubious founder, one who might deserve the label "pornographer" in the pernicious as well as the hygienic sense.

The meaning of "pornography" traveled a surprising distance during the nineteenth century, largely on account of historical amnesia on the part of those who used the word. Forgetfulness of the past is the most deplorable feature of twentieth-century arguments about the subject, but the trait was already visible in 1896, when Algernon Charles Swinburne wrote to his close friend Theodore Watts-Dunton, announcing a literary rediscovery. An omnivorous reader with a taste for obscurities, Swinburne was always burrowing through the neglected shelves of libraries. This time, he had dusted off a copy of *Le Paysan perverti* ("The Depraved Peasant") by the forgotten French novelist and pundit Nicholas Edme Restif de la Bretonne (1734–1806); some comments on Shakespeare had so forcibly struck Swinburne that he transcribed them for Watts-Dunton's benefit. "Is not the appreciation of Shakespeare simply marvellous in a contemporary countryman of Voltaire's?" The novel as a whole, however, was a different matter:

> Yet I do not say I should recommend this his most famous work (as I believe it is) as a prize for proficiency in French to be competed for by English schoolboys. I cannot count the rapes, and nobody but the gifted author could possibly remember how to unravel the complicated webs of reduplicated and intertangled incest. And the moralist who treats the most atrocious and unnatural crimes and outrages of this kind (or rather of these two kinds, now combined and now distinct) as pardonable if regrettable lapses or momentary aberrations from the narrow way, which need not trouble the most sensitive conscience for more than a moment of atoning penance, winds up, apparently in conscientious earnestness, with the elaborate model of a communal association founded on principles and regulated by statutes which would have been rather too rigid for a colony of Spartans disgusted

with the licentious luxury of their native Lacedaemon. What a wonderful time—and country—it was!

A very different time and country, at least, from late Victorian England. Restif's blithe alternation between licentiousness and stern moralism, in which he seemed to sense nothing odd, mystified Swinburne, for whom the two attitudes were utterly irreconcilable. "Rape, incest, and the pox," he marveled, formed the basis of *Le Paysan perverti*, yet the book also contained chapters full of "good sense, just reasoning, right feeling, and . . . true prophetic insight." The conundrum was impossible: "And this critic, to whom we can find and cite no parallel before the coming of Coleridge and Lamb, was the writer who assumed, with modest dignity and manly confidence, the honourable title of 'The Pornographer.' "[29]

Restif was a puzzle to his contemporaries as well as to posterity. Meanly born, largely self-educated, he rose to prominence in the France of Louis XVI, weathered the Revolution, and survived to greet the dawn of the nineteenth century, meanwhile pouring out a seemingly inexhaustible flood of tracts, novels, and memoirs. His fiction, as Swinburne's response to his best-known work suggests, is licentious in the manner of Tobias Smollett or Restif's countryman Choderlos de Laclos. His name is often linked with that of the Marquis de Sade, though not so much on moral grounds (nothing in Restif comes close to Sade's excesses) as because they were bitter enemies, each accusing the other of corruption; both also imagined themselves to be social reformers. Indeed, when Restif called himself "The Pornographer," he was invoking his reforming side, not his literary one. And from his own point of view, he had no reason to apologize. "The Pornographer" was Restif's favorite title, and he took it to be strictly honorable; he had, in fact, invented it—at least he thought he had.

In 1769, Restif published a little book entitled *Le Pornographe* ("The Pornographer") which, in good eighteenth-century style, bore an exhaustive subtitle: *A Gentleman's Ideas on a Project for the Regulation of Prostitutes, Suited to the Prevention of the Misfortunes Caused by the Public Circulation of Women*. Near the end of his life, still in apparent ignorance of Athenaeus, he explained the neologism: "*Pornographer*," he wrote, "is made up of two Greek words: *porne*, prostitute, and *graphos*, writer; it means *a writer on prostitution*."[30] Swinburne's astonishment that a man could call himself "The Pornographer" with dignity and confidence reflects neither Restif's perversity nor Swinburne's misunderstanding; it is the byproduct of the tangled history of a word.

Restif's pride in *The Pornographer* was somewhat justified; though there is no evidence that any government ever saw fit to implement its program, it was the first published proposal for the management of an age-old institution. In forty-five "articles," Restif outlined the operation of state-run brothels called *Parthenia*, where every aspect of the trade (except the sexual act) would be strictly supervised. He allowed broad liberty to the residents in the *Parthenia*—such as the right to refuse patrons who displeased them—but in the end it was male desire that ruled, even if its means sometimes became ludicrous. Restif viewed the regulation of prostitution as only a part—and a rather trivial one—of a general program for cleaning up urban life. In the conclusion to *The Thesmographer* (1789), he put prostitution in its place:

> O public administrators! Forbid carriages in cities; allow horses to go only at walking pace; prohibit dogs and birds; admit only those dogs which are absolutely necessary; punish with disgrace and a fine all men and women who make idols of their cats; establish the *Parthenia* from *The Pornographer*, so that no *fille publique* appears in the streets or at the window; make their base condition useful after its fashon. . . .[31]

Window-dressing was Restif's chief aim; for him, prostitution was no more serious a problem than crowded streets, and "public girls" were hardly distinguishable from house pets. From the perspective of later works on The Pornographer's subject, his recommendations were both impracticable in substance and offensively flippant in tone.

Slight though it was, however, *The Pornographer* remained for sixty years the only significant work of its kind. As late as 1836, Restif's first important successor, the irreproachable Alexandre-Jean-Baptiste Parent-Duchâtelet (1790–1836), reluctantly placed it "at the head" of all discussions of prostitution, though he had to lament its reflection of his precursor's inveterate "levity, which characterizes his numerous publications."[32] No one could accuse Parent of that failing; his two hefty volumes *On Prostitution in the City of Paris, Considered with Regard to Public Hygiene, Morals and Administration*, the fruit of eight years' research, were so fiercely serious that, in effect, they invented their subject all over again. Parent's credentials, like his style, were impeccably dreary: a doctor and a member of the Paris Municipal Sanitation Department, he had made his reputation with several monographs on sewers and drains. The very look of *On Prostitution*, with its aggressively scientific organization and plethora of charts and tables, would have stifled any doubts as to its author's intentions. Yet in introducing his subject, Parent felt obliged to confront those priggish souls who might find it (and him) scandalous. In a rare burst of eloquence, he made a provocative analogy:

> If I have been able, without scandalizing anybody, to enter cess-
> pools, to handle putrid substances, to spend part of my time in
> refuse dumps, and to live, as it were, in places that the majority
> of men would close off as degraded and disgusting, why should
> I blush to open up a cesspool of another kind (a cesspool filthier,
> I assure you, than all the rest), in the reasonable hope of doing
> some good by examining it in all its aspects?[33]

Parent's death at forty-six, in the year *On Prostitution* was published, invites some doubts about the physical side-effects of his probing. But he remained, as he insisted, morally unstained.

Indeed, the underground quality of both his lines of work inspired in Parent an intensity of self-righteousness that the most straitlaced of his readers could hardly have rivaled. Touching pitch had not defiled him: "Because I devote myself to research on prostitutes, must I necessarily be stained by contact with these unfortunate women?"[34] And should anyone accuse him of licentiousness, Parent had a crescendo ready: "The usefulness, I would almost say the necessity, of undertaking this labor has shown me that I must speak frankly; I have done so. I am treating a serious subject and addressing sober people; it has been my duty to call things by their names and to march straight toward my goal."[35] The leering smirk of his foremost predecessor must have haunted Parent as he wrote these repetitive self-defenses; if, two generations after *The Pornographer*, an air of lewd frivolity still clung to writing about prostitution, Parent was determined to dispel it.

Usefulness, necessity, frankness, sobriety—the assertion of these staid attributes calls up, like ghosts at noon, their opposites: frivolity, luxury, innuendo, drunkenness. Parent's tactics had the lamentable potential of reminding his readers—who might not have thought of it on their own—that there were other stances he could have taken, other ways his book could be read. Parent had many reasons for laying such heavy emphasis on his detached attitude and hygienic intentions, but one of them surely was that these were the only things that distinguished him from Restif or any other old-time roué. He had visited brothels at least as often as they and knew much more than they could have known about the private habits of prostitutes among themselves. Point of view was everything: prostitution itself had not changed much since Restif's day, but this modern aficionado, with notepad in hand and constable by his side, carried in his head a different desire. Perhaps it was the invisibility of this difference—invisible, that is, unless he declared it—that led Parent to wax so eloquent on the subject of his mental cleanliness. Perhaps it was this reason, too, that caused him to return obsessively to his pet analogy between sewers and prostitution.

Parent's reinvention of pornography quickly came to seem like invention; Restif's *Pornographer* was forgotten, and a new field of study was founded, with Parent as its leader. In England, traditionally the belated imitator of French innovations, Parent's volumes spurred what one recent commentator has called "a flurry of local surveys," including Michael Ryan's *Prostitution in London, with a Comparative View of That of Paris, and New York* (1839) and J. D.

Talbot's *The Miseries of Prostitution* (1844).[36] For the most part, these
early works were hasty, ill-informed, derivative of Parent and of
each other. They were superseded for once and all, in 1857, by
William Acton's *Prostitution, Considered in Its Moral, Social and Sanitary Aspects, in London and Other Large Cities: with Proposals for the
Mitigation and Prevention of Its Attendant Evils*, the first thoroughly
researched pornographic study in English. Acton's facts and figures,
along with his recommendations, were original; but his title and
methods harked back to Parent, as did his rhetoric.

Today, Acton (1814–75) is chiefly famous, or infamous, for his
remark, in a book published the same year as *Prostitution*, that the
"majority of women (happily for them) are not very much troubled
with sexual feelings of any kind."[37] However typically Victorian
this statement may be, or revealing of Acton's personal illusions,
the attitude it implies is not that of *Prostitution*. There, Acton adopts
Parent's stance of reasoned, scientific detachment, dispensing with
his predecessor's nervous assurances that unsavory research need
not taint the researcher. Twenty years after Parent, the burden of
reproach had fallen upon the hypocritical public:

> It is high time for us to get the better of "a fear that starts at
> shadows." The word RECOGNITION may sound very dreadful, and
> be regarded by many as the precursor of a coming deluge of
> continental immorality. But what is the real fact? Is not recog-
> nition already accorded by society? Who are those fair creatures,
> neither chaperons nor chaperoned, "those somebodies whom no-
> body knows," who elbow our wives and daughters in the parks
> and promenades and rendezvous of fashion? Who are those painted,
> dressy women, flaunting along the streets and boldly accosting
> the passers-by? Who those miserable creatures, ill-fed, ill-clothed,
> uncared for, from whose misery the eye recoils, cowering under
> dark arches and among bye-lanes? The picture has many sides;
> with all of them society is more or less acquainted.[38]

Acton showed none of Parent's skittishness about his own reputation. He opposed the French system of licensing prostitutes but
strongly advocated the Contagious Diseases Act (1864), which au-

thorized justices of the peace to order the medical examination of women suspected of prostitution. The jurisdiction of the first Act was confined to eleven garrison towns; the second (1866) strengthened the first, and the third (1869) extended it to cover six additional municipalities. In the 1870 edition of *Prostitution* and till the end of his life, five years later, Acton propagandized vigorously for the extension of the Act to cover the whole population, in civilian as well as military areas. But popular resistance (and apparent ineffectiveness) won out; the Acts were repealed in 1886.[39]

By Acton's time, Restif's levity had become inconceivable, and even Parent's self-defensiveness was passé. Occasionally, however, as if his subject demanded it, Acton turned distinctly Parentesque:

> What we have to do is to close the approaches to this deadly swamp—to drain it, and to fill it up, and at the same time to disinfect its foul malaria streams, and prevent them from overflowing into purer soil—to diminish its power for mischief—to stop aggregations to it—to withstand its extension. To do all this, we must take its measure, probe its depths, and accurately experience and understand its nature. We must look at it ourselves, and call the attention of others to it; we must discard euphemisms, and call it by its true name; we must prescribe the method of treatment, appoint its limits, and subject it to rule. What is this but recognition?[40]

Though in Acton's version the scene had turned somewhat tropical, Parent's unruly metaphors were still in operation: vile, insidious fluidity that clear eyes and straight talk would render harmless. Indeed, perhaps impelled by his metaphors, three years after the publication of *Prostitution*, Acton triggered a lively public debate by writing a letter to the *Lancet*, later reprinted in *The Times*, complaining about the "wretchedly imperfect" drainage of a house he had rented at Brighton.[41]

When hygienic pornography reached the United States, it brought its metaphors along. In his *History of Prostitution* (1858), Dr. William W. Sanger, resident physician of Blackwell's (now Roosevelt) Island, introduced his subject with a declaration which, to a specialist, must have sounded hackneyed: "Though benevolence may at times lead its devotees through scenes where moral purity is shocked, and to neighborhoods where filth and obscenity violate the very air they breathe, there is no contamination to those whose motives are good."[42] "Has not the hour arrived when truth will speak trumpet-tongued, and when her voice must be heard?" Dr. Sanger went on,[43] ignoring the fact that, across the Atlantic, truth had been trumpeting for more than twenty years. However, despite his threadbare rhetoric, Sanger's methods—much like Parent's and Acton's—were sound, and his research was thorough. He went somewhat further than his precursors in directing attention to the causes of prostitution as well as its effects, and he introduced a new dimension into pornographic literature—history.

Actually, the title of Sanger's book is misleading, since a third of it is a statistical study of prostitution in contemporary New York City. But the first chapters intend to give a full survey of the oldest profession from the earliest times until the present moment. In this, Sanger departed from Restif, Parent, and Acton, for all of whom prostitution was eternally rooted in human nature; for them prostitution had no history, since though its trappings might have changed with time, its essence was always the same. Like a good American, Sanger imagined that this social evil could be not only controlled but eradicated. He was therefore able to conceive of prostitution as a truly historical phenomenon—one that had passed through various phases of development and would reach an end. No doubt unwittingly, however, Sanger's optimism had the peculiar effect of compromising his patently sincere moral probity. It brought him up against a much older form of pornography than the hygienic kind.

When he came to the Roman part of his *History of Prostitution*, Sanger first threw up his hands in horror. "The walls of respectable houses," he wrote, mindful of the Pompeiian excavations, "were covered with paintings, of which one hardly dares in our times to mention the subjects. Lascivious frescoes and lewd sculptures, such as would be seized in any modern country by the police, filled the halls of the most virtuous Roman citizens and nobles." This indignation was commonplace but irreproachable; shortly thereafter, however, Sanger's imagination ran away with him:

> A young Roman girl, with warm southern blood in her veins, who could gaze on the universal pictures of the loves of Venus, read the shameful epigrams of Martial, or the burning love-songs of Catullus, go to the baths and see the nudity of scores of men and women, be touched herself by hundreds of lewd hands, as well as those of the bathers who rubbed her dry and kneaded her limbs—a young girl who could withstand such experiences and remain virtuous would need, indeed, to be a miracle of principle and strength of mind.[44]

Nothing more deplorable could have been dreaded by the cataloguers of the Museo Borbonico than that they might inspire in their readers overheated fantasies like this. Yet this dream came not to a woman or a child or a poor man but to a medical doctor, who retailed it under the same injunctions to purity the cataloguers themselves had employed. Dr. Sanger was not personally to blame; he did his best under impossible conditions. Already by the time he wrote, the pornographic field had been staked out, and he merely tumbled into one of its many boobytraps.

Though the metaphors were different, in its fundamental structure the dilemma that faced Dr. Sanger was the same as that which plagued the first cataloguers of obscene antiquities. In both cases, a subject of study was dangerous and valuable at once: attention had to be paid to matters which, if they had lacked hygienic or historical worth, would properly have been kept out of sight. Both kinds of early pornographers felt compelled to dig up things that had lain buried for centuries—not only exposing them, but also making them public to an extent never possible before. At the door of a brothel, or of the Naples Museum, guards could inspect visitors; in the middle of the eighteenth century, when Restif's *Pornographer* and the first Pompeiian catalogues were published, limited literacy combined with the high price of books to guarantee that the potential danger of certain subjects would never turn actual, because only proper eyes would see them. A century later, theoretically at least, anyone had access to such books. Writers no longer enjoyed the luxury of external restraints on their audience; now, if risky things were to be talked about, and if the old hegemony of mature, affluent men was to be maintained, the restraints had to be internal—that is, somehow set up within the books themselves.

To some extent, the nineteenth-century development of professional specialization served as a replacement for crumbling barriers of sex and class. So long as surveys of prostitution appeared only in medical journals, and so long as Roman depravity was exposed only in tomes that no one but well-to-do antiquarians would buy, the gentlemanly enclosure remained unbreached. But it was characteristic of early pornographers that, though they shielded themselves behind these walls, they strove at the same time to break through them. Acton's plea for "RECOGNITION," in shrill capitals, is a case in point: he wrote as a doctor, but his campaign could not succeed unless it was joined by a larger audience than the medical one. He therefore ran the risk of promoting the evil he sought to cure, as a reviewer of *Prostitution* saw:

> Although a scientific investigator may be called upon to detail the results of his experience, and although the *littérateur* may find his end in giving photographic representations of filth and low debauchery, and although this may stimulate the really good to exert themselves for the amelioration of vice, yet, to the sensual, the vicious, the young and inexperienced, these scientific books thus popularized are too liable to be converted into mere guidebooks to vice, or to afford amusement to the prurient fancy of the depraved; and thus, as it were, they hold a candle to the devil, by suggesting means and appliances for vicious indulgences which otherwise might never have been thought of. . . .[45]

The same specter haunted the authors of Pompeiian guides and catalogues: the best way of insuring that these books would do no harm would have been to leave them unwritten—an alternative never mentioned by writers on most subjects, but invoked by early pornographers with an earnest persistence that made it impossible not to ask the question "Why did you write this?"

Few other books present themselves so emphatically as acts of will; in few other books is the author's motive of such central importance. All such works were the products of what Michel Foucault calls "an institutional incitement" to speak about sex, "and to do so more and more; a determination on the part of the agencies of power to hear it spoken about, and to cause *it* to speak through explicit articulation and endlessly accumulated detail."[46] The ultimate aim of this incitement, according to Foucault, was neither a censorship nor a taboo but a "policing" of sex, its regulation through "useful and public discourses."[47] To make the discourse of sex public was to make it susceptible of control; to risk danger was to define danger and render it beneficial by gauging and channeling its energies. The two forms of pornography we have been looking at in this chapter played important roles in staking out a "specific field of truth" about sex;[48] by choosing not to keep silent, their authors took unwitting part in "the multiplication of discourses concerning sex in the field of exercise of power itself"[49]—a multiplication that has continued at a dizzying rate to the present day.

In this case, however, the impersonal, infallible movements of Foucaultian "power" are less pertinent than the confusions and contradictions that beset the early speakers of pornography and that still bog down anyone who ventures upon that miry field. Foremost among these is the bewildering interplay of speech and silence: from the point of view of the early pornographers, it was a good thing that centuries of silence had been broken, yet by speaking out they burdened themselves with the impossible task of regulating both what they said and who heard them. Certain things never talked about before had to be mentioned now, but only in certain ways and to certain people; if this discourse became general, the consequences would be far worse than those of silence. Professional jargon and lumps of Greek and Latin were of some help; most pornographers, however, put their trust in something less palpable—the intention of the writer and the attitude of the reader.

They make a dreary chorus, these tirelessly repeated exhortations to sobriety and detachment. Like any protesting too much, they have the effect of holding their opposites always in view, refusing to let writer or reader forget that intoxication and arousal are equally possible—indeed, easier and more amusing—states of mind. Such reiterated declarations also shift the site of value and danger away from the representation itself and onto the ineffable subjectivities of the representer and his audience. The effect was the same in both genres of original pornography: prostitutes and Pompeiian relics became, in themselves, morally neutral, impotent to do good or ill. All depended instead on how they were portrayed and on how the portrayal was received. The same statue might be a cadaver for one observer, lewd flesh for another; if any control was to be imposed, or any evaluation made, the intangible realm of the author's and reader's intentions had to be entered, since the object before one's eyes gave no clue as to its impact.

In the mid-nineteenth century, writers on prostitution or ancient art could be relatively sure that their books would not fall into improper hands. Even so, as the reviewer of Acton's *Prostitution* said, a well-to-do, well-educated man might also be prurient and depraved. The best hope an author had of enforcing an attitude in his readers—a faint hope, but the best one—was to demand it of them explicitly. The demand was treacherous, however, and not merely because the author could not hover at the reader's elbow to make sure it was fulfilled. It flew like a boomerang; the reader had to imitate the author, whose calm and serious frame of mind also had to be asserted. Yet, as Acton's perceptive reviewer went on to ask, who would ride herd on the author?

The extent of prostitution is very imperfectly known, and Mr Acton has rendered a service by discussing the subject, and furnishing us with an account of the evil. It is, nevertheless, to be regretted that the author should have allowed himself to introduce sensational matter into his history of a most repulsive subject; letters from Belgravian mothers and their respondents, culled from the *Daily Telegraph* and *The Times*, were quite unnecessary.

Still more objectionable are highly coloured autobiographies of women of loose character, or picturesque descriptions of evenings spent at Cremorne and elsewhere.[50]

The evening at Cremorne had been Acton's own. He visited the notorious Chelsea gardens, "on a pleasant July evening," with the stern intention of taking notes on "the demeanour of London prostitution," and nothing in his rather disgruntled account would suggest any lapse from sobriety on his part. Nevertheless, in contrast with the rest of *Prostitution*, Acton's style in this passage tends toward lushness, as if he found it a relief to turn from gray statistics to the evocation of actual sights and sounds:

> As calico and merry respectability tailed off eastward by penny steamers, the setting sun brought westward hansoms freighted with demure immorality in silk and fine linen. By about ten o'clock, age and innocence, of whom there had been much in the place that day, had seemingly all retired, weary with a long and paid bill of amusements, leaving the massive elms, the grass-plots, and the geranium-beds, the kiosks, temples, 'monster platforms,' and 'crystal circle' of Cremorne to flicker in the thousand gas-lights there for the gratification of the dancing public only. On and around that platform waltzed, strolled, and fed some thousand souls—perhaps seven hundred of them men of the upper and middle class, the remainder prostitutes more or less *prononcées*.[51]

A writer's pleasure animates this scene, which goes on for three more pages in a modern edition—pleasure taken and pleasure offered. Aside from the slight chance that an unimaginably ignorant reader, somehow encountering *Prostitution*, might have learned from it that Cremorne existed and immediately hailed a hansom, Acton could hardly be accused of providing occasion for vice. Yet his claim to absolute sangfroid put him in a vulnerable position. Like his fellow pornographers—and, like them, probably unaware—he invited an inspection of his motives and feelings at every moment. He had required detachment from his reader and used himself as the model to follow; if he slipped even once, he was compromised.

The stance was impossible to sustain. The very fact that a writer had chosen obscenity as a subject, instead of something innocuous, would impugn him. But "pornography" as a field of discourse was mined from the start with impossibilities, not the least of which was that it turned writers and readers alike into amateur psychologists, who never asked what an object was, only what was meant by it. From the start, "pornography" named a battlefield, a place where no assertion could be made without at once summoning up its denial, where no one could distinguish value from danger because they were the same. The reason we now use a relative neologism—and a learned one at that—to designate a class of objects most commentators take for eternal is that "pornography" names an argument, not a thing. We have always had obscenity, at least as long as we have had a scene of public, reportable life that requires a zone of darkness to lend sense to it by contrast. But the zones got jumbled about a century ago, as one dark area after another was reclaimed from forgottenness, mapped, and thrust into the light. "Pornography" had its origins, around the middle of the nineteenth century, in the two specialized fields we have considered in this chapter. They were the first to dig up the obscure old word and to begin the exploration of its manifold, maddening ambivalences. Even among specialists, however, the word "pornography" was never common, and if it had remained their property, the world at large would not have learned it. But those specialists were part and parcel of their culture; the tensions they responded to reached outward into the world around them—tensions that found their proper forum when "pornography" ceased to be a technical term and went fully public.

It was when contemporary art joined in the pornographic battle that the modern concept of "pornography" had its origin. From Chapter 3 until the end of this book, that will be our subject. Now, however, we need to investigate the various ways "pornography" was dealt with in the pre-pornographic era—those centuries before the nineteenth, when obscenity existed in plenty but did not yet go by its modern name. The development of the modern concept entailed the wholesale reorganization of the past to make room for a category the past had not recognized. The project was begun at the Secret Museum and in its catalogues: the Romans had displayed their "pornographic" objects in what seemed the most unlikely places; modern classifiers had to rip them from their Roman street corners and entrance halls and group them under a single heading. Gradually, the project of regrouping was undertaken with the relics of all ages, giving rise eventually to the twentieth-century fantasy that pornography has always been a fact of life, and that the past always dealt with it as we do.

CHAPTER TWO

THE PRE-PORNOGRAPHIC ERA

THOUGH THE NINETEENTH CENTURY invented "pornography," it did not invent the obscene. All cultures known to us, even the most ancient, distinguish classes of acts and objects according to some opposition of public against private, proper against improper, or clean against dirty. There has never been a society—until our own—in which all representations were available equally to any observer at any time. That we are rapidly approaching such a condition (or have reached it) is the result of complex social transformations: rising literacy, increasing urbanization, and the accelerating incitement to control all things, especially the forbidden, by making them subjects of discourse. Ironically, in the movement toward promiscuous representation, "pornography" stands not as a roadblock but as an important stage of progress—a sort of shadow zone between highly selective darkness and indiscriminate light. It is by no means an unequivocal gain that all things should be displayed to everybody; nevertheless, it seems undeniable that this is the direction in which Western culture has been heading for the last two centuries at least. If we wish to understand the post-pornographic age we live in, we should first encounter the pre-pornographic age, the time (most of human history) when the standards of who should see what were very different from those our great-grandparents have bequeathed us.

Although it was the rediscovered obscenity of ancient Rome that first received the label "pornography," classical Greek culture, too, had passed on its share of controversial artifacts, including great numbers of explicitly painted vases and, in literature, the scurrilities of Old Comedy. For the Greeks themselves—at least for the Athenians of the fifth and fourth centuries B.C.—the "sexual and excremental realms," in the words of a modern scholar, were subject to restriction according to a "basic idea of shame and modesty, but without dirtiness."

> Indeed, one might say that the Athenians . . . viewed sexuality in almost all of its manifestations as an essentially healthy and enjoyable fact of life. There is no indication of the kind of guilty, inhibited, and repressive feelings so characteristic of later societies in regard to this area of human life. The Athenians of this era may not have been uninhibited children of nature, but their inhibitions concerning human sexuality were certainly less muddled by complicated feelings of shame and guilt than our own.[1]

Though there is a degree of disgruntled modern nostalgia in this judgment, unfortunately it seems to be true—unfortunately, because it repeats the single greatest cliché about Greek civilization at its height. Arguments of this kind were occasionally used to exonerate the Romans, but half-heartedly, since the obscene relics of Pompeii were hardly necessary to show that Imperial Rome had been licentious; surviving literature proved it abundantly. With the exception of Aristophanes and fragments from other comic playwrights, however, Greek literature was distinguished by a stately decorum that rendered it harmless, even uplifting, to the tenderest of minds. As Matthew Arnold said of Homer in 1860—polishing up a truism—the grand Greek style "is something more than touching and stirring; it can form the character, it is edifying."[2]

Already a generation before Arnold, this opinion was hackneyed enough for Byron to make a brilliant parody of it:

> They look upon each other, and their eyes
> Gleam in the moonlight; and her white arm clasps

Round Juan's head, and his around her lies
    Half buried in the tresses which it grasps;
She sits upon his knee, and drinks his sighs,
    He hers, until they end in broken gasps;
And thus they form a group that's quite antique,
Half naked, loving, natural, and Greek.[3]

Byron had a habit of mocking cultural shibboleths and getting in trouble for it. In this case, he expresses a well-educated, cynical man's weariness with worn-out encomiums on the sunny innocence of the Greeks, who obviously, if only because they were human, could not have lived the pristine lives imagined by later commentators. The Greeks, in fact, were thoroughly familiar with obscenity, both sexual and scatological, though they confined it to special times and places; it belonged to certain festivals and the comic performances associated with them. Gross words and actions were satirical, employed "as a means of abuse, criticism, and degradation" directed at public figures, current events, or even the gods."[4] Obscenity might also have an apotropaic aim, intended to ward off evil spirits by demeaning or threatening them. There was no danger that such matters would be indiscriminately displayed, yet even at the peak of Greek civilization, voices were raised calling for stricter control.

In the fourth century B.C., Plato's *Republic* outlined the government of an ideal state, whose laws included the careful management of all forms of representation, written, pictorial, and dramatic. Discussing the early education of citizens, Socrates strongly objected to the "ugly and immoral" stories told by Hesiod and Homer, in which the gods were said to have practiced all sorts of violence and chicanery on one another as well as on mankind. Such stories were not only "false," they also invited imitation: "We shall not tell a child that, if he commits the foulest crimes or goes to any length in punishing his father's misdeeds [as Cronos did to Uranus, and Zeus to Cronos], he will be doing nothing out of the way, but only what the first and greatest of the gods have done before him."[5] Because the earliest ideas a child takes in were likely to become "indelibly fixed," special care had to be exercised to insure that the stories told to small children conveyed wholesome lessons. Adults, though they might suffer less drastic harm, also stood to gain nothing from hearing these lies; so Socrates quickly moved to forbidding them throughout the Republic:

> The poet will only be allowed to say that the wicked were miserable because they needed chastisement, and the punishment of heaven did them good. If our commonwealth is to be well-ordered, we must fight to the last against any member of it being suffered to speak of the divine, which is good, being responsible for evil. Neither young nor old must listen to such tales, in prose or verse. Such doctrine would be impious, self-contradictory, and disastrous to our commonwealth.[6]

Socrates did not specifically mention sex, though his indictment of pernicious myths would presumably include the amorous escapades attributed to Zeus; these, too, would encourage imitation, thanks to the celestial rank of their perpetrator. The effect in all cases would be disruptive of good social order, and therefore "disastrous to our commonwealth."

Socrates' austere argument has little enough in common with the hysteria over pornography that erupted more than two thousand years later. He did, however, lay the groundwork for his successors in several ways. He implied that the falseness of myths—his fundamental reason for banning them—was no count against their power; indeed, it seemed to give them access to a deeper level of the mind than reason can reach. Like the painter, the poet appeals

> not to the highest part of the soul, but to one which is equally inferior. So we shall be justified in not admitting him into a well-ordered commonwealth, because he stimulates and strengthens an element which threatens to undermine the reason. As a country may be given over into the power of its worst citizens while the better sort are ruined, so, we shall say, the dramatic poet sets up a vicious form of government in the individual soul: he gratifies

that senseless part which cannot distinguish great and small, but regards the same things as now one, now the other; and he is an image-maker whose images are phantoms far removed from reality.[7]

The mental faculty which responds to painting and drama is in every way inferior to reason, yet that very inferiority gives it dangerous strength. This is particularly true in the theatre, where reason is put to sleep:

There is in you an impulse to play the clown, which you have held in restraint from a reasonable fear of being set down as a buffoon; but now you have given it rein, and by encouraging its impudence at the theatre you may be unconsciously carried away into playing the comedian in your private life. Similar effects are produced by poetic representations of love and anger and all those desires and feelings of pleasure or pain which accompany our every action. It waters the growth of passions which should be allowed to wither away and sets them up in control, although the goodness and happiness of our lives depend on their being held in subjection.[8]

The analogy between the individual and the state is consistent: both contain lower orders, dangerous because they are low and hence immune to reasonable appeal. Nothing can be done about these riffraff except to restrain them; they are incorrigible, and whatever speaks directly to them must be banned.

Ironically, in the pornographic age, Plato himself became the target of criticism that exactly followed the structure he had formulated, though with a sexual emphasis missing from his own attack on poetry. Certain of his dialogues seemed to advocate what was known as "Greek love" and therefore posed a threat to the moral integrity of boys who were taught Plato in school. An amusing instance of the confusions that could arise from the touchy problem is the collaboration of Benjamin Jowett (1817–93) and John Addington Symonds (1840–93) on Jowett's translation of the *Sympos-*

ium, the most scandalous Platonic dialogue in this regard. In his ongoing project of translating Plato, Jowett came to the *Symposium* in the summer of 1888 and went through it word by word with Symonds, whom he had tutored at Oxford. Apparently, unaware that Symonds took an intense personal interest in the subject,[9] Jowett proposed to write an essay which would accompany the dialogue, explaining that pederasty in Plato was a "matter of metaphor." "What he means I cannot imagine," Symonds wrote to his friend Henry Graham Dakyns. "The fact is that he feels a little uneasy about the propriety of diffusing this literature in English, & wants to persuade himself that there can be no harm in it to the imagination of youth."[10] To Jowett, Symonds wrote patiently but with fervor, dissuading him from the project and pointing out that, for certain readers (a "species," Symonds called them, with "predetermined temperaments"), Platonic pederasty was very far from a figure of speech:

> It is futile by any evasion of the central difficulty, by any dexterity in the use of words, to escape from the stubborn fact that natures so exceptionally predisposed find in Plato the encouragement of their furtively cherished dreams. The Lysis, the Charmides, the Phaedrus, the Symposium—how many varied and unimaginative pictures these dialogues contain of what is only a sweet poison to such minds!

"It is indeed impossible," Symonds concluded, "to exaggerate the anomaly of making Plato a text-book for students, and a household-book for readers, in a nation which repudiates Greek love. . . ."[11] Whatever Jowett may have thought of his former pupil's enthusiasm, his translation was published without the explanatory essay.

Plato's notion of the seductive power of representations had undergone some curious changes between his day and Symonds's; in the later version, it also acquired a heavy overlay of special pleading. Yet, at bottom, Symonds's thinking was just as Platonic as Plato's own: for susceptible minds, representations of certain sorts had irresistible power, metaphoric or not. The power could not be reasoned away, because it did not operate on the higher faculties; it struck deeper and lower, into the realm of passion and dreams. Some such Platonic conception, often wildly distorted and crudely expressed, has supported most discussions of pornography in the nineteenth century and ours. Greek philosophy, however, also offered a second view of the impact of fiction on life, one which attributed equal potency to the representative arts but regarded their effects as beneficial rather than suspect. Aristotle's *Poetics*, the most influential single document in the history of Western criticism, has very little to say about the moral influence of art on its audience; virtually the whole of it is summed up in the famous statement that, through "pity and fear," tragedy achieves "the proper purgation of these emotions."[12] "No passage, probably, in ancient literature," as a late-Victorian scholar remarked with some exasperation, "has been so frequently handled by commentators, critics, and poets, by men who knew Greek, and by men who knew no Greek."[13]

The haggle has centered on the word *katharsis* ("purgation"), which has been interpreted as everything from a religious metaphor to a no-nonsense medical term. Testily conceding that the "hygienic" sense "appears to be what Aristotle meant," two influential modern critics have nevertheless come down firmly on the side of the "moral" or "lustratory" view, which is not only honored by history but also comes closer to "what most of us would like to say." In this reading, *katharsis* would imply "the purification or aesthetic depersonalization of our usually selfish emotions," rather than merely "the purgation or expulsion of something harmful, the emotions themselves."[14] The technicalities of the debate are immaterial here, as probably everywhere else; the contrast between Aristotle and Plato, however, is provocative. It arose at the very outset of Western thinking about the nature and effects of representations—Aristotle was Plato's pupil—and it has staked out the range of such thinking ever since. For Plato, all representations are at least potentially harmful, because they distract attention from the real world, which itself is merely the shadow of the ideal. Representations are shadows of shadows, and when real life imitates them (when the viewer of a theatrical comedy becomes a buffoon at home), chaos results. Aristotle re-

gards the encounter with representations as a self-contained experience: the audience of a tragedy does not carry pity and fear out
of the theatre, but endures and has done with them while the play
is going on. Both Plato and Aristotle concede great, irrational power
to drama and all the other arts, but the one sees this power as
continuous, the other as intermittent. Plato makes art out to be
something like poison, slowly accumulating in the system and stran-
gling it. In the Aristotelian view, art is homeopathic medicine, to
be taken as needed and put back on the shelf.

The century-long argument over pornography has inherited, usually in ignorance of the source, the terms and structure of this much
more ancient, permanently inconclusive debate. It is possible to
say that those who would ban pornography take a Platonic position,
while those who regard it as harmless—or deny it any influence
whatever—veer toward the Aristotelian side. Moreover, both fac-
tions take a stand with respect not merely to a special class of books
or pictures called "pornographic," but also, by implication, to *any*
representation, of whatever kind, in whatever medium. The vaguely
defined region of emotion and fantasy that both Plato and Aristotle
saw as the site where art took effect has shrunk down, in discussions
of pornography, to a zone of "sexuality"—apparently more specific
but really no better understood, and endowed with the same blind
susceptibility attributed to it by the Greeks. Plato and Aristotle
realized clearly enough what most modern commentators never
knew or have forgotten: that if certain kinds of portrayals can arouse
the urge to imitate them in life, then all portrayals must, to some
degree, possess the same capability. The power of representations
derives from the nature of representing, not from the thing or action
represented in any particular case. The practice of treating this
power as if it belonged to only a special class of images leads directly,
as the history of "pornography" has shown, into a hopeless muddle.

Though Roman civilization left behind a plethora of pornography
for later ages to fret about, in the areas of philosophy and aesthetics
it produced nothing to compare with Plato and Aristotle. The most
significant Roman document of literary criticism, Horace's *Art of
Poetry* (ca. 18 B.C.), is hardly more than a grab bag of practical

advice for poets and dramatists. Horace did, however, make a pair of pronouncements that would come to have a bearing on the pornography debate—four enigmatic lines, ceaselessly quoted and reinterpreted over the centuries, that caused later commentators as much distress as anything in the Greeks:

aut prodesse volunt aut delectare poetae
aut simul et iucunda et idonea dicere vitae

. . .

omne tulit punctum qui miscuit utile dulci
lectorem delectando pariterque monendo

Poets would either delight or enlighten the reader,
Or say what is both amusing and really worth using.

. . .

He wins every vote who combines the sweet and the useful,
Charming the reader and warning him equally well.[15]

The twin slogans *prodesse et delectare* and *utile dulci* haunted Western thinking about art well into the nineteenth century. On the one hand, Horace seemed to suggest that pleasure and usefulness were separate, capable of combination but not requiring it for artistic success. On the other, he implied that the greatest art provided both in equal measure, somehow making them identical. John Dryden propounded the former view in 1671, maintaining that the aim of tragedy is, "by example, to instruct," while "in comedy it is not so; for the chief end of it is divertisement and delight. . . ."[16] In 1802, William Wordsworth took the latter view to an extreme: "We have no knowledge, that is, no general principles drawn from the contemplation of particular facts, but what has been built up by pleasure, and exists in us by pleasure alone."[17] Before, after, and between them, every possible point along the range was occupied by some authority or other; the question, never settled, was under constant debate and approached with a constantly shifting roster of presuppositions.

The pleasure that poetry—and, by analogy, all the arts—was

supposed to offer remained throughout most of Western history a special, intellectual form of delight. It was pleasure taken in elegant diction, beautiful structure, or fine ornamentation; not until the mid-eighteenth century do we find a prevailing tendency to let the immediate impact of the represented object supersede in force and value the effects of the style and decorum of the representation. This sense of aesthetic propriety, as distinct from (though usually in accord with) moral decency, also harked back to Horace, who advised a would-be playwright to avoid "indecent remarks" and "dirty jokes" on social, not moral grounds:

> The better-class patrons may take offense (the freeborn,
> The knights, the wealthy) and refuse to award the crown,
> As it were, unwilling to see in a favorable light
> What the roast-beans-and-chestnuts crowd finds so entertaining.[18]

Comedy, the classical genre reserved for obscene words and gestures, had already been for Aristotle an inferior species, in both subject matter and appeal; verbal and pictorial obscenity has retained traces of its comic, low-class associations ever since. Classical comedy also specialized in satire, often of the most offensive kind, directed at notables who might even be present at the performance. Not until the nineteenth century did grossly sexual and excremental references lose their satirical aura. Strange as the Roman fondness for explicit sexual representations appeared to the staid cataloguers of Pompeii, the entire Western tradition agreed with Roman culture in certain fundamental ways that did not alter till "pornography" was born: except for some very specific religious usages, blunt sexual references were abusive, funny, and low.

The Romans excelled in abuse. Their poets hit a peak of obscene polemic that Western literature would not reach again (and then only palely) until the end of the seventeenth century. Catullus, Martial, and Juvenal regularly accused their enemies of practices which modern languages have no words for; the Romans, however, seem to have regarded obscene invective as a specialized field of literacy or oratorical expertise, in which technical prowess was the first consideration. A specially interesting example is Catullus' notorious Carmen 16, with its stunning opening lines, *"Paedicabo ego vos et irrumabo,/Aureli pathice et cinaede Furi. . . ."* Until the last twenty years, no attempt whatever was made to render this bizarre threat accurately into English. F. W. Cornish, editor and translator of the Loeb text (still a standard trot), simply omitted the lines and called the poem a "fragment," with no indication that he, not the vicissitudes of time, had done the hatchet work. Recent translators have been bolder, though hardly less inaccurate. The version by C. H. Sisson (1967) gives the first line as "All right, I'll bugger you and suck your pricks"—blunt enough, but as a later scholar has pointed out, exactly wrong about the meaning of *irrumabo*.[19] In 1970, Reney Myers and Robert J. Ormsby evaded that problem while retaining the grossness with "I'll fuck you both right up the ass,/Gay Furius, Aurelius. . . ."[20] But accuracy and obscenity have been captured in equal measure only very recently, by Amy Richlin: "I will bugger you and I will fuck your mouths,/Aurelius, you pathic, and you queer, Furius. . . ."[21] The lengths to which classical scholarship will go are sometimes amazing.

Though one modern commentator has referred to Carmen 16 as "homoerotic," even he has had to admit that the threat in the first line (repeated in the last) "would subject his victim to the absolute depths of degradation and infamy."[22] The exact nature of the threat is made still more problematic by its continuation:

> I will bugger you and I will fuck your mouths,
> Aurelius, you pathic, and you queer, Furius,
> who have thought me, from my little verses,
> because they are a little delicate, to be not quite straight.
> For it is proper for a pious poet to be chaste
> himself, but there is no need for his little verses to be
> so. . . .[23]

Whatever Catullus' private habits or intentions were, in this poem he seems to threaten degradation to anyone who assumes too direct a connection between his poetry and his person. Aurelius and Furius, having made this mistake, are liable to assault. Yet, of course, their liability is also announced in a poem, which presumably would be subject to the same caveat. Catullus has set a tricky trap for the simpleminded: if Aurelius and Furius read this poem as they read his "delicate" verses, he will have proven them fools, carrying out his threat without having to touch them.

Modern scholarship, taking full advantage of contemporary license, has cast considerable light on the nature of Greek and Roman obscenity. The prevailing sense now is that classical civilization was intriguingly different from our own, in this regard as in most others, and that we should suspend our modern prejudices in order to understand it correctly. Well into the twentieth century, however, the emphasis fell on the opposite side: students of the classics were urged to see the similarities between ancient life and their own, to draw useful parallels, and to contemplate the eternal truths of the human condition. This approach was satisfactory for dealing with tragedy and epic—Freud applied it with great effect when he devised the Oedipus complex—but it met a stumbling block in sexual satire and invective, notably such terms as *irrumare*, for which English has no exact equivalent. The OED lists a single instance, from Henry Cockeram's *English Dictionarie, or an Interpreter of Hard English Words* (1623), of "irrumate," defined by Cockeram as "to sucke in," the same reversal of the Latin meaning that Sisson would perform three centuries later. A Victorian gentleman, however, might still find refuge in the classics when his native language failed. In the anonymous sexual autobiography *My Secret Life*, printed in the 1880s though in progress for decades before that, the author resorts to memories of Catullus in order to describe an acrobatic three-way session with the prostitute "H." and her young friend Harry. "He did not irruminate me with skill," the account winds up, "and after a little time we ceased and his prick drooped."[24] Though he misforms the English verb, he gets the Latin sense right; given his skittish attitude toward homosexual encounters, it also seems likely that the scornful, demeaning connotations of *irrumare* were on his mind, at least while writing.

Until late in the nineteenth century, classical literature constituted the most plentiful, readily available source of the kind of explicit sexual portrayal we have come to know as "pornography." So long as a classical education remained the privilege of gentlemen, however, it was subject to the same tacit restrictions that helped to defuse the volatile contents of Pompeiian catalogues and hygienic studies of prostitution. There were occasional murmurs of protest, but most men of genteel upbringing would have agreed with Macaulay's confident assertion, in 1841:

> The whole liberal education of our countrymen is conducted on the principle, that no book which is valuable, either by reason of the excellence of its style, or by reason of the light which it throws on the history, polity, and manners of nations, should be withheld from the student on account of its impurity.

"There is certainly something a little ludicrous," Macaulay admitted, "in the idea of a conclave of venerable fathers of the church rewarding a lad for his intimate acquaintance with writings" like those of Aristophanes and Juvenal. But, on the other hand, reality was far more corrupting than any poem:

> A man who, exposed to all the influences of such a state of society as that in which we live, is yet afraid of exposing himself to the influences of a few Greek or Latin verses, acts, we think, much like the felon who begged the sheriffs to let him have an umbrella held over his head from the door of Newgate to the gallows, because it was a drizzling morning, and he was apt to take cold.[25]

Despite the fears of Jowett and others, this blithe attitude prevailed throughout most of the century, at least in England.

Across the Atlantic, however, where the goal of universal education was taken more seriously and approached at a faster rate, the dangers lurking in the classics became apparent quite early. Only ten years after Macaulay's smug remarks, Dr. Sanger of Blackwell's Island included in his catalogue of incitements to prostitution "the bad effects of, so called, classical studies":

Are they not oftentimes acquired at the risk of outraged delicacy or undermined moral principles? Mythology, in particular, introduces our youth to courtesans who are described as goddesses, and goddesses who are but courtesans in disguise. Poetry and history as frequently have for their themes the ecstasies of illicit love as the innocent joys of pure affection. Shall these branches of study be totally ignored? By no means; but let their harmless flowers and wholesome fruits alone be culled for youthful minds, to the utter exclusion of all poisonous ones, however beautiful.[26]

Sanger neglected to indicate how this culling should be managed, except to suggest that all translation of the more outrageous classics, like Catullus and Martial, cease at once.[27] This would do no good, however, if the whole population, girls included, were to become fluent in Greek and Latin, as might have been the case if a gentleman's traditional education had simply been extended unchanged to both sexes and all classes. In fact, the risky classics were made innocuous not so much by gelding as by altering the curriculum to keep them out.

In 1841, Macaulay was able to declare it "unquestionable" that "an extensive acquaintance with ancient literature enlarges and enriches the mind," rendering its possessor "useful to the state and to the church";[28] but a generation later this truth no longer seemed self-evident. The steady advance of science, with its palpable, practical benefits and quick accessibility to all students, cast increasing doubt on the value of the traditional curriculum, which began to look more decorative than useful. "This distinctive character of our own times," said Thomas Henry Huxley in 1880, "lies in the vast and constantly increasing part which is played by natural knowledge"—that is, scientific information. "Not only is our daily life shaped by it; not only does the prosperity of millions of men depend on it, but our whole theory of life has long been influenced, consciously or unconsciously, by the general conceptions of the universe which have been forced upon us by physical science."[29] In the face of this glaring fact, humanists like Matthew Arnold nevertheless asserted that "the monopoly of culture" belonged to them alone, thanks to their classical erudition. For Huxley, the claim was absurd:

> Scholarly and pious persons, worthy of all respect, favour us with allocutions upon the sadness of the antagonism of science to their medieval way of thinking, which betray an ignorance of the first principles of scientific investigation, an incapacity for understanding what a man of science means by veracity, and an unconsciousness of the weight of established scientific truths, which is almost comical.[30]

In the Renaissance, when the humanistic curriculum was first laid down, it did in fact comprise "the best that has been thought and said in the world"—Arnold's definition of culture. But the world had changed immeasurably since the days of Erasmus, and by not changing with it, by clinging to the same old texts with their ridiculously antiquated view of the universe, humanism had become hopelessly obsolete.

Replying to Huxley in a lecture three years later—significantly enough, delivered during a tour of the United States—Arnold could do no better than to redefine "literature": it is "a large word," he said; "it may mean everything written with letters or printed in a book."[31] Scientific texts, therefore, might be "literature," as might any book in any language. When it came to the specific question of Latin and Greek, having already obscured the issue, Arnold merely summoned up a vague and rather sneering vision of the future:

> Women will again study Greek, as Lady Jane Grey did; I believe that in that chain of forts, with which the fair host of the Amazons are now engirdling our English universities, I find that here in America, in colleges like Smith College in Massachusetts, and Vassar College in the State of New York, and in the happy families of the mixed universities out West, they are studying it already.[32]

The future, however, failed to oblige. Though a certain number of women did and do study the classics, the old curriculum has steadily dwindled away, until in modern universities—even those of the strongest "humanistic" bent—Latin and Greek are minor, marginal specialties.

The split between science and the humanities, profoundly influential on the development of twentieth-century culture, was already apparent in the interchange between Huxley and Arnold; the weakness of the humanist's stance was embarrassingly clear. No doubt Huxley was correct in implying that the classics were useless emblems of a self-perpetuating elite; in that view, their disappearance from the standard curriculum would be a sign of triumphant democratization. Other, less heartening factors, however, also dictated what Terry Eagleton has called "the rise of English," the replacement of Greek and Latin by native literature. Imperialism, of course, marched in step with it; in Eagleton's interpretation, the decline of religion as a pacifier of the masses also required an ideological substitute, something soothing and easily intelligible to the growing number of women and middle-class men attending universities. "English" filled the bill exactly—especially since, as it is customarily taught even today, literature deflects attention from specific grievances:

> Since literature, as we know, deals in universal human values rather than in such historical trivia as civil wars, the oppression of women or the dispossession of the English peasantry, it could serve to place in cosmic perspective the petty demands of working people for decent living conditions or greater control over their own lives, and might even with luck come to render them oblivious of such issues in their high-minded contemplation of eternal truths and beauties.[33]

The decline of the classics would indicate no real change in the dominant ideology, only its retrenchment. An unanticipated effect of these developments, however, was that Greek and Roman "pornography," once shielded from common view by barriers of class and gender, acquired new safeguards in the form of remoteness and obscurity. Either way, the danger was warded off; it is probably no accident that the decline of classical studies, which Gilbert Highet sees as beginning in earnest about 1880,[34] coincided closely with the first real surge of public controversies over "pornography" in modern art and fiction.

Though the national literatures of western Europe offered little to compare with the extravagances of Greek comedy or Roman satire, even "English" was hardly free of risk. Chaucer and Shakespeare in particular, but also Swift, Pope, Milton, and even the King James Bible, presented to later generations the peculiar problem of works which formed essential parts of the literary heritage but which nevertheless, in the words of Dickens's Mr. Podsnap, might "call a blush into the cheek of a young person." By 1864, "Podsnappery" could be made the target of merciless satire: despite his habit of loftily dismissing every unfamiliar fact—"I don't want to know about it; I don't choose to discuss it; I don't admit it!"— Mr. Podsnap runs into constant, comical trouble in his efforts to protect this hypothetical institution called "the young person":

> It was an inconvenient and exacting institution, as requiring everything in the universe to be filed down and fitted to it. The question about everything was, would it bring a blush into the cheek of the young person? And the inconvenience of the young person was, that, according to Mr. Podsnap, she seemed always liable to burst into blushes when there was no need at all. There appeared to be no line of demarcation between the young person's excessive innocence, and another person's guiltiest knowledge. Take Mr. Podsnap's word for it, and the soberest tints of drab, white, lilac, and grey, were all flaming red to this troublesome Bull of a young person.[35]

We have met the creature before: transposed two thousand years back in time, she is Dr. Sanger's imperiled Pompeiian virgin; she is also the inflammable reader who might get the wrong impression from hygienic and art-historical "pornography." But though her most familiar incarnation is Victorian, she was in existence long before Victoria and outlasted her.

The foremost historian of expurgated English books dates the first such publication 1724, though the practice did not become widespread until the end of the eighteenth century.[36] It flourished throughout the nineteenth and came to a rather abrupt though incomplete end with the First World War. For the most part, "pornography" did not fall within the province of the expurgators; they were concerned with books which were objectionable only in part, and which could be cleaned up by cutting out a few passages or altering a few words. The method was well suited to anthologies, another eighteenth-century invention, designed for newer members of the reading public—the middle class, and particularly women— who had no desire for complete editions and no need for the apparatus of scholarship. In collections of the "flowers" of the great poets, expurgation could be performed simply by omission, without altering any texts. This was Samuel Johnson's approach in the series of fifty-two *Works of the English Poets* (1779–81), which he selected and for which he wrote his famous prefaces, later published separately as *Lives of the English Poets*. Johnson, however, trimmed only one of his authors on moral grounds—the notorious Rochester, whose works he sent to George Steevens "to castrate." Rochester, as we shall see, was a very special case; Johnson's criteria for the other fifty-one poets were simply excellence and beauty. Even Matthew Prior, who would later be compared in looseness to Juvenal,[37] got by unscathed, as James Boswell reports:

> I asked whether Prior's Poems were to be printed entire; Johnson said they were. I mentioned Lord Hailes's censure of Prior, in his Preface to a collection of *Sacred Poems*, by various hands, published by him at Edinburgh a great many years ago, where he mentions, "those impure tales which will be the eternal opprobrium of their ingenious authour." JOHNSON. "Sir, Lord Hailes has forgot. There is nothing in Prior that will excite to lewdness. If Lord Hailes thinks there is, he must be more combustible than other people."[38]

It seems that the Scots—on account of either combustibility or evangelicalism—practiced expurgation far more assiduously than the English until the very end of the eighteenth century.[39]

The English soon caught up, however, and when they did they gave a name to the practice that has stuck with it ever since—"bowdlerization." The name derives from that of the Bowdler family, most of whom seem to have tried their hands at it, particularly Dr. Thomas Bowdler and his sister Henrietta Maria, the first edition of whose *Family Shakespeare* was anonymously published in 1807. Expanded in 1818 (to include more plays, not fuller texts), it went through many printings throughout the nineteenth century before becoming anathema in the twentieth, when the very name of Bowdler is synonymous with the cringing squeamishness supposedly characteristic of the Victorians. The example of Mr. Podsnap should suggest, however, that even in the depths of the Victorian age, the bowdlerizing sensibility never fully carried the field. There were always those who, like Dickens, were ready to satirize the habit of gutting the world's literature to suit the susceptibilities of imaginary virgins. And even at its worst, bowdlerism failed to focus with absolute singlemindedness on indelicate sexual references. These were its favorite targets, but the scissors also got applied to blasphemy, vulgarity, and lines that were merely felt to be inappropriate to the character speaking them. Shakespeare—the bowdlerists' (and the Bowdlers') foremost victim—also did not suffer his first surgery at Victorian hands; for centuries, his texts had been handled with a cavalier disregard for integrity that modern scholars find shocking.

Even today, liberal cuts are made in any version of Shakespeare intended for the stage; from the seventeenth through the nineteenth century, these practical expurgations sometimes disposed of half the play. Not only that, entirely new scenes and characters were also introduced to please the changing tastes of audiences. The most famous instance is Nahum Tate's 1681 castration of *King Lear*, which includes among other protobowdlerizations a complete rewriting of the last scene, so that Cordelia does not die but survives to marry Edgar. Joseph Addison had already attacked this over-

sensitive revision in 1711—"*King Lear* is an admirable Tragedy . . . as *Shakespear* wrote it; but as it is reformed according to
the chymerical Notion of Poetical Justice, in my humble Opinion
it has lost half its Beauty"[40]—though fifty years later, Johnson
defended it:

> A play in which the wicked prosper, and the virtuous miscarry,
> may doubtless be good, because it is a just representation of the
> common events of human life; but since all reasonable beings
> naturally love justice, I cannot easily be persuaded, that the ob-
> servation of justice makes a play worse; or, that if other excellen-
> cies are equal, the audience will not always rise better pleased
> from the final triumph of persecuted virtue.[41]

Usually a champion of textual accuracy, Johnson printed *Lear* in
Shakespeare's version but approved of Tate's for performance; the
prettified *Lear* held the stage well into the nineteenth century.

Typical as the Bowdlers' cut-and-paste tactics may seem of Victorian hypocrisy, they had old and numerous precedents, and they
cannot be categorically distinguished from excisions made for reasons far removed from prudery. Indeed, for many Victorians, the
pruning of the archive was an act to be proud of. Bowdlerization,
after all, was required only because the past had been crude; if
Victorian delicacy (or squeamishness) had prevailed in earlier ages,
there would have been no need for latter-day scissors. The nineteenth-century campaign to clean up the past was not merely a self-
delusive reflex of cowardice. It was motivated at least in part by
the belief that the present, for all its faults, was the brightest, most
vigorous time history had yet seen, above all a more decent time
than even the immediately preceding age. Our own century has
been unique in regarding increased license, sexual or other, as a
gain; the Victorians saw progress rather in terms of advancing order,
control, and propriety. The reorganization of the library, the pruning or quarantining of works that gave offense, seemed to its per-
petrators a wholesome act of housekeeping. Nevertheless, the
Victorians brought to the task a sense of the danger inherent in

books and pictures that made prior ages seem sophisticated by comparison. We may chalk it up to simple prurience and prudery, but it remains true that the triumph of Bowdlerism was also impossible prior to the nineteenth century because representations in general had not yet come to possess the special power, for both good and ill, that was later attributed to them. The focus of that power, the specific realm of the "sexual," had not yet been fully demarcated or assigned a leading role in the conduct of human life. By overvaluing both sex and representations, the nineteenth century created a category which had not existed, or only in rudimentary form, in any past age. Imposing their own vision on the past, the Victorians of course distorted it, but we succumb to our own distortions if we suppose that Victorian repressiveness merely sought to clamp down a lid on freedom.

Shakespeare was the special *bête noire* of the Bowdlers and their cohorts; Chaucer followed the Bard a close second. This "well of English undefyled," as Edmund Spenser called him near the end of the sixteenth century,[42] seemed hardly so potable to later ages; but cautious editors had the advantage that Chaucer wrote in a language almost as foreign to the common reader as Greek or Latin. Noel Perrin places the earliest bowdlerization of Chaucer's Middle English in 1831, though a trimmed translation had appeared forty years earlier.[43] By the mid-twentieth century, any student willing to take the slight trouble to master Chaucer in the original had unobstructed access to his bawdiest passages; since its first edition in 1962, the *Norton Anthology of English Literature*, the most popular such text in undergraduate survey courses at American universities, has included the full text of the Miller's Tale, complete with marginal explications. These, however, do observe a certain decorum. Beside Chaucer's unequivocal line "And prively he caughte her by the queinte," the editors define "queinte"—which has an obvious modern cognate—as "*pudendum*," no doubt dispatching generations of freshmen to unabridged dictionaries.[44] Translations of Chaucer, too, though freer (and therefore more accurate) than they were a century ago, retain patches of reticence. Nevill Coghill's widely read translation of the *Canterbury Tales*, for example, renders the

same line as "He made a grab and caught her by the quim"—
"quim" being obsolete slang used routinely by the author of *My
Secret Life* but unlikely to be found on the tip of most modern readers'
tongues.[45]

From the seventeenth century onward, two conceptions of the
past prevailed, complementing and contradicting each other. Past
ages were earthy, genuine, close to nature; they were also dirty,
rude, and brutal. In virtually the same breath, Chaucer could be
praised for the first set of attributes, censured and censored for the
second—as by John Dryden, who in 1700 called him "a man of a
most wonderful comprehensive nature," but who limited his own
translations of the *Canterbury Tales* to those which "savour nothing
of immodesty."[46] Chaucer himself, however—like Shakespeare—
followed classical rules of decorum, confining gross references to
low characters and comic scenes. There was no mingling of noble
and bawdy, no confusion of the realms to which each belonged,
and apparently no anxiety that a naive reader might fall into im-
propriety on account of either. At the end of the *Canterbury Tales*,
Chaucer does disclaim his "translacions and enditynges of worldly
vanitees," and "many a song and many a leccherous lay; that Crist
for his grete mercy foryeve me the synne";[47] but this not uncommon
gesture withdraws absolutely everything he wrote, except a few
pieces of strictly devotional nature. Even in self-condemnation,
Chaucer made only the wholesale distinction between worldly and
religious writings; not until many centuries later would the worldly
come to possess an array of subdivisions.

John Wilmot, second Earl of Rochester (1647–80), made the same
kind of retractation, repenting on his too-early deathbed and seeking
solace, as his last counselor reported, in the hope "*that as his life had
done much hurt, so his death might do some good.*"[48] Of all the poets in
the English literary tradition, Rochester came closest to earning the
title of pornographer; even Johnson sent his poems to be "castrated,"
and a complete edition was not published until 1968.[49] The bowdlerizers never molested Rochester, for the simple reason that no
amount of snipping would tame him. Unlike any other English
poet, he totally lacked redeeming features; besides, his oeuvre was

in such a state of confusion that sorting out true from false attributions seemed a hopeless task. Nevertheless, editions of Rochester's poetry, or of poems said to be his, continued to be printed at regular intervals during the century after his death, and his inclusion in Johnson's editon of 1779 suggests that he was then still felt to deserve a niche, however small, in the pantheon. After Johnson, for almost another century, interest in Rochester fell off to zero. Not only did few new editions of his poetry appear, but he was also hardly mentioned, except to be condemned in passing. "Silence," however, as the historian of Rochester's critical reputation has remarked, can be "as significant as comment."[50] In the middle of the nineteenth century, Rochester began to emerge from obscurity, though now his work was looked upon as "a valuable record of Restoration society"[51]—a slowly accrued benefit that took the edge off his indecency.

The ups and downs of Rochester's fame make an interesting barometer of public taste in the English-speaking world during the last three centuries. In his own time, Rochester was a notorious rake even in a court whose libertinism is proverbial. If he did perform all the escapades attributed to him, his death at thirty-three is no wonder, since every imaginable form of debauchery was attached to his name. Among his more innocuous pranks—this one fairly well authenticated—was the month or so he spent in London, in the summer of 1676, disguised as "Alexander Bendo," physician and astrologer, whose advertisements claimed cures for everything from scurvy to female complaints, especially the latter. He may have undertaken this masquerade in order to escape arrest on a charge of murder and to win King Charles's forgiveness; if so, he succeeded on both counts, though later ages have never been able to understand how a British nobleman could conceive of dressing up as an Italian quack—and, having done so, get away with it.[52] In one respect, however, Rochester was a conventional aristocrat: he never arranged for publication of any of his writings, letting them circulate in manuscript for the delectation of his friends and the outrage of his enemies. The first printed edition of his poems appeared only after his death, in an evident effort to cash in on his notoriety without fear of reprisal; it was full of spurious poems which, on account of their outspokenness, could plausibly pass as his. Had he seen the volume, Rochester would probably have disdained protest.

All later editions of Rochester's poetry in a sense violate its primary intention, since his poems were never meant to pass beyond the high-born and high-living circle he moved in. To thrust them before a public composed of all classes and degrees of sophistication is in fact to make them more pernicious than their author ever designed. And though Rochester far exceeded Chaucer and Shakespeare in bawdiness, he followed, just as they had, the classical convention restricting such matters to the contexts of comedy and satire. All of Rochester's most objectionable poems are so fiercely satirical that it would take an obsessive reader indeed to find them titillating. Among the most extreme, "A Ramble in St. James's Park" was omitted even from the 1926 Nonesuch Press edition, the fullest till its time,[53] though the New York police nevertheless seized and supposedly destroyed all imported copies.[54] The poem's invective against an unfaithful mistress is truly scarifying:

> May your depravèd appetite
> That could in whiffling fools delight,
> Beget such frenzies in your mind
> You may go mad for the north wind,
> And fixing all your hopes upon 't
> To have him bluster in your cunt,
> Turn up your longing arse t' th' air
> And perish in a wild despair![55]

Nothing in Pope or even Swift comes close to this in vindictiveness; to find a parallel, we would have to return to Catullus, Juvenal, and Martial, who were no doubt in Rochester's classically educated mind as he wrote. The only way to bowdlerize Rochester was to silence everything but a few harmless lyrics—which was duly done throughout the nineteenth century and well into the twentieth.

So far, we have been considering works which, for one reason or another, presented nineteenth-century editors and translators with problems similar to those encountered by surveyors of prostitution and cataloguers of Pompeii. In all these cases, the cultural inheritance had to be reorganized, moving certain objects or words into a shadowy zone of recent invention. Little attempt was made to comprehend why this zone, which should always have been in existence, had been so newly staked out; it was generally assumed that the artists of the past had simply been either naive or incompletely civilized. Very seldom was it supposed, even by the most Podsnappish of bowdlerizers, that works which would scandalize a present-day reader had had the same effect on their contemporaries or were intended by their authors to raise blushes. If Shakespeare was occasionally crude, his audience more than matched him; the rapport between artist and public was assumed to have been—and probably had been—complete. Only in the nineteenth century itself do we begin to find frequent instances of artists deliberately affronting their audiences, treading upon ground they knew to be forbidden. The establishment of a restricted area is itself the boldest invitation to trespass; before the nineteenth century, when no barriers were yet completely manned, there was no strident temptation to leap over them. So long as grossness had a home and stayed there—primarily in satire and comedy—it could be freely displayed to a select audience without inspiring much outrage. But when this sense of propriety was lost, when it began to seem possible that anything at all might be shown to anybody, new barriers had to be erected against a threat that was probably already invincible.

Nothing in the official archive qualified as what we would call "pornography," and none of it was given that label by nineteenth-century commentators. The knotty problem of intention, which befuddled the hygienic pornographers, was absent from discussions of classical, medieval, and the bulk of Renaissance literature. The young person, that troublesome Bull, might turn scarlet on reading Chaucer, but if she did it was her problem (or virtue), not his. The indubitable value of such writings, ratified by the centuries, guaranteed that if cuts were made here and there, or if certain works in their entirety were withheld, all would be well. As early as the sixteenth century, however, the world had begun to see books and pictures which inspired no such confidence. Pornographic by any standards, including our own, these works posed no question of value: they laid claim to none, and not until much later in their history was any attributed to them. Because they did not belong to the canon of literature, susceptible minds had little need of protection from them; scarcity and obscurity provided all the necessary safeguards. Only in the nineteenth century—the same era that gave them their name—was any serious notice taken of their existence. Yet they persisted, in reputation if not in fact, and they offer the most provocative instance we possess of the difference between the pre-pornographic age and the age that invented "pornography."

"The story for our purposes begins with Aretino," remarks the pioneering historian of this shadowy genre.[56] Nowhere in European literature prior to Pietro Aretino (1492–1556) do we encounter the combination of explicit sexual detail and evident intention to arouse that became, three hundred years later, the hallmark of the pornographic. If any individual deserves to be called the originator of pornography, Aretino does; yet as is so often the case in the history of this ungovernable subject, this origin, too, was equivocal. As Giorgio Vasari, Aretino's contemporary, tells the story, it was threefold:

> Giulio Romano caused Marc'Antonio to engrave twenty plates showing the various ways, attitudes, and positions in which licentious men have intercourse with women; and, what was worse, for each plate Messer Pietro Aretino wrote a most indecent sonnet, insomuch that I know not which was the greater, the offence to the eye from the drawings of Giulio, or the outrage to the ear from the words of Aretino. This work was much censured by Pope Clement; and if, when it was published, Giulio had not already left for Mantua, he would have been sharply punished for it by the anger of the Pope. And since some of these sheets were found in places where they were least expected, not only were they prohibited, but Marc'Antonio was taken and thrown

into prison; and he would have fared very badly if Cardinal de'Medici and Baccio Bandinelli, who was then at Rome in the service of the Pope, had not obtained his release. Of a truth, the gifts of God should not be employed, as they very often are, in things wholly abominable, which are an outrage to the world.[57]

Though Giulio Romano did the original drawings and Marc'Antonio the engravings, it was Aretino's *Sonetti lussuriosi*, added in 1524, that made the collection infamous. For centuries thereafter, forgetting that Aretino had come third in line, posterity would know the whole product as *Aretino's Postures*.

Threatened with reprisals, the poet remained unrepentant. In an open letter to Battista Zatti, dedicating the sonnets to him, Aretino gave a surprisingly modern-sounding account of their origin:

on seeing them [the drawings] I was inspired by the same feeling that prompted Giulio Romano to draw them. . . . And I dedicate the lust they commemorate to you to spite the hypocrites since I reject the furtive attitude and filthy custom which forbids the eyes what delights them most. What harm is there in seeing a man mount a woman? Should the beasts be more free than us?[58]

Authorities differ on the number of drawings and sonnets in the original pamphlet; Vasari says twenty, but most other sources give sixteen, perhaps expanded later, by other hands, to as many as thirty-six. For a work so frequently mentioned as this, it remains remarkably obscure: though the sonnets survived the centuries, the engravings are known even today only in fragments. In his pseudonymous *History of Prostitution*, Paul Lacroix gave the most plausible explanation:

To all appearances, they [the engravings] were next brought into France, where they were put to use to make several successive reprintings. These were barely adequate to the unbridled libertinism of the sixteenth century, but fortunately they have left no trace, since the destiny of such abominable books is not to survive the person who owns them.[59]

The "fortunately" is disingenuous; Lacroix would dearly have loved to own, or even get a glimpse of, this legendary abomination. But it seems to be true that shocked executors—and sometimes the owners themselves, in a revulsion of feeling—were responsible for the high mortality rate of such books and pictures. Not before the middle of the nineteenth century was a systematic campaign begun (in which Lacroix took a significant part) to rescue them from oblivion.

In addition to getting credit for the first known example of what a modern observer would call "hard-core" pornography, Aretino was an extraordinary figure in all other ways, a mystery to his contemporaries as well as to later historians. The self-styled "Scourge of Princes," he bragged about his friendship with virtually every crowned head of his time, including Henry VIII of England; he edited and published his own letters, featuring those in which he thanked these notables for gifts of everything from clothing to vegetables. He supplemented the sonnets with the *Ragionamenti* (1534–36), a series of dialogues examining in crude detail what Aretino considered womankind's three estates—nun, wife, and whore.[60] But he also wrote a number of pious works, which seem as sincere as his gutter productions. For students of the Italian Renaissance (a favorite mid-nineteenth-century subject), he became a star example of the contradictions that made the epoch fascinating. In his seven-volume *Renaissance in Italy* (1875–86), Symonds included Aretino among the "pornographic pamphleteers and poets" who inhabited the decadent cinquecento.[61] "The man himself incarnated the dissolution of Italian culture," Symonds intoned.[62] In Aretino's own day, however, this dire fact had gone exasperatingly unremarked:

Nobody thought of addressing him without the prefix of *Divino*. And yet, all this while, it was known to everyone in Italy that Aretino was a pander, a coward, a liar, a debauchee, who had wallowed in every lust, sold himself to work all wickedness, and speculated on the grossest passions, the basest curiosities, the vilest vices of his age.[63]

Faced with the impossibility that Aretino had also written such works as *I tre libri della Humanità di Christo*, Symonds could only throw up his hands: "These books, proceeding from the same pen as the 'Sonetti lussuriosi' and the pornographic 'Ragionamenti,' were an insult to piety."[64]

Symonds concentrated his ire on the *Ragionamenti*; with a well-developed sense of "pornography" and its latter-day connotations, he likened the public reception of these "Pornographic Dialogues" to that greeting Zola's *Nana* in 1881, the difference being that Aretino had written "with a licentious, and not an even ostensibly scientific" aim.[65] On the same page, however, historical accuracy compelled Symonds to contradict himself: "We have abundant and incontrovertible testimony," he grudgingly admitted, "to the fact that his 'Dialoghi,' when they were first published, passed for powerful and drastic antidotes to social poisons." A late-twentieth-century reader is unlikely to find in the *Dialogues* anything corresponding to his more specific understanding of the pornographic. From its mock dedication to Aretino's pet monkey—which is invited to "take these pages of mine and tear them up, for great lords not only tear up the pages dedicated to them but even wipe themselves with them"[66]—all the way through its last set of dialogues on how to be a successful whore, the book is far too bitterly polemical to be accused of licentious intent. Here, for example, Nanna, the world-weary prostitute, instructs her daughter, Pippa, in the tricks of the trade:

And what a murderous job it is for a woman working at pleasure to get a man who wants to have his balls scratched and tickled. And what a bore it is always to keep his nightingale awake and erect, and besides, having to hold your hands on the shores of his ass! Then let one of these whore-torturers come and tell me that money can pay for such filthy, stinking patience. I'm not telling you all this, my dear daughter, so that it will disgust you— on the contrary, I want you to know how to do everything better than any other bitch—but I have touched all the keys to show you that we don't steal the few pennies they give us. No, we buy it dearly at the price of our honesty and are driven to it by our poverty.[67]

The bitter tone and concentration on unpleasant physical detail render the *Ragionamenti* dubious as an aphrodisiac; to a modern reader, the dialogues seem much more like the social satire their contemporaries took them to be.

Nevertheless, from at least the seventeenth century onward, Aretino's name became synonymous with the sort of book or picture (or combination of the two) that spurred sexual arousal. As late as 1824, an ephemeral magazine called *The Voluptuarian Cabinet* printed the prospectus of a male brothel offering these allures:

> A lady of 70 or 80 years of age can at pleasure enjoy a fine robust youth of 20; and to elevate the mind to the sublimest raptures of love, every boudoir is surrounded with the most superb paintings of Aretino's Postures after Julio [sic] Romano and Ludovico Carracci, interspersed with large mirrors, also a side-board covered with the most delicious viands and richest wines.[68]

It is unknown whether this establishment ever opened its doors, but the advertisement shows that, four centuries after the "luxurious sonnets" were published, readers of a certain sort were still expected to respond to Aretino's name, probably without having seen the notorious engravings he embellished. In the seventeenth century, virtually the only name attached to representations of sexual activity had been Aretino's; this monopoly endured, with some rivalry from Rochester, until the middle of the eighteenth, when competition arose in the form of John Cleland's *Memoirs of a Woman of Pleasure*, more familiar as *Fanny Hill*. Before then, however, the tiny handful of explicitly erotic modern works were all associated with Aretino, by either authorship, attribution, or imitation.

Seventeenth-century references are so numerous as to be striking by their very redundancy. Lady Castlemaine, one of the mistresses of the libertine Charles II, was reputed to know "more postures than Aretino."[69] The obscene farce *Sodom* (1684), long ascribed to

Rochester but probably by his obscure contemporary Christopher
Fishbourne, opens on "an Antechamber hung round with *Aretins
Postures*."[70] Rochester himself, in his guise of Alexander Bendo,
disclaimed any connection: "I have seen physicians' bills as bawdy
as Aretine's dialogues; which no man that walks warily before God
can approve of."[71] Sometimes shorthand would suffice. In William
Wycherley's *The Country Wife* (1675), Horner, newly returned from
France, announces that "I have brought over not so much as a
bawdy picture, new postures, nor the second part of the *Ecole des
filles*. . . ."[72] The last of these, a French imitation of the *Ragionamenti*, was first published about 1655 and went through numerous
editions and translations in the following fifty years. It gave rise,
in 1668, to the next recorded instance, after Aretino's account of
his inspiration to write sonnets, of a man's sexual arousal by representations.

On January 13 of that year, Samuel Pepys added this minor
entry to his voluminous diary:

> Thence homeward by coach and stopped at Martins my book-
> seller, where I saw the French book which I did think to have
> had for my wife to translate, called *L'escholle de Filles*; but when
> I came to look into it, it is the most bawdy, lewd book that ever
> I saw, rather worse then *puttana errante*—so that I was ashamed
> of reading it.[73]

The book's mild-sounding title might have misled Pepys at first,
but there was no excuse for his returning less than a month later
to buy it "in plain binding (avoiding the buying of it better bound)
because I resolve, as soon as I have read it, to burn it, that it may
not stand in the list of books, nor among them, to disgrace them
if it should be found."[74] The predictable climax came the following
night, after Pepys had entertained a group of friends:

> We sang till almost night, and drank my good store of wine; and
> then they parted and I to my chamber, where I did read through
> *L'escholle des Filles*; a lewd book, but what doth me no wrong to

read for informations sake (but it did hazer my prick para stand all the while, and una vez to decharger); and after I had done it, I burned it, that it might not be among my books to my shame. . . .[75]

Two centuries later, Lacroix would lament that books of the Aretinian kind customarily went that way; yet even in 1828, the charm that had seduced Pepys, mythical by then, still held. *The Festival of the Passions*, a novel published that year, describes a man's discovery of a woman masturbating while reading: "he informs her of what he has seen, and requests her to show him the book, which instead of one of devotion proves to be *The Amours of Pietro Aretin*. Familiarities are now hazarded and permitted, and the lady shows herself a thorough libertine"[76]—as she would have to be, with such a book in even one of her hands.

The most remarkable facts about hard-core pornography before the nineteenth century are how little of it there was and how obsessively those few works fed off one another. Like some specialized form of magnet, Aretino's name attracted to itself the supposititious authorship of anything that at all resembled his sonnets and dialogues. A good example is *La Puttana Errante*, a combination of the two forms, which was probably first published in 1660 and had its title immediately stolen by a short-lived English periodical, *The Wandering Whore*. *Puttana* advertised itself as Aretino's, though he had nothing to do with its composition, and its true authorship remains uncertain.[77] "Aretino"—or "Aretine" or "Aretin"—became synonymous all over Europe with the portrayal of sexual acrobatics; no doubt the name was invoked far more often than Aretino's works were actually seen, as an abbreviated reference to an attitude that seemed unique to him. The effect of this groundbreaker and his imitators on seventeenth-century sexual practices is impossible to determine, though it seems to have been nonexistent; despite the Aretinians, as Roger Thompson sums it up, "the missionary position ruled."[78] Aretino's notoriety seems to have derived from the fact that no one before him, and very few writers in the three centuries after, regarded the sexual act as an arena for diversity and experimentation.

Not, of course, that lust was never recognized as a special form of desire, or that techniques of lovemaking were never discussed in print. But "Aretino" became the label for a new and so far uncommon approach to the mechanics and hydraulics of sex, their consideration from an evaluative, analytic point of view. To illustrate sex acts graphically, with the intention that the illustrations be imitated in flesh, is a very different matter from damning or eulogizing lust in the abstract, moralized way taken by all of Aretino's precursors and most of his successors. As David Foxon has laconically suggested, the very possibility that sex might be handled in this calculated fashion, however few people actually did so, reflects a certain intellectualization of the subject, first appearing in the early seventeenth century and making great strides thereafter.[79] It also shows that one could now conceive of "sex" in its own right, sorting it out from the moral, legal, and religious contexts in which it had hitherto been embedded. Not until very late in the nineteenth century would the sifting be completed, leaving us today with a notion of sex as something like advanced calisthenics. "Pornography" as the twentieth century has known it requires this understanding of sex for its very existence. Indeed, most of the arguments about pornography in our era have had as their usually tacit subtext the fundamental question of the separability of sex from all other mental and spiritual activities. Purveyors of pornography, and those who regard it as harmless, tend to consider sex in an Aretinian manner, as a self-contained activity with no necessary impact on the other aspects of its participants' lives. Opponents take the older view that there is no such thing as "sex" pure and simple, that it is so complexly interwoven with the rest of life as to be separable only by fraud or violence.

Full-fledged Aretinians are still rare today, perhaps because their point of view lurches into absurdity as soon as its first implications are drawn. The author of *My Secret Life*, a century ago, went about as far in that direction as it was possible in his time to go, devoting eleven large volumes, complete with index, to physical descriptions of sex almost wholly detached from any context. Yet he was traditional enough in one important sense: he confined his escapades not only to a separate life, but also to a class of partners utterly distinct from his own. He trafficked in whores, with an occasional shopgirl or day laborer thrown in; though he distinguished himself by singlemindedness and stamina, in social respects he was no different from all the generations of privileged men before him. Even for Aretino, the only suitable milieu in which to try out inventive postures was that of the bawdyhouse, and the titles of the protopornographic works that came in his wake—*The Wandering Whore, The Whore's Rhetorick, Memoirs of a Woman of Pleasure*—reveal their agreement with him. The hysteria of the early hygienic pornographers was due in part to their eagerness to dissociate themselves from a venerable tradition of whore writing, all of it jocular, lewd, and mostly underground. To write about prostitution soberly, to insist that all right-thinking people must read about it, violated the boundaries that had stayed in place throughout Western history. Until the nineteenth century, licentiousness had had its proper time, place, and level; "pornography" came into being when that time-honored distribution was failing and had to be replaced.

Until the nineteenth century, too, decorum had prevailed in books as well as in real life. Aretinian subliterature, never plentiful, had remained a hole-and-corner genre, furtively printed and sold, seldom outlasting the life of its wary purchaser. Some of it is "pornographic" in the modern sense, but none of it threatened to reach the indiscriminate public feared by the high-minded pornographers we examined in Chapter 1. That troublesome Bull of a public, blurring the old lines by being able to buy books and read them, threatened to turn every home into a brothel. It would derange the canon of literature by failing to distinguish *Paradise Lost* from any pulp romance; it would neglect to note the difference between the word and the deed. It would, in short, make "pornography" an issue to cry from the rooftops.

CHAPTER THREE

ADVENTURES OF
THE YOUNG PERSON

ALL THE VARIETIES of pictures and writing we have looked at so far, from medical studies of prostitution to Aretino's Postures, were shielded from promiscuous publicity by a wide array of accidental or deliberate safeguards. Some, like hygienic surveys and museum catalogues, were too technical for general circulation; others, like the obscene classics, were accessible only to the privileged few who had a command of Greek and Latin; still others were impossibly rare, like Aretino and his seventeenth-century imitators. In the ordinary course of things, Dickens's Podsnappish "young person" would never catch sight of such obscurities. Those relics of the licentious past that did come under her gaze—the Bible, Chaucer, Shakespeare—might have been securely bowdlerized; but even if they were not, they carried a lulling patina of veneration that served to take the edge off their inflammatory qualities. Virtually anything, of course, then as now, could abet sexual arousal in special conditions. At the end of the nineteenth century, Krafft-Ebing, Freud, Havelock Ellis, and others began amassing evidence—now overwhelming in volume—that the unlikeliest objects and actions were eroticized by someone, somewhere, at least once. To earlier pastors and masters, however, sexuality seemed hardly so pervasive. Despite their comical hysterics, pre-Freudian observers had, if anything, a too precise idea of the sexual. They recognized the act and the relevant bodily parts; they failed to see the omnipresence of

67

sexuality which, oddly enough, in the twentieth century has helped to deprive sex of its terrors. They also lacked a confident sense of the line between the figurative and the real. The most troublesome thing about the Young Person—I call her "she" because Dickens did, though boys and men could be equally obstreperous—was that she persisted in taking representations for reality. Monkey-see-monkey-do was her only imperative.

The contrast between the nineteenth-century view and our own is exemplified by Peter Gay, when he comments that, to the minds of Victorian censors, attorneys, and reformers, "a sensual lyric poem by Algernon Swinburne, a sober manual on contraception by Robert Dale Owen, and a pornographic story by Anonymous were all the same, all certain to corrupt and deprave the innocent. The most arresting and most controversial obscenity trials of the century were, therefore, not of pornographic productions at all, but of candid, realistic erotic poems, plays, and novels."[1] It is true that the Victorians neglected to distinguish "pornography" from the candid, the realistic, and the erotic, as their great-grandchildren have learned to do. But Victorian hamhandedness was not the simple result of fear or prurience. In fact, the history of "pornography" during the last century has been a long, often painful process of winnowing out, discovering that within the initially undifferentiated mass of "the obscene" there are thickets of shades and discriminations. Those "arresting" obscenity trials were the laboratories where such subtleties were tested and confirmed. We would be unable today to separate the erotic from the pornographic if trials had not been conducted. It is a mistake to mock our ancestors because they were blind to nuances which only their labor has enabled us to identify at a glance.

"Subdivision, classification, and elaboration," wrote George Augustus Sala in 1859, "are certainly distinguishing characteristics of the present era of civilisation."[2] The taxonomic mania raged upstairs and down. In 1861, Isabella Beeton's hugely popular *Book of Household Management* required that an ordinary housemaid be adept at the use of no fewer than ten different brushes, each with its specialized shape and function;[3] in the more abstract sciences, authorities were indefatigably at work discriminating strata, ethnicities, classes, and species. The realm of representations was subjected to the same surveillance. Hygienic and art-historical pornography were twin byproducts of the urge to subdivide—to locate and label prostitutes as well as to compartmentalize the relics of Pompeii. The spotting (and blue-penciling) of the past's indiscretions obeyed an identical imperative; the Victorians were the first to recognize, or to think they were doing so, that earlier times had been gross not only in their manners, but also in their habit of letting evil subsist cheek by jowl with good. The nineteenth century has, of course, come under a similar charge from the twentieth.

The nineteenth century was also the great age of exhibitions, libraries, and museums. In the eighteenth century, rich "virtuosos" like Richard Payne Knight and his friend Charles Townley assembled vast collections of everything from Roman sculpture to skewered beetles; but these were private hobbyhorses, ridden alone and displayed to a few choice visitors. The British Museum and Library were established in 1753, the Louvre in 1793, after its royal residents had been disposed of; the United States followed with the Library of Congress in 1800 and the Smithsonian in 1846. Increasingly, such institutions became the resting places of less-imposing private collections, sometimes containing items which, as Paul Lacroix lamented, would otherwise have been destroyed by scandalized heirs. As the nineteenth century wore on, it grew more and more unlikely that obscene artifacts would end, after their owner's death, in fiery oblivion. Selective conflagrations continued to occur, but they were steadily replaced by the decision to foist things off upon curators, letting them make distinctions.

Curators faced dilemmas that executors were not heir to; they were forbidden to destroy what came to them, no matter how distasteful they might find it. We have seen a paradigm of their response in the Museo Borbonico; other museums and libraries found similar solutions. A favorite was to omit dangerous objects and books from printed catalogues, allowing their preservation to be known only privately, by those supposedly immune to corruption. This way was taken by the library of the British Museum, whose "Private Case," established in the 1860s, obtained its first published catalogue, the *Registrum Librorum Eroticorum* by "Rolf S. Reade" (an anagram of Alfred Rose), only in 1936.[4] The *Enfer* ("hell," a pun on *enfermé*, "locked up") of the Bibliothèque Nationale in Paris, founded under Napoleon, was unusual in listing its risky holdings openly; until 1913, however, when a separate catalogue of "erotica" was published, these were concealed according to the method of Poe's "Purloined Letter"—hidden in plain sight by being distributed without special mark throughout the library's file.[5] The nineteenth-century librarian's understanding of the peril lurking in books was much looser than our own. Again, one's first impulse is to dismiss the matter as a symptom of prurient prudery, finding incitements to lust in every nook and cranny, no matter how remote. It was attacked as such in its own time, with evident justice. But another way of regarding the ubiquity of dangerous representations in the nineteenth century is to consider that our concept of "pornography" was then rudimentary and at the start of a long process of development. The Victorians understood "sex" well enough; what they failed to grasp fully—though they learned it and taught it to us—was that the corrupting power of a book or picture varies hugely, depending on how it conveys its impression and how those impressions are received.

The development of the modern concept of "pornography" was aided from an out-of-the-way quarter, the bibliophiles who privately collected and catalogued "erotic" works. Bibliophily—or, in its more advanced stages, bibliomania—was another product of the nineteenth century's obsession with lists, charts, and genealogies; it is still active today, though in shrunken and less flamboyant form. Bibliophily can be distinguished from mere love of books by its relative neglect of contents—let alone such elusive qualities as style and structure—in favor of publication date, binding, paper, and especially scarcity. Like their virtuosic precursors, bibliophiles tend to regard a book as the sum of its tangible attributes, as if books were butterflies or seashells. Bibliophily in the nineteenth century was an expensive addiction, indulged in by gentlemen who possessed the money and leisure it required. They formed international clubs like the Société des Amis des Livres, based in Paris; they issued annuals and newsletters, detailing their findings for one another's benefit; they amassed great private collections, most of which, in due course, ended up burdening public librarians. Above all they classified, and in the process they helped to bring "pornography" into being.

Many of the most assiduous nineteenth-century bibliophiles specialized in what would today be called "pornography," though the collectors themselves rarely used that newly coined, already tricky word. They preferred older, vaguer labels like "curious," "erotic," or "forbidden"; sometimes they went in for circumlocution, as in the title of Jules Gay's *Bibliographie des ouvrages relatifs à l'amour* ("Bibliography of Works Relating to Love," 1860), which G. Legman has called "the first published bibliography of erotic and facetious literature."[6] Or else they sought refuge in Latin, as in Henry Spencer Ashbee's three volumes written under the pen name "Pisanus Fraxi," *Index Librorum Prohibitorum* (1877), *Centuria Librorum Absconditorum* (1879), and *Catena Librorum Tacendorum* (1885). The first of these titles is a jocular echo of the Roman Catholic *Index;* the others, "A Company of a Hundred Hidden Books" and "A Chain of Books to Be Passed Over in Silence," are reminiscent of the contemporary and equally self-canceling project of the Secret Museum. Books of Ashbee's favorite kind had in fact, before the advent of the erotic bibliophiles, been "hidden," "passed over in silence," or simply burned, making them scarce and hard to come by. Explicit sex, we may assume, made such books rare; but for Ashbee and his colleagues, rarity was the first attraction.

Henry Spencer Ashbee (1834–1900) is the most famous of the Victorian bibliomanes, thanks to Legman's ingenious case that he wrote *My Secret Life*[7] and to Steven Marcus's psychoanalysis of him in *The Other Victorians.*[8] Ashbee provides ideal terrain for the sleuth in the unconscious, because as Marcus demonstrates, his obsessive scholarly apparatus masks profound confusion about the real appeal of the books he registers. If we take for granted that sex must have been Ashbee's overriding interest, we are bound to find confusion in a passage like this, from the preface to *Index Librorum Prohibitorum:*

> My object is to collect into a common fold the stray sheep, to find a home for the pariahs of every nation. I do not then hesitate to notice the catchpennies hawked in the public streets, as well as the sumptuous volumes got up for the select few, and whose price is counted in guineas. I embrace indeed that which should be avoided as well as that which should be sought. In this work will be found books in every branch of literature, and I have purposely selected works as various as possible, in order to show through what widely spread ramifications erotic literature extends, and what a vast field has to be traversed.[9]

Ashbee's rhetoric is not very different from that of the hygienic pornographers; indeed, the word "erotic" comes as rather a shock after the description of what seems to be a selflessly humanitarian enterprise.

The discrepancy between Ashbee's stance in his introductions and commentaries and the rank nature of his subjects might reflect confusion, but it is consistent confusion. In the "Preliminary Remarks" to *Centuria*, he returns to the same issue:

> I have been censured by some of my friends for having admitted into my former volume many worthless books, bad in point of art, rubbish in fact. I plead guilty to the accusation, and beg to remind my readers that in so doing I acted in conformity with the programme which I had sketched out. I do not retract what I have advanced, I go even further. What we want are not bibliographies of good and standard works, such as "no gentleman's library should be without," but of rare, forgotten, insignificant, deceitful, or even trivial and pernicious books. A good book, like a great man, will penetrate, sooner or later, will eventually make its mark, and obtain its proper place. Worthless books, on the other hand, are stumbling-blocks to the student; they exist, and are constantly obtruding themselves in his path; he must conse-

quently be grateful to the bibliographer who shall have taken the trouble to wade through this literary garbage, shall have estimated it at its real value, and shall give a terse but reliable account of it.[10]

It remains an open question why books of this kind had not already found their "proper place"—that is, oblivion. Parent-Duchâtelet would recognize the rhetoric, no doubt with a blush. Ashbee employed the same strategies, down to imagery of waste products and sewage, as had been used a generation earlier by his unwitting precursors in the pornographic field.

Ashbee's bibliographies were published in limited editions—250 copies seems to have been the total printing of each volume[11]—and their elaborate format made them too expensive for any but the richest purchasers. They were also privately distributed, so that the danger of their falling into improper hands was slight. Ashbee addressed himself to a highly specialized audience that presumably shared his values; nevertheless, like the cataloguers of the Secret Museum, he felt obliged to defend himself against possible charges of corrupting effect. His quotations and summaries were full of obscene language, but "in my own text I never use an impure word when one less distasteful but equally expressive can be found." "The passions," furthermore, "are not excited": "My extracts on the contrary will, I trust and believe, have a totally opposite effect, and as a rule will inspire so hearty a disgust for the books they are taken from that the reader will have learned enough about them from my pages, and will be more than satisfied to have nothing further to do with them."[12]

Ashbee's criteria of sex and scarcity come close to defining "pornography" in the modern sense, but they do not do so exactly. Only one work by the Marquis de Sade, for example, is included in Ashbee's bibliographies, though Sade's other books are frequently mentioned in commentaries. They were probably too well known, at least by repute, to qualify as "pariahs." Most of the recent publications, like *L'Ecole des Biches* (1868) and *Kate Handcock* (1882) fill the pornographic bill well enough; but others, like *History of the Sect of Mahárájas, or Vallabhácháryas, in Western India,* published in 1865 by the respectable house of Trübner & Co., seem to have been included only because accounts of exotic sexual customs bulk large in them. The population of admissible books shows a geometric rise through time: none at all before the sixteenth century, very few then and in the seventeenth, steadily more as the eighteenth century advanced, and an explosion in the nineteenth. As Ashbee delved further back in history, his standards for inclusion grew more vague. The eighteenth century saw *Nocturnal Revels* (1779) and *The Genuine and Remarkable Amours of the Celebrated Author, Peter Aretin* (1776), but it also had room for the earnest Richard Payne Knight's *Discourse on the Worship of Priapus,* as well as several pseudomedical tracts in indecipherable neo-Latin. Anticlerical diatribes were still being written in Ashbee's day, but they had glutted the market in the seventeenth and eighteenth centuries; Ashbee included as many as he could get hold of, because they regularly focused on the illicit congress of priests and nuns. *The Nunns Complaint Against the Fryars* (1676) might have promised some delectation to Ashbee's select readership, though it is considerably less likely that *Reasons Humbly offer'd for a Law to enact the Castration of Popish Ecclesiastics* (1700) would have done the same. Treating the earliest days, Ashbee became catholic to a fault. He listed nothing by Rochester except the extravagantly lewd *Sodom,* which he took to be authentic and on which he spent several pages thick with quotations. But he devoted equal attention to *Satan's Harvest Home* (1749), an unremittingly indignant assault on prostitution male and female.

The intricate insanity that spawned Ashbee's bibliographies is nowhere more apparent than in the needless defense of his undertaking against imaginary charges of depraving vulnerable readers. Over and over again, he damned the very things he was immortalizing. "Better were it," he declared in the "Preliminary Remarks" to *Catena,* "that such literature did not exist. I consider it pernicious and hurtful to the immature but at the same time I hold that, in certain circumstances, its study is necessary, if not beneficial."[13] Like a photographic negative of bowdlerization, erotic bibliography would protect the world from pernicious literature by highlighting it instead of blotting it out; the benefit would be the same. Fraudulent as this reasoning is, Ashbee and his fellows evidently believed in it. At least, they felt obliged to proclaim the belief, even in pages intended only for their friends.

Ashbee's confusion about his motives for compiling bibliographies of the erotic, and about what they should include, is more than matched by a puzzling indecision as to whom he is addressing in them. Sometimes he blithely declares that the reader must make his own judgment on the value of such work; sometimes he announces that "the real desideratum" is a bibliography which, "confining itself to the worthless and deceitful, points out what should be avoided"[14]—a custodial function performed, the implication is, by no one before Ashbee himself. His books are "not intended for the general public, but for students"[15]—an excuse for leaving all quotations in their original languages, as the wary cataloguers of Pompeii also did. Yet the imaginary specialist, mature, male, and cultivated as he is supposed to be, can hardly have needed a warning like Ashbee's comment on *The Pearl*, a "Journal of Facetiae and Voluptuous Reading" published between July 1879 and December 1880:

> Scenes follow fast upon each other as cruel and as crapulous as any to be found in *Justine* or *La Philosophie dans le Boudoir*, and, it must be owned, far more pernicious, for the enormities in those works are generally enacted in unfrequented forests, in imaginary châteaux, in unknown convents, or in impossible caverns, whereas in the tales before us they are brought close home to us, and occur in Belgravian drawing-rooms, the chambers of our Inns of Court, or in the back parlours of London shopkeepers.[16]

It is almost as if, in these passages and others like them, Ashbee had lost sight of his sobersided "student" and had turned into a veritable Podsnap, fearful that the Young Person might get hold of such books and mistake them for real life.

Unlikely as the Podsnappish role was for a man of Ashbee's elitist attitude and outré tastes, he was compelled to adopt it by one of the sources of value he sought to adduce for the books that fascinated him. Scarcity alone would have satisfied the pure bibliophile, and lewdness the pure sensualist; but Ashbee was driven upon shaky ground by his claim that "erotic literature" could be viewed "from a philosophic point of view—as illustrating more clearly than any other human nature and its attendant foibles."[17] Ashbee ascribed this opinion to his friend and fellow erotomane James Campbell Reddie, but, at least when the mood was on him, Ashbee shared it. He was even able to make the implausible assertion that "erotic novels, falling as they generally do into the category of domestic fiction, contain, at any rate the best of them, the truth, and 'hold the mirror up to nature' more certainly than do those of any other description."[18] We may, with Steven Marcus, dismiss this notion as "ludicrous";[19] it certainly has the earmarks of wish fulfillment. More interesting, however, is the fact that, though the resemblance might have been misleading, much of Ashbee's "erotic literature," especially its more recent examples, did look like "novels" and even bore that label. "Domestic fiction" was, in Ashbee's day, a virtual synonym for "novels"; and this was the special province of the readers whom Ashbee's subjects (and his own accounts of them) would be bound to deprave and corrupt.

In a famous attempt at a definition of pornography, Marcus has proposed that accurate representation of reality, though present to some degree in pornographic works, is accidental to a genre whose "governing tendency in fact is toward the elimination of external or social reality." The ideal pornographic work would be set in "pornotopia," a never-never land where time and space measure nothing but sexual encounters, where bodies are reduced to sexual parts, where even those parts are merely counters in a game of increasingly unlikely recombination.[20] Sade's "novels" approach this ideal state more nearly than any others,[21] but no known work actually achieves it. For us, a century after Ashbee, the pornotopian model might define rather well what we mean by "hard-core" pornography; but for Ashbee and his contemporaries, who had not yet learned to make such distinctions, the zone of conflict lay just

where the impossible verged on the plausible, where works of "crapulous" fantasy might be mistaken for "domestic fiction."

The books in Ashbee's bibliographies that we would unhesitat-
ingly label "pornography" were not recognized as such by him.
Not only did he avoid the word, he also failed to see any essential
difference, for his purposes, between *Curiosities of Flagellation* (a
fantasia of 1875) and an eighteenth-century anticlerical tract. He
saw that "sex" was the principal subject of both volumes, he saw
that both were scarce, and he flung them together accordingly. We
may attribute Ashbee's lack of discrimination to an overcharged
libido, but if he possessed this disorder, so did most of his generation
and those before and after him. When they condemned books, they
also overlooked such matters as tone, style, and intention; they,
too, saw "sex," and that meant danger. Very few of Ashbee's books,
furthermore, ever became public enough to rouse a furor or stage
a trial. The greatest *causes célèbres* of the nineteenth and early twentieth centuries focused on books that situated themselves on the
line between pornotopian fantasy and realistic fiction. Even for
Ashbee, the exact location of this line posed a problem; it nearly
drove his contemporaries mad.

The Young Person was shielded from the corrupting influence
of Ashbee's bibliographies by their limited circulation and, especially, high price. The same defenses engirdled most of the books
Ashbee listed. *The Mysteries of Verbena House* (1882), for example,
was published in an edition of only 150 copies at the incredible
price of four guineas, despite its mere 143 pages and four colored
lithographs—"obscene and of vile execution," according to Ashbee.[22] At about that time, the average yearly income of a lower-
middle-class English family was estimated at £110;[23] if the absurd
idea of buying *Verbena House* had ever occurred to such a family's
breadwinner, it would have consumed two weeks' wages. In the
United States, salaries were generally higher, though even in New
York—then as now among the most expensive American cities—
an estimate of 1883 placed the highest average wage of skilled
artisans at eighteen dollars a week.[24] A lewd Manhattan plumber
would have had to work a week and a half for *Verbena House*.

This is an extreme case, but it is clear that the kind of "hard-core" pornography we now would place at the bottom of the social scale belonged at the top a century ago. Its quality was no higher than what we are familiar with today, but its circulation was confined to that class of "safe" readers who were granted easy admission to the age's other Secret Museums. It therefore figured hardly at all in public controversies; there was, literally, no harm in it. We possess very little evidence on the circulation of written or pictorial obscenity at lower social levels, since no one made the effort to preserve and catalogue it. Such material no doubt existed, but it continued to follow the Aretinian path into oblivion. Dr. Sanger of Blackwell's Island, however, in enumerating the causes of prostitution, gives us an account of a classic scam, as it was practiced in the New York of 1858:

Boys and young men may be found loitering at all hours round hotels, steam-boat docks, rail-road depôts, and other public places, ostensibly selling newspapers or pamphlets, but secretly offering vile, lecherous publications to those who are likely to be customers. They generally select young and inexperienced persons for two reasons. In the first place, these are the most probable purchasers, and will submit to the most extortion; and, in the second, they can be more easily imposed upon. The venders have a trick which they frequently perform, and which can scarcely be regretted. In a small bound volume they insert about half a dozen highly-colored obscene plates, which are cut to fit the size of the printed page. Having fixed upon a victim, they cautiously draw his attention to the pictures by rapidly turning over the leaves, but do not allow him to take the book into his hands, although they give him a good opportunity to note its binding. He never dreams that the plates are loose, and feels sure that in buying the book he buys the pictures also. When the price is agreed upon, the salesman hints that, as he is watched, the customer had better turn his back for the moment while taking the money from his pocketbook, and in this interval he slips the plates from between the leaves and conceals them. The next moment the parties are again face to face, the price is handed over, and the book he has seen before is handed to the purchaser under a renewed caution, and is carefully pocketed. The book-buyer leaves, and at the first opportunity the prize is covertly drawn forth to be examined more minutely, and the unwary one finds that he has paid several dollars for some few printed pages, without pictures, which would have been dear at as many cents.[25]

The technique is timeless; nowadays it would more likely be applied to drugs than to obscene pictures. Even at this low level of operation, however, Dr. Sanger's young dupe must have been rather well-heeled, if he had several dollars to throw away on the street.

In Sanger's view, the crime of fraud was less grievous than the others that might have been committed had the pictures been handed over. He wasted little indignation, however, on "directly obscene publications" like these; at least as dangerous, and more susceptible to control, was "a class of voluptuous novels which is rapidly circulating."

Some are translations from the French; but one man, now living in England, has written and published more disgustingly minute works, under the guise of honest fiction, than ever emanated from the Parisian presses. He writes in a strain eminently calculated to excite the passions, but so carefully guarded as to avoid absolute obscenity, and embellishes his works with wood-cuts which approach lasciviousness as nearly as possible without being indictable. It is to be regretted that publishers have been found, in this and other cities, who are willing to use their imprints on the title-pages of his trash, and sell works which can not but be productive of the worst consequences. Those who have seen much of the cheap pamphlets, or "yellow-covered" literature offered in New York, will have no difficulty in recalling the name of the author alluded to, and those who are ignorant of it would only be injured by its disclosure.[26]

Braving the risk of injury, I would suggest that the author alluded to was G. W. M. Reynolds (1814–79), phenomenally prolific novelist and journalist, and uncrowned monarch of a literary subculture that caused the establishment far more anxiety than anything perpetrated by Ashbee and his friends. The principal work Sanger had in mind was probably *The Mysteries of London*, a voluminous novel published in 312 weekly pamphlets (each with one or more daring woodcuts) between 1845 and 1850. There is no doubt that, in his heyday of the 1840s and '50s, Reynolds was the most popular writer of English in the world. Though a "de luxe" edition of the *Mysteries of London* was published in the United States as late as 1900,[27] he had fallen into almost total obscurity even before his death. The reasons for his fall are not far to seek; an encyclopedia of 1936, in its very brief entry on Reynolds, summed them up: "His novels were extremely sensational, and most of them were mere pot-boilers, not intended to be literature."[28]

In Chapter 2, we considered one view of the evolution of "literature": as an *ad hoc* discipline, devised in the late nineteenth century for the purpose of accommodating the lower middle class to prevailing values. Reynolds and his ilk would never fit into such a program. Interest in them has revived in recent years, but mainly on account of the sociological value that accrues, as Ashbee and the Pompeiian cataloguers knew, to anything if it remains in existence long enough.[29] In their own time, though their vast circulation was vaguely known, only alarmists like Sanger paid attention to them—until, about 1860, a curious and alarming role reversal began to show itself. Under the leadership of Wilkie Collins and Mary Elizabeth Braddon, the respectable novel was being invaded by subjects and techniques that, prior to the 1860s, had been the property of Reynolds and his fellow hacks. This new brand of fiction went by the name "sensationalism"; to many observers, it reflected both the degradation of public taste and the general leveling of culture brought about by advancing literacy and affluence. The furor over "sensation novels," which raged from 1860 till about 1875, formed a sort of curtain raiser for the more violent controversies about "pornography" that would occupy the following decades.

During most of the nineteenth century—from Sir Walter Scott's *Kenilworth* in 1821 until, ironically, Braddon's own *Sons of Fire* in

1895—the English novel market was dominated by the artificial standard of three volumes at 31s.6d. The price was cheaper than that of exotics like *Verbena House*, but still beyond the reach of most middle-class readers, not to mention those below them. Cheaper reprints of the more successful titles were issued after a suitable interval—rather like the sequence of hardbound and paperback today—and a reader who desired to keep au courant could subscribe to circulating libraries like Mudie's, which exercised their own form of censorship.[30] Even the subscribers to Mudie's, however, had to pay a guinea a year for the privilege of reading current fiction. This fee, too, was prohibitive for the vast majority of potential readers, who contented themselves with penny-a-number shockers or else with no fiction at all. The advent of the "sensation novel" did nothing to upset these economic barriers, but it seemed to offer distressing evidence that, under the confusing pressures of modern life, the respectable public was adopting the crude tastes of the masses.

"The poor will enjoy themselves in their own way," commented an anonymous reviewer of "Penny Novels" in 1863;[31] his air of amused condescension was shared by other genteel writers, on the rare occasions when they glanced into the literary underworld. No such easy tolerance, however, went to higher-quality novelists like Florence Marryat, who were seen to be sliding toward "that Avernus of fiction which the penny novel may be taken to represent."[32] The link between the poorly understood realm of the penny dreadful and the new phenomenon of the sensation novel was plain to most observers, though they responded to it with differing degrees of outrage.

Among the most hysterical was William Thomson, Archbishop of York, who made himself briefly notorious by delivering a speech to the Huddersfield Church Institute, October 31, 1864, on the innocuous-seeming subject of "The Church's influence as a source of reading." Thomson characterized sensation novels as:

> tales which aimed at this effect simply of exciting in the mind some deep feeling of overwrought interest by the means of some terrible passion or crime. They went to persuade people that in

almost every one of the well-ordered houses of their neighbours there was a skeleton shut up in some cupboard; that their comfortable and cosy-looking neighbour had in his breast a secret story which he was always going about trying to conceal; that there was something about a real will registered in Doctors' commons and a false will that would at some proper moment tumble out of some broken bureau, and bring about the *dénouement* which the author wished to achieve.

The effect of such reading was dire:

> They taught them [workingmen] not to trust to appearances— that there was behind a great world of crime, wickedness, and misery to which they alone possessed the key. Now it was this claim to superior truth that gave them their first attraction; they satisfied a certain kind of spirit of inquiry. . . . This style of reading was thoroughly false and dangerous for another reason— on account of what he would call its fatalism. Always they would observe in this kind of fiction some great passion was supposed to take possession of a man; it was love, or jealousy, or what not, and it was enough to state that the man was stricken by this passion to be sure that his destruction was settled beforehand by the writer of the fiction, and that there was no possibility of escape. If he was not greatly mistaken, this tone had strongly reacted upon society itself, and in some of the great crimes perpetrated he seemed to see the influence of this kind of feeling.[33]

The vocabulary is different, but we can recognize in the Archbishop's apprehensions the same belief in the impact of fiction that would later support denunciations of pornography and the sensationalism of film and television.

Few commentators on sensationalism were as timid as Archbishop Thomson, though of course his fears applied to "workingmen," not sophisticated readers. A modern observer may wonder how anyone at all could have been corrupted by the works of Collins, Braddon, and company. For the most part, they are creaky melodramas, relying on bigamy and murder to advance their plots but hardly advocating those deeds as ways of spicing up real life. Yet the sensation novel was in fact subversive of good order. Lady Audley—founder of a populous race that soon came to be known as "sensation heroines"—is blonde, beautiful, and an ideal ornament for any drawing room. She is also an adulteress and an attempted murderess. Her "secret" (hereditary madness) exculpates her to some degree; she has also, however, been left in penury by an absconded husband, and when Sir Michael Audley woos her, only an idiot would refuse. *Lady Audley's Secret* does not exonerate its heroine—she dies raving in Belgium—but Lady Audley's example, if young ladies of 1862 had been inspired to follow it, would have spawned some remarkable upheavals.

Nothing so drastic happened: reality refused to imitate representations, despite the anxieties of those who felt it had no choice. In historical perspective, the impact of sensation novels has practically nothing to do with their content; what matters is that they were hastily written, sloppy, and brazenly imitative of one another—products of the printing press rather than the pen. Though these works came forth in the standard expensive format, they were "vulgar," a charge brought against them at least as often as that of immorality and hardly separable from it. Sensation novels were ephemeral, mass-produced articles, slapdash in construction because no one was expected to linger over them, all much alike because so long as steady appetite and supply endured, a new one could be picked up the moment the old was put down.

They were, that is, an early instance of the invasion of art by the leveling influences of technology, the loss—next to universal in the twentieth century—of what Walter Benjamin calls art's "privileged character."[34] Commenting on "Fiction Fair and Foul" in 1880, John Ruskin ascribed the corruption of contemporary fiction, which in his view extended far beyond the confines of "sensationalism," to the same urban influences that Wordsworth had indicted eight decades earlier: "the thoroughly trained Londoner can enjoy no other excitement than that to which he has been accustomed, but asks for *that* in continually more ardent or more virulent concentration; and the ultimate power of fiction to entertain him is by varying to his fancy the modes, and defining for his dulness the horrors, of Death."[35] Urbanization collaborated with advancing technology and literacy to produce, by the middle of the nineteenth century, a reading public very different from that for which any of our early pornographers wrote their books. It was an anonymous, amorphous public, in which distinctions of sex and class could no longer be relied upon to determine who would read what. It had no taste and no discretion; it liked its amusements strong, and it responded to them with infantile, brutal immediacy. Such, at least, was the image of this new public that haunted the imagination of authoritative commentators, however little it may have corresponded to reality. Dickens's Young Person and Archbishop Thomson's workingman were only two versions of the same bugaboo: a reader whom no one knew and who could not be trusted.

This reader's favorite opiate was novels, which he (especially she) devoured without regard for quality and moral effect. From its beginnings in the early eighteenth century, the novel had been the preeminent middle-class art form—though to call it "art" at that early date is anachronistic, since the novel's elevation to equal stature with poetry and painting did not occur until the middle of the Victorian age. Many early novelists took their craft seriously and expected great things of it; Henry Fielding's preface to *Joseph Andrews* (1742), in which he defines the novel as a "comic epic-poem in prose," is a famous case in point.[36] But for most commentators, and for a large proportion of the burgeoning reading public, novels remained a mere diversion. They were thought of as the pastime of a certain class of women and girls, mostly belonging to the urban bourgeoisie, whose newfound leisure and pretensions to gentility had liberated them from work and left them little to do but read. The classics were closed to them, and history and philosophy were too demanding. It was to this rapidly growing class that, during the first century of its existence, the novel was principally addressed. Despite the artistry of Fielding, Richardson, Jane Austen, and a few others, the novel would continue to be regarded as an inferior genre until the arrival of Sir Walter Scott.[37]

The chief difference between the novel and the poetry and prose romances which had preceded it was the novel's adherence to characters, settings, and events that resembled real life—that is, something similar to the reader's own experience. Aristocratic audiences might be pleased by farfetched allegories embellished with gorgeous turns of phrase, but middle-class readers preferred plainly told stories about people with whom they had something in common. In the nineteenth century, this adherence to the probable would acquire the title "realism" and spawn a series of legal and critical battles. Long before it was officially named, however, the novel's portrayal of life as the reader might live it was seen to be characteristic of the new genre and characteristically pleasing to its readership. Truth to life, admirable though it might be in theory, harbored dangers. Writing at the dawn of the English novel, in 1750, Samuel Johnson delivered a classic warning. "In the romances formerly written, every transaction and sentiment was so remote from all that passes among men, that the reader was in very little danger of making any applications to himself"; such confections might do no one any good, but they did no harm. The new "familiar histories," in contrast, brought their lessons directly home. Though their potential for good was enormous, the risk was even greater:

> But if the power of example is so great, as to take possession of the memory by a kind of violence, and produce effects almost without the intervention of the will, care ought to be taken, that when the choice is unrestrained, the best examples only should be exhibited; and that which is likely to operate so strongly, should not be mischievous or uncertain in its effects.

The novel possessed this "power" because it was "written chiefly to the young, the ignorant, and the idle"; Johnson did not specify who should be entrusted with regulating the power, though he seemed to impose that duty upon the novelists themselves. A century before the invention of "pornography," Johnson staked out the field where it would operate:

> It is justly considered as the greatest excellency of art, to imitate nature; but it is necessary to distinguish those parts of nature, which are most proper for imitation: greater care is still required

in representing life, which is so often discoloured by passion, or deformed by wickedness. If the world be promiscuously described, I cannot see of what use it can be to read the account; or why it may not be as safe to turn the eye immediately upon mankind as upon a mirror which shews all that presents itself without discrimination.[38]

Such arguments were stale even in 1750; in the last chapter, we saw their origins in Plato and Horace. What was new in Johnson's time, and would grow in intensity during the century after him, was the anxious, proprietary air taken by the custodians of public taste and morality. Johnson's reading public was extremely small; books were scarce and expensive, and the danger he diagnosed was slight. But if we move ahead a century, into an age when prostitution was publicized, obscene artifacts were catalogued, and erotic books were saved from destruction; if we add that, by then, virtually everyone could read whatever fell into his hands, with no guide to monitor his response; if we expand Johnson's class of young, ignorant, and idle readers to include practically the whole population—we can see how Dickens's Young Person came into being and why, fragile though she was, she terrified all her superiors.

Warnings of the Johnsonian kind are still being issued today, in a different vocabulary but with little change in their presuppositions. Nowadays, perhaps, they have grown a bit tiresome even to those who accept them on principle; but in the century after Johnson, what is most striking about these alarms is their increasing desperation, as if, perversely, each announcement of danger only made the danger more acute. In 1791, for example, the Reverend Edward Barry virtually echoed Johnson in his *Theological, Philosophical, and Moral Essays;* everything is the same, except for Barry's luridness:

Among the many incentives to seduction, that of novel reading most assuredly ranks as one; not but flowers may sometimes be selected—but weeds, pernicious fatal weeds, too often choak up the garden;—the greater part of such writings are studiously contrived to interest, to agitate, and to convulse the passions, already but too prone, by a sympathy of sentiment, to lead the mind astray. The very mummery of tale, which *swindled* tears from the eyes, and transport from the heart, which gave sensations it could not relieve, has left a train of gunpowder in the soul, and in such a posture, that one chance spark of fire might be sufficient to blow up reputation, and make a bankrupt of virtue. Obscene books and prints create and inflame, in no small degree, impure desires. . . .[39]

Sixty years later, Dr. Sanger would make Reverend Barry sound calm; but even Sanger seems levelheaded next to this outcry of 1888:

The only acquaintance which the writer of this article has with Zola's novels is from two pages of one of the most notorious of them placed open in the window of a well-known bookseller in the City of London. The matter was of such a leprous character that it would be impossible for any young man who had not learned the Divine secret of self-control to have read it without committing some form of outward sin within twenty-four hours after. In this case a boy, apparently about fourteen years old, was reading the book. The writer immediately went into the shop, and accosting the manager in a loud voice, demanded that he should "step outside and see this boy reading this infernal book in your window." The shop was full of customers, and the manager naturally looked thunder-struck. Half-an-hour afterwards, when the writer passed, the book was gone.[40]

The infernal book was probably a censored translation of Zola's *La Terre* ("Earth"); the anonymous "writer of this article" published his championship of virtue in the *London Sentinel* and was quoted by Samuel Smith of Flintshire in the House of Commons. The parliamentary debate, spurred by the efforts of the National Vigilance Association, led the following year to the trial and imprisonment of Henry Vizetelly, whose firm had published the offending translation.

The career of the Young Person was a glorious one. She made her debut as early as 1692, when a writer for the *Athenian Mercury* warned against "the softening of the Mind by Love" and advised that "Young People wou'd do better, either not to read 'em [romances] at all, or to use 'em more sparingly than they generally do, when once they set about 'em."[41] She attained her apotheosis (by then "she" was also "he") in the hysteria over masturbation that followed the same curve as that of concern with the dangers of realistic fiction. According to its most recent historian, the literature of masturbation began about 1710, with the English *Onania, or the Heinous Sin of Self-Pollution;*[42] it obtained its classic embodiment in Samuel-Auguste-André-David Tissot's *L'Onanisme, Dissertation sur les Maladies produites par la Masturbation* ("Onanism: Essay on the Ailments Produced by Masturbation"), first published in 1758 and innumerably reprinted. Relying heavily on *Onania*, Tissot also drew on the ancient theory of the humors, bodily fluids that since Galen had been supposed to govern everything from excretion to thinking. Semen was not one of the traditional humors, but Tissot promoted it to that status in a ghastly passage:

> A robust wet-nurse, who would be killed by extracting several pints of blood from her in a twenty-four hour period, can provide the same amount of milk to her child four or five hundred days in a row without apparent discomfort, because of all the humors, milk is the least laborious to produce. Furthermore, it is almost a foreign humor, while blood is an essential one. There is another essential humor, seminal liquid, which so strongly influences bodily powers and the perfection of the assimilative processes maintaining them that Doctors through the centuries have unanimously believed that to lose one ounce of this humor would be more debilitating than to lose forty ounces of blood.[43]

To masturbate meant, according to a clear if barbaric logic, to waste this precious fluid, along with the energy expended in orgasm. Performed in childhood, masturbation rechanneled the life force that should have gone toward healthy physical and mental development. Its result was weak, sickly, and impotent adults.

The economic metaphor was plausible enough when applied to boys, especially if one believed—as Tissot apparently did not, though the myth was widespread—that the male was allotted a predetermined number of ejaculations in his lifetime. It worked less well for girls, yet Tissot found that the damage wrought by female masturbation was even more severe. In boys, the most common effects of masturbation (and the signs by which watchful parents could recognize indulgence in this secret vice) were disturbance of the stomach, weakening of the lungs, slackening of the nervous system, and "monstrous enfeeblement of the organs of generation."[44] In girls and women, however, these afflictions were joined by a horrifying list of specifically female complaints:

> Besides all the symptoms I have already reported, women are particularly liable to attacks of hysteria or frightful vapors; incurable jaundice; cruel cramps in the stomach and back; sharp pains in the nose; acrid white discharges [leukorrhea], a continual source of bitter pain; falling and ulceration of the womb, along with all the disabilities produced by these two ailments; lengthening and scabbing of the clitoris; and finally to uterine fury, which deprives them at once of modesty and reason and puts them on the level of the lewdest brutes, until a despairing death snatches them away from pain and infamy.[45]

Tissot obtained much of his information from *Onania*, but he claimed to have observed at least some of these dire effects himself. He might also have observed (he does not say) the "spending" of women in orgasm, a myth so attractive to male commentators that the author of *My Secret Life* recorded witnessing it at close range dozens of times.[46]

Even if women were assumed to "spend," however, and were therefore subject to the same physical economics as men, the symptoms of female masturbation entailed some provocative differences. Decay, madness, and eventual death came to both sexes; but while men were thought simply to drain away, like a cask that has sprung a leak, masturbating women picked up new vitality on the way to the grave. The pain and ugliness that Tissot attached to the white discharges and lengthened clitoris of the female masturbator do not disguise the resemblance of these sick attributes to healthy symptoms of being male. It is as if, by spending sexual energy in her own behalf, a woman endeavored to become a man; her own body punished her accordingly. The penultimate state of the autoerotic woman—"uterine fury" (*fureurs utérines*); the phrase is first recorded in English in 1728—was more like a crescendo than a tailing off. While impotence identified the masturbating male, his female counterpart experienced an access of power so tremendous that it shattered all restraints. Just before she died, she became indistinguishable from the stereotypical prostitute, with the significant difference that her only client was herself. Both the prostitute and the masturbating woman took resources that might have been profitably invested— in children and the maintenance of a home—and spilt them, adding to the poisonous effluvia of modernity that alarmed Parent and his followers. But while the prostitute was "on the town" (in Victorian parlance both English and American) or a *fille publique* (as the French said), the masturbating woman endangered no one with disease or depravity. She was not contagious; her force did not dissipate, it consolidated.[47]

Tissot's little book was tremendously influential for at least a century after it was published; not all authorities agreed with him, but he was cited as definitive as late as 1870, and he set the tone for discussions of his subject well into the modern era. During a "half-century of terrorism," as Peter Gay calls it,[48] from about 1850 to 1900, Tissot's old warnings were heeded with a violence that probably would have appalled him, as it does any modern observer. Penile rings for little boys—spiked on the inside, to insure pain, even bloodshed, if the penis swelled during sleep—were on sale around the turn of the twentieth century, though they were no doubt advertised much more widely than they were used. When all else failed, girls were sometimes subjected to clitoridectomy,[49] a measure which, in addition to its sickening cruelty, indicates the extremes to which males felt themselves driven when their purpose was the emasculation of the female.

Mutilation of children's bodies was rare, and even during the heyday of masturbatory hysteria, terror among adults was far from universal. Yet the fact of its occurrence, and of its close coincidence with the earliest controversies over "pornography," suggests that the Young Person, though she was called a waif in need of protection, actually was the opposite—a frightening dynamo, anarchic and profligate in her actions, opportunistically spilling over every dam erected by male hegemony, seeking not the advancement of civilization but its dispersal, reversion to chaos, the origin, a time without structure. Weirdly overdetermined, she condensed into a single image the inchoate energies latent in women, children, and the vague conglomerate known as "the poor"—the three adversaries that "pornography" was invented to hold at bay. The matter was not so simple, however, as the oppression of these groups by a privileged minority. No doubt they were oppressed, but then they always had been; what was new in the nineteenth century was the discovery of unprecedented ways in which they threatened their oppressors. As far as pornography is concerned, the threat was perceived principally in sexual terms; yet "sex" itself was an image, a vivid substitute for other dangers that, barely perceived in any case, could not be so readily represented.

At bottom, the issue was and remains political, if we take the word in its broadest sense to designate all the relations of power and the lack of it that govern human beings in their living together. The apparently disparate developments we have considered so far—accelerating urbanization, literacy, and availability of books and pictures; preservation of the past in museums and libraries; advancing gentility, as more and more people laid claim to freedom of choice; not least the swelling urge to tabulate and therefore regulate whatever existed or might come to be—cast a bewildering maze of shadows. The blackest of them was the Young Person, black because she was so very white, depraved on account of her innocence, displaying the fearsome ability to ignore mutual exclusion which, just a generation after Dickens devised her, Freud would attribute to the unconscious. She never lived, of course; no actual person exactly embodied her. Yet phantom though she was, she had greater impact and aroused more furious discussion than any merely living being could achieve.

It was the novel that excited the strongest fears for (or of) the Young Person. The novel was the universal entertainment of its day, accessible to both sexes and all classes, bearing none of the built-in barriers that restricted the circulation of other potentially harmful books. As book prices declined and literacy advanced, the possible audience for any novel came close to equaling the entire population—most of which was composed of Young Persons in one guise or another. In the mid-1870s, Anthony Trollope bragged that, in England, novels were being read "right and left, above stairs and below, in town houses and in country parsonages, by young countesses and by farmer's daughters, by old lawyers and by young students." Many of these novels were Trollope's, and he took pride in their ubiquity. But he also recognized the power and the risk:

> If such be the case—if the extension of novel-reading be so wide as I have described it—then very much good or harm must be done by novels. The amusement of the time can hardly be the only result of any book that is read, and certainly not so with a novel, which appeals especially to the imagination, and solicits the sympathy of the young. A vast proportion of the teaching of the day,—greater probably than many of us have as yet acknowledged to ourselves,—comes from these books, which are in the hands of all readers.[50]

Trollope was confident about the beneficial effects of reading novels, especially his own, but others who witnessed the same phenomenon were less sanguine. They feared that the habit of private imaginative stimulation—not very different from masturbation and possibly leading to it—would cause the Young Person to forget that reality and fiction were not the same.

Then as now, the structure of the fear, the knee-jerk scenario it conjured up, stood firm in the virtual absence of evidence that such responses ever in fact occurred. Like the horrors wrought by masturbation, the pernicious effects of fiction required no witnesses; they simply *had* to be real, because they were so fervently wished for. Now and then, a case did arise in which some real-life crime was said by the perpetrator to have been inspired by fiction. Rare as these events were, they won huge publicity, as if the exception itself made the rule. A provocative case was that of sixteen-year-old Angélina Lemoine, who was tried (and acquitted) at Paris in 1859 for the murder of her illegitimate child, sired by the family coachman. Questioned on her reading, Angélina admitted that she had been allowed access to "the serialized novels in her mother's newspapers," along with many other novels, including George Sand's. These fictions had apparently made her discontented with the dullness of her existence; illicit sex (across class boundaries, too) had been her way of fictionalizing real life, and pregnancy was "the only way to complete my novel."[51]

Wish fulfillments like Angélina's served also to fulfill the wish of scandalized observers that fiction should be so powerful, and the Young Person so pliant. The scarcity of such direct imitation did not deter commentators from invoking its necessity; the insistence that fiction could be of good effect led automatically to the recognition that it might just as easily produce evil. Ideally, the novelist's discretion should have been reliable. It should have been, in Trollope's words, "a matter of deep conscience," calling for scrupulous self-restraint:

> The regions of absolute vice are foul and odious. The savour of them, till custom has hardened the palate and the nose, is disgusting. In these he will hardly tread. But there are outskirts on these regions, on which sweet-smelling flowers seem to grow, and grass to be green. It is in these border-lands that the danger lies. The novelist may not be dull. If he commit that fault he can do neither harm nor good. He must please, and the flowers and the grass in these neutral territories sometimes seem to give him so easy an opportunity of pleasing![52]

On the whole, until the last quarter of the nineteenth century, the English and American novel exercised this form of precensorship.

In France, however, they managed things differently. Both at home and overseas in translation, it was the French novel that first announced its refusal to be governed by care for the Young Person's welfare. Increasingly as the century advanced, novelists everywhere pursued other goals—the demands of their art or the allure of hitherto unexplored subjects—which drew them not only into Trollope's "border-lands" but even into the "regions of absolute vice." With the collapse of external restraints, this novelistic rebelliousness generated a crisis: if everyone was reading novels, and if novelists no longer cared what harm they did, the only recourse was to haul books into court.

CHAPTER FOUR

TRIALS
OF THE WORD

THERE HAS BEEN CENSORSHIP as long as there have been signs and representations. At no time in human history has the power to portray the world in words or pictures been granted unrestricted exercise; some contrary power has always grappled with it, endeavoring to set limits on what may be displayed to whom. By comparison with other forms of censorship, campaigns against "pornography" have been distinguished by their relative innocuousness and ineffectuality: paper has been burned by the ton, but few bodies have been broken; and works decried as "pornographic" one day have very often—with a rhythm peculiar to this subspecies of censorship—been proclaimed masterpieces the next. Today, in the postpornographic era, efforts to censor pornography no longer seem to resemble programs of political or religious censorship. The latter have climbed to ever higher levels of cruelty and thoroughness, while the former dwindle away to protest marches and instantly unconstitutional municipal ordinances. Yet censorship has the same nature no matter in whose name it is invoked or by what means it moves. Once "pornography" was labeled and its threat identified, the methods employed to control it were borrowed unchanged from the long tradition of political and religious persecution that preceded "pornography" and outlives it.

In the fourth century B.C., Socrates was condemned to death for corrupting the youth of Athens; in the first century A.D., Ovid was exiled from Rome for offending Caesar Augustus; in the fourteenth century, the Albigensians were purged from southern France.[1] These instances of pre-pornographic censorship (hundreds of others could be cited) all followed the same pattern: dangerous thoughts were suppressed by action against both words and flesh. Before the invention of the printing press, the speaker and his speech were so nearly allied that to dispose of the one was the directest way of silencing the other. After the invention of movable type in the mid-fifteenth century, an astonishing explosion of print—perhaps twenty million books were produced in Europe between 1450 and 1500[2]—made the alliance immediately obsolete, though the old procedure continued to be followed, as it does today. Futility, however, was already guaranteed five hundred years ago. Once printed, a writer's words acquired a life independent of his and much larger; only neglect can kill a printed book. Then as now, the fact that censorship has been attempted is sufficient to insure that the censored thing will survive.

The first figure to take advantage of this fact was Martin Luther, who had he been born two centuries earlier, would have followed the Albigensians into oblivion. But Luther lived in the new age of print: his protesting Theses, posted on the door of the Augustinian chapel at Wittenberg on October 31, 1517, were quickly translated from Latin into German and disseminated; within fifteen days, the whole country knew of them.[3] In a sense, Luther made himself the first media personality; along with his words, images of his face—most copied from engravings by his friend Lucas Cranach the Elder—traveled far beyond the range his body could have reached, spreading the message.[4] At about the same time, enterprising hacks like Aretino were able to employ similar tactics in the interest of self-aggrandizement. In John Addington Symonds's jaundiced opinion, Aretino attained what notoriety and influence he had in sixteenth-century Italy because his "acute common sense enabled him to comprehend the power of the press, which had not as yet been deliberately used as a weapon of offence and an instrument of extortion."[5] Though their aims were utterly different, both Luther and Aretino realized that the new medium of print gave a writer's words immunity to all old forms of censorship. Even if the writer himself should die, his words would continue.

The most striking fact about official censorship, at least until the end of the eighteenth century, was its clumsiness. Much more effective than the efforts of any governmental or religious agency were private acts like Pepys's destruction of *L'Ecole des Filles*. Such individual acts virtually wiped Aretino's Postures from the face of the earth; the presence of his *opera omnia* on the Roman Catholic *Index* only sold more copies. Prior to the eighteenth century, no distinction was made between books banned for their political or religious content and those prohibited on moral grounds. Speaking of this earlier period, one would be incorrect to separate the realms of the political, the religious, and the moral in any schematic way: politics and religion ran together, since the interests of the church were often, officially or not, those of the state; and morality, public and private, belonged under both jurisdictions. Insofar as obscenity attracted the attention of censors, it usually did so in tandem with abusive polemic. This was the proper place of gross sexual reference for the Greeks and Romans; it remained there until the Victorians, sifting out "the sexual" from other modes of being, sought to identify in "pornography" an object worthy of censorship but free of obvious political or religious power.

The three concerns were still closely linked in 1763, when John Wilkes's indictment for seditious libel led immediately to an indictment for obscenity as well. Wilkes (1727–97), a gentleman, Member of Parliament, and something of a rake, attracted governmental censure first for his radical paper the *North Briton*, in number 45 of which, carried away by rhetoric against the King's ministers, he called George III a liar. A search of his home, where on his private press he was printing a collected edition of the *North Briton*, brought a second indictable discovery—*An Essay on Woman*, a lame, unfinished, obscene parody of Pope's *Essay on Man*. In customary eighteenth-century fashion, a blizzard of charges and counter-charges ensued, blurring the facts forever. Wilkes probably wrote only part of the poem; his printer had probably been bribed; the search was illegal in any case. Nevertheless, the Earl of Sandwich read the poem before a no doubt bemused House of Lords, while the Reverend John Kidgell gave the public a full account of it in his piously prurient pamphlet *A Genuine and Succinct Narrative of a Scandalous, Obscene and Exceedingly Profane Libel, Entitled, An Essay on Woman*. Expelled from the House of Commons, Wilkes fled to France; he returned in 1768, was reelected to Parliament, and remained embroiled in public controversy till the end of his life.

Wilkes's defense against the obscenity charge is provocative because it hinged on the question of what constituted publication, as differentiated from private amusement. The anonymous *Letter to J. Kidgell* (probably written by Wilkes's friend John Almon[6]) maintained that Wilkes was innocent on this count, because he had given strict orders that *"the public was never to see"* the obscene products of his leisure.[7] Wilkes insisted that the proof sheet had been stolen, and that in fact Kidgell and his Tory cohorts had "published" *An Essay on Woman*, "for the sheet *seems* to have gone backwards and forwards, from hand to hand; which by the strict letter of the law is called *publication*."[8] The poem had presumably circulated in manuscript before any attempt to print it; that custom dated back centuries, for obscene and respectable works alike. In the eyes of Wilkes's opponents, however, the very existence of printed copies (though supposedly never more than twelve) made a qualitative difference. Wilkes's defense failed; *An Essay on Woman*, finished or in proof, had been published and therefore joined sedition and blasphemy as a matter of public debate.

Only a few years earlier, a book had appeared which, even by modern standards, indubitably was "published." The first volume of John Cleland's *Memoirs of a Woman of Pleasure* was advertised in November 1748; the second was on sale in March of the following year, and by November, at least sixty sets (at sixpence each) had been sold.[9] Posterity would come to know the novel as *Fanny Hill* and would still be putting it on trial more than two hundred years later. In its own time, however, the most remarkable thing about Cleland's novel was what a small fuss it raised. This staple of the pornographic "pharmacopoeia," which the author of *My Secret Life* would haul down from the shelf as if it were a patented aphrodisiac,[10] whose title would become virtually synonymous with "pornography," passed through eighteenth-century bookshops almost unnoticed. Complaints were lodged against Cleland, and he was required to give an account of himself to the Secretary of State's office; nothing more seems to have been done, however, perhaps because Cleland disowned the novel, pleaded the distress of a gentleman fallen on hard times, and added a caveat that in retrospect looks prescient: "My Lords the Bishops . . . can take no step towards punishing the Author that will not powerfully contribute to the notoriety of the Book, and spread what they cannot wish supprest more than I do."[11] By the time of the official inquiry—made more than eight months after the completed work had first been advertised—an expurgated version was already available. Oddly, though copies of the unexpurgated text survive, the abridgment seems to have been lost.[12]

The contrast between the contemporary notoriety of Wilkes's poem—now practically forgotten—and the obscurity of Cleland's novel—still widely read as a "classic" of pornography—suggests not only that the past submits to constant revision by the present, but also that neither Cleland nor his book possessed sufficient political prominence to elicit censure from the authorities. England would not acquire a statute directed specifically against obscenity until the Obscene Publications Act of 1857; before then, though obscenity was indicted often enough, it remained subordinate to the other offenses that more forcefully attracted public attention. In 1787, George III issued a royal Proclamation urging his subjects to suppress "all loose and licentious Prints, Books, and Publications, dispensing Poison to the Minds of the Young and Unwary, and to punish the Publishers and Vendors thereof";[13] policing, however, continued to be carried on by private agencies like William Wilberforce's Proclamation Society, later superseded by the Society for the Suppression of Vice, founded in 1802. Between that date and 1857, the Society instituted 159 prosecutions, all but five of which ended in conviction.[14] These were small-scale efforts, which attracted little notice and evidently had small effect, despite their high rate of success. One reason was that although individuals could be prosecuted for displaying obscene material in public places, before 1857 the courts had no legal power to order the destruction of those materials.

Censorship was much more effectively exercised upon theatrical performances than upon books and prints. For over two hundred years, from the passage of the Stage Licensing Act in 1737 till its repeal in 1968, British theaters were required to obtain the approval of the Lord Chamberlain's office for any play they intended to produce, in advance of production. There is no doubt that the licensing of plays had a crippling effect on British drama in the eighteenth and nineteenth centuries. In a modern critic's words, the "censors' defense of the social order evolved at the expense of the drama," depriving it of "personal or social satire, of participation in religious or moral debate, and, above all, of engagement in political controversy."[15] The operations of the Examiner's office also illustrate, by contrast, how clumsy and confused campaigns against "pornography" were, even after legislation had been passed to support them. For two centuries, the licensing of plays functioned quietly, smoothly, and, until very late in its existence, without determined opposition. The policing of obscenity, meanwhile, began in haphazardness and developed into chaos; at no point did it fail to meet resistance, usually just as muddleheaded as the efforts of censorship themselves. The adoption of the term "pornography" to designate morally censorable material did nothing to remedy the confusion; indeed, legal discussions of pornography fell at once into a monotonous routine of haggling about what "pornography" was supposed to mean.

In France, the course of censorship was even more erratic than in England; it depended on the disposition of the monarch and his ministers, and underwent total suspension (theoretically, at least) in the libertarian phase of the Revolution. Rigor was restored under Napoleon's First Empire, but to English and American eyes, French rigor continued to seem indistinguishable from license. This prejudice, not quite extinct yet, was endemic and had no necessary correspondence to reality; it is true, however, that from a very early date, French art and literature displayed a freedom of sexual reference unmatched in English. François Rabelais (ca. 1494–1553) practiced a thoroughly traditional, though unusually vigorous blend of scatology and satire in his *Gargantua and Pantagruel* (1532–52), parts of which were condemned by the Sorbonne on their first publication. Sir Thomas Urquhart (1611–60) translated the first three of Rabelais' five books into racy, idiomatic English; Peter Anthony Motteux completed the project in 1693–94, and for three centuries thereafter, until the appearance of W. F. Smith's scholarly, annotated edition in 1893, *Gargantua* in quaint English or quainter French endured as a semi-respectable classic. It was old and strange enough, couched in sufficiently bizarre late-medieval terms, to leave the Young Person cold. But it was also unrestrained in its obsession with bodily functions, making it the kind of book an adult male might read without reproach only if he took certain precautions. Rabelais in this special context was so familiar to the English public of 1855 that Anthony Trollope could portray Archdeacon Grantly, on a dull weekday morning, postponing the composition of Sunday's sermon to lock his study door, take "from a secret drawer beneath his table a volume of Rabelais," and amuse himself with "the witty mischief of Panurge."[16] The adjective "Rabelaisian" is first recorded in English in 1857, but the sense of it was no doubt in oral circulation long before that.

Above and beyond such underground books as *L'Ecole des Filles*, works like the Abbé Prévost's *Manon Lescault* (1731) and Choderlos de Laclos's *Liaisons dangereuses* (1782) inured English readers to the idea that anything written in French—especially "French novels"—was suspect. A literature that could canonize the history of a prostitute written by an ecclesiastic, along with a manual of seduction by one who wrote from firsthand knowledge, was clearly very un-English. Syphilis had been known as "the French pox" as early as the sixteenth century (the French retaliated with *le vice anglais*, flagellation), but this ancient national stereotype took on a powerfully political tone in the wake of the Revolution of 1789 and the decades of turmoil that followed. From a British point of view, radical political opinions went hand in hand with a fondness for things French, especially French fiction. The pairing remained close throughout the nineteenth century and may help to account for the tardiness with which the masterpieces of French realism were translated into English. In Balzac's case particularly, hostility arose from what one modern commentator calls "the fear of seeing take place in England what had already taken place in France"—revolution.[17] Though there might not seem to be anything politically inflammatory about the fiction of Balzac and his realist successors, inflammation of all kinds was to be withheld from the British reader. French literature was damned first of all on moral grounds; but below the surface of moral outrage—and usually not very far below—political anxiety lurked.

In France itself, they managed things differently; they hardly managed them at all. Among the worst horrors spawned by the Revolution were the works of Donatien-Alphonse-François, Marquis de Sade (1740–1815), whose crazy career well illustrates the contrast between French censorship and its English counterpart. Sade turned to writing as a serious occupation only in his forties, in 1782, when he had already been in prison for nearly four years on account of crimes that, a century later, would acquire the label "sadistic." As imprisonment would also do for Genet in the twentieth century, it gave Sade the isolation his peculiar genius required; without reserve, he was able to vent his anger against God, the state, womankind, his relatives—all the forces which had sent him to prison in the first place. After completing his "atheistic credo," the *Dialogue between a Priest and a Dying Man*,[18] Sade moved on to his pornotopian epic, *The 120 Days of Sodom*, on which he was still making notes three years later. By then transferred from Vincennes to the Bastille, Sade set to work with amazing speed and regularity, revising his notes into a narrative and inscribing it on strips of thin paper barely five inches wide, pasted together at the ends to form a scroll almost forty feet long. He worked three hours a night for more than a month, covering both sides of the scroll with tiny, meticulous handwriting. But, ironically, the liberation of the Bastille in July 1789 resulted in the loss of Sade's masterpiece. Convinced that the manuscript had been destroyed, he spent the rest of his writing career, in *Justine* (1791/97), *Juliette* (1797), *The Crimes of Love* (1800), and numerous other works, attempting "to reconstitute, in one form or another, the elements he had expounded in *The 120 Days of Sodom*."[19] In fact, however (though Sade would never know this), the *Sodom* scroll had been recovered from his cell by a certain Arnoux de Saint-Maximin, through whom it passed into the estate of the Villeneuve-Trans family. In the 1930s, nearly a century and a half after Sade lost it, *The 120 Days of Sodom* was published.[20]

Sade went to the grave in ignorance, but rumors that his magnum opus survived were in circulation throughout the nineteenth century. Ashbee, for example, who had not himself seen the strange manuscript, gave an accurate account of its appearance as reported to him by "two gentlemen."[21] Accident and reticence suppressed *Sodom;* Sade's other works, however, despite their "crapulous" character, went through numerous editions in Sade's lifetime and after. The 1791 edition of *Justine* was reprinted six more times in the subsequent decade alone—always at Paris, though the title pages claim a variety of other origins, from London to "Philadelphie."[22] Sade appears to have gained no profit from these clandestine publications, none of which bore his name; indeed, afraid of prosecution, he consistently and vehemently denied that he had written either *Justine* or its sequel, *Juliette*, which were nevertheless universally attributed to him. It is likely that Sade's final imprisonment—at Sainte-Pélagie, later in the madhouse of Charenton, where he died—was at least in part motivated by his supposed authorship of the libelous pamphlet *Zoloë et ses deux acolytes* (1800), in which Napoleon and Josephine, along with practically every other eminent figure of the day, were ridiculed.[23]

Sade was never prosecuted as a pornographer. Strictly speaking, he hardly could have been: in his time, the word *pornographer* was available only in the honorific sense invented and jealously guarded by his archenemy Restif. But Sade's greatest outrage was his fusion of religion, politics, and sex into a single, absolute ethic of transgression—an achievement recognized, however dimly, by his contemporaries as well as by those twentieth-century commentators, mostly French, who have revered him as the prophet of our disorder. No one has ever condemned Sade's books chiefly as a source of lascivious excitation; they are literally too extreme, in all directions, for that rather mild rebuke. Instead, they won him a reputation as the epitome of evil, evil so profound and pervasive that it wiped out all boundaries. That reputation, which persists, has little to do with Sade's deeds; in life, the original sadist was fairly innocuous by any standards, and certainly by those of his time and station. In imagination, however, the imprisoned author was at liberty to imagine the inversion of all values, sexual and other, that govern civilized behavior; not only that, he fervently advocated their inversion. Sade's books are uniformly, unrelentingly, stupefyingly didactic: their subtitles, from *Sodom*'s "School of Libertinism" (possibly a glance at *L'Ecole des Filles* and Aretino's instructive dialogues) through those of *Justine* and *Juliette* (respectively "The Misfortunes of Virtue" and "The Fortunes of Vice"), unmistakably declare that these works are not mere entertainments but handbooks—for young persons and adult males alike.

The following of Sade's instructions might lead to either anarchy or fascism; opinions differ. In any case, the complete overthrow of the existing order would ensue if Sade's program were carried out. It is this necessity which makes Sade dangerous, even now. And it can hardly be an accident that, just as the first movements were being made toward isolating "sex" as a zone apart from religion and politics, a writer arose who emphatically proclaimed the identity of the three, even employing the new one, "sex," as the detonator of the other two. Nor is it accidental that Sade chose what he was pleased to call the "novel" to convey his apocalyptic message. In "Reflections on the Novel," prefixed to the 1800 edition of *The Crimes of Love*, Sade invoked Lovelace's rape of Clarissa and her subsequent death—the least happy of endings—to point a prescient moral:

'Tis therefore Nature that must be seized when one labors in the field of fiction, 'tis the heart of man, the most remarkable of her works, and in no wise virtue, because virtue, however becoming, however necessary it may be, is yet but one of the many facets of this amazing heart, whereof the profound study is so necessary to the novelist, and the novel, the faithful mirror of this heart, must perforce explore its every fold.[24]

Novelistic "realism" would not be propounded until more than half a century had passed, and Trollope's warning against the temptation to tread upon "regions of absolute vice" would be issued a generation later yet. The gauntlet, however, had already been thrown down.

Everything about Sade's works was so offensive that his challenge to the limits of the novel—a small matter by comparison—was easily overlooked. The French conception of where those limits lay, though certainly laxer than the English, was nevertheless rigid enough; it was embodied in a law of 1819 condemning "outrages to public and religious morals and to good manners."[25] The imprecision of this language allowed the law to be enforced in the most "vacillating and arbitrary" fashion, especially under Napoleon III's Second Empire (1852–70). The licensing of plays, suspended since the Revolution, had been reestablished in 1850, with the direct purpose, even more obviously than in England, of silencing those who would criticize the current régime. Press censorship, too, was widely exercised, though in such a "ludicrously fumbling and ineffective" manner that it was hardly perceived as a threat. In surprising contrast to England, where philistinism was first diagnosed and supposedly most at home, the prevailing public attitude in mid-nineteenth-century France was uniformly hostile to all forms of unorthodoxy; the "innovating artist," as a modern historian has remarked, "was as great a danger to society as the faithless wife or the socialist working man."[26]

The stifling atmosphere of Second Empire France spawned the first reasonably coherent school of artists and writers to obtain a feeling of solidarity from its deliberate opposition to ruling social values. These were the practitioners of "realism"—another new word, to both French and English, in the early 1850s.[27] The reluctant, reticent head of the school was Gustave Flaubert (1821–80), who had that honor thrust upon him thanks to both the nature of his work and the distinction granted his first published novel,

Madame Bovary, when it was put on trial in 1857 for outrages to public morality and religion. The trial of *Madame Bovary* is of prime significance in the history of "pornography," although that word, still rather specialized and not yet wholly pejorative, was nowhere used in it. In about equal measure, the prosecution and the defense set the tone for all the trials of pornography that would be staged in the subsequent century. Indeed, it is quite remarkable—and either curious or depressing, according to one's point of view— how thoroughly Flaubert's trial prefigured what was to come. Either it was an extraordinary omen, or else history has been stupidly refusing to learn from itself for more than a hundred years.

Flaubert began work on *Madame Bovary* in 1851, but the first installment did not appear in print till October 1, 1856, in his friend Maxime DuCamp's *Revue de Paris*. Flaubert's extreme meticulousness has become legendary; he devoted himself with near-maniacal fervor to finding exactly the right word for every context, sometimes spending days on the composition of a single paragraph. It must have come as a shock, after five years of such labor, to receive from DuCamp a chatty, breezy letter advising that Flaubert should allow DuCamp and his staff to make some judicious cuts: "You have buried your novel under a heap of details which are well done but superfluous: it is not seen clearly enough, and must be disencumbered—an easy task." After scrawling "Gigantesque!" on Du-Camp's letter, Flaubert responded, refusing to allow any changes whatever. Negotiations ensued, the end result of which was that Flaubert's language would be left alone, but that a single passage near the end of the novel (about a page and a half in modern editions) would be entirely excised. The passage—Emma's extended liaison with Léon behind the closed curtains of a meandering cab—was "impossible" according to DuCamp, and Flaubert grudgingly agreed to let it go.[28] But the novelist can hardly have been prepared for the editorial note prefixed to the installment of December 1, in which the offending cab ride would otherwise have occurred: "Here the editors found it necessary to suppress a passage unsuitable to the policies of the *Revue de Paris;* we hereby acknowledge this to the author."[29]

Flaubert had expected the cut, though not the disclaimer or the request that further cuts be permitted in the sixth and final installment, scheduled for mid-December. First he threatened to halt publication, then to take the *Revue* to court; eventually, he consented to censorship, but with a note of his own: "Considerations which it is not in my province to judge compelled the *Revue de Paris* to omit a passage from the issue of December 1; its scruples having been again aroused on the occasion of the present issue, it has thought proper to omit several more. Consequently, I hereby decline responsibility for the lines which follow. The reader is asked to consider them as a series of fragments, not as a whole."[30] Governmental action against *Madame Bovary* had already begun in November, thanks in part to complaints by readers but also to the over-liberal cast of the *Revue*, which had received warnings before. As late as December 31, Flaubert wrote to Edmond Pagnerre: "I am a pretext. The government is out to destroy the *Revue de Paris*, and I have been chosen as its instrument."[31] Whatever the actual motive, the case of *Madame Bovary* came to trial on January 29, 1857, planting a milestone along the road that would lead from the neglectful silence of the past to the noisy confusion of the future.

Court proceedings were conducted with great formality: a statement by the Imperial Advocate, Ernest Pinard, then a counterstatement (four hours long) by the defense attorney, Antoine-Marie-Jules Sénard. Though it was completed in a single day, the debate managed to touch on every issue that the next century would argue about. Admitting that the language of the 1819 law was "a little vague, a little elastic,"[32] Pinard went on to explain the prosecution's peculiar difficulty. To read the whole novel aloud to the jury would be impracticable, but to read only the "accused passages" would make him liable to the charge of stifling debate by restricting the range of discussion. Pinard proposed an equally peculiar solution to this problem: he would first "tell the whole novel without reading it," then the accused passages; this, presumably, would put them in context. Frequently reminding the jury that "I am telling the story, not quoting," Pinard proceeded to spin out a hodgepodge of paraphrase and interpretation. As he wobbled uncertainly between the present tense and the past—between reporting the events as fictional and reporting them as real—he subtly transformed *Madame Bovary* into the story he wished it to be, the story it might have been under some other treatment than Flaubert's. "The lovers reach the farthest limits of sensual delight!" he cried at one point—just the sort of bombast Emma herself has read in the pulp romances that prepare the way for her downfall. Flaubert, listening in the courtroom, must have felt an odd mingling of dismay and ironic self-justification.

Pinard concluded the first phase of his attack by replacing Flaubert's subtitle, *Provincial Customs*, with a new one: *The Story of a Provincial Woman's Adulteries*. This was perfectly appropriate to the tale Pinard had told, though less so to Flaubert's original, since it completely submerged Madame Bovary's individuality and brought the controversial word "adultery" (worse yet, plural) into a prominence Flaubert never gave it. The prosecutor's next phase, quotation, confined itself to four "scenes, or rather four tableaux," chosen from an implied multitude. In view of the double charge—offenses against both "public" and "religious" morality—the quoted passages were classed accordingly, two of each kind. Now, instead of fusing reportage with interpretation in a blurry form of paraphrase, Pinard read from the novel verbatim for a stretch, interposed a paragraph of commentary, returned to the novel, and so on back and forth. Whatever the jury of 1857 may have thought, the effect on a modern reader is curious: not only does Flaubert's prose possess a dignity and power lacking from Pinard's, but the prosecutor's shrill, indignant tone also makes it seem as if he ought to disqualify himself from reading such books, thanks to his overheated imagination.

A typical example is Pinard's treatment of a brief passage in Part Two, chapter nine, in which Emma has just returned from her first adulterous liaison with Rodolphe. As Flaubert described the scene:

> But when she saw herself in the mirror she wondered at her face. Never had her eyes been so large, so black, nor so deep. Something subtle about her being transfigured her.
>
> She repeated: "I have a lover! a lover!" delighting at the idea

as if a second puberty had come to her. So at last she was to
know those joys of love, that fever of happiness of which she had
despaired! She was entering upon a marvelous world where all
would be passion, ecstasy, delirium.[33]

Pinard's response was emphatic: "And so from the moment of this
first transgression, this first fall, she glorifies adultery, she sings
the hymn of adultery, its poetry, its delights. That, gentlemen,
seems to me much more dangerous, much more immoral than the
fall itself!" The reading of a subsequent "lewd" passage drove Pinard
to even greater heights (and back into the past tense): "Was her
beauty ever so striking as on the day after her fall, the days that
followed her fall? What the author shows you is the poetry of
adultery, and I ask you once again if these lewd pages are not
profoundly immoral!!!"

We shall probably never know how those three printed excla-
mation points were enacted in the courtroom, but there is no doubt
that Pinard found himself in an awkward position and did not acquit
himself with skill. On the one hand, he was required to condemn
Madame Bovary for specific, if rather vague reasons; his lawyer's
guile therefore went to work making the novel look as offensive as
possible. On the other hand, however, he was obliged to assume
for the purpose a point of view very different from his own—that
of the Young Person, French style. In his summing-up, Pinard
sketched a classic profile of that troublesome Bull:

Who reads M. Flaubert's novel? Men engaged in economics and
social studies? No! *Madame Bovary*'s slight pages fall into the slightest hands, those of young girls and, sometimes, married women.
Well! When their imagination has been seduced, when that seduction has reached down to their hearts, when their hearts have
spoken to their senses, do you think that cool, reasoned argument
will withstand the seduction of both senses and feelings?

Pinard concluded the case for the prosecution with a wholesale
indictment of literary realism—one that Sade might have applauded
because, half a century before, he had invited it:

This moral code does not stigmatize realistic literature for painting the passions. Hatred, vengeance, love—all our lives are grounded in them, and art should paint them, but not without limits and standards. Art without rules is art no longer; it is like a woman who would shed all her clothing. To impose upon art the single standard of public decency is not to enslave but to honor it. Nothing grows great without standards. There, gentlemen, you have the principles we profess and the doctrine our conscience upholds.

The jury, as it turned out, would agree with these principles, though it would acquit Flaubert for reasons that Pinard himself had suggested. Despite his efforts, the unfortunate prosecutor had not been able to conceal his admiration for the book he was assigned to condemn. Commenting on the suppressed cab ride, Pinard had made a crucial distinction:

Gentlemen, I would draw your attention to two things: an admirable picture as far as talent is concerned, but an execrable picture from the point of view of morality. Yes, M. Flaubert knows how to embellish his pictures with all the resources of art, but without art's restraints. No gauze for him, no veils—he gives us nature in all her nudity and crudity!

At least in the eyes of the public prosecutor, Flaubert had taken up Sade's mandate: the province of realism was to be the entire heart of man, and since within that heart (as Pinard admitted) virtue occupied only a tiny, guarded corner, realism was bound to explore the rest, the dark part. In effect, the prosecution supplied the defense with sufficient grounds for a winning argument.

But the defense went further. The clever Sénard (a well-known lawyer who had been a friend of Flaubert's father) began with inflated praise not of *Madame Bovary* but of Flaubert himself. Pinard had said next to nothing on that subject, beyond the implication that it takes a lewd man to write a lewd book. In discussions of this kind the transition from the work to its author is virtually automatic; in Flaubert's case, the link worked all to the advantage of the defense. "M. Gustave Flaubert," intoned Sénard, "is a man of serious character, inclined by nature toward sad and weighty things. He is not the man whom the Public Prosecutor, by means of fifteen or twenty lines bitten off here and there, has just introduced to you as a maker of lewd tableaux. No; he is by nature, I repeat, the gravest, the most serious, and at the same time the saddest man you could conceive of." Such a man, of course, would never have intended to arouse lewd thoughts; while Pinard had focused on the ineffable Young Person, Sénard ran to the other absent entity that both sides in the pornography debate have always preferred to the text in front of them—the author's intentions. But, just as the prosecution had deduced its imaginary victim from the pages of *Madame Bovary*, so the defense had to resort to the same source for clues as to what Flaubert really had in mind. "Merely by restoring a phrase or two," Sénard went on, "by placing beside those few quoted lines the few lines that precede and follow them, his book will soon regain its proper tone, and at the same time it will let you see its author's intentions."

Sénard's view of those intentions was as alien to the truth as Pinard's vision of a deliberate design to debauch. Objecting to the prosecution's invented subtitle, the defense came up with one of its own:

No! the second title of this work is not *The Story of a Provincial Woman's Adulteries*. If you absolutely must have a second title, it is: the story of the education too often given in the provinces; the story of the risks to which it may lead; the story of degradation, of knavery, of suicide considered as the consequences of an original error, an error itself prepared for by the first wrongdoings into which young women are often lured; the story of an education, the story of the deplorable life to which this education is too often the preface.

In his dedication of *Madame Bovary* in volume form to Sénard, Flaubert remarked, no doubt with irony, that by "becoming part of your magnificent defence, my work has acquired for myself, as it were, an unexpected authority."[34] Unexpected, indeed—whatever fate Flaubert may have anticipated for his novel, he certainly never dreamed of its playing a role in this uplifting little scene, imagined by Sénard: "For my own part, I understand perfectly how the father of a family might say to his daughter, 'Young woman, if your heart, your conscience, religious feelings, and the voice of duty are insufficient to keep you on the right path, look, my child, at how much worry, suffering, sadness, and grief attend the woman who goes searching for happiness outside her own home!' "

Sénard was determined to portray *Madame Bovary* as a handbook of bourgeois respectability; that he succeeded is eloquent testimony to the power of resourceful interpretation. The demolition of Pinard's case was a much easier task, since the Prosecutor's very ability to distinguish the lewd from the chaste had already proven his familiarity with lewdness. Sénard went so far as to accuse the prosecution, along with the editors of the *Revue de Paris*, of having turned a wholesome book into a pernicious one by mutilating it. His prime example was the notorious cab ride, omitted from the *Revue* and darkly alluded to, though not quoted, by Pinard. From a proof sheet ("procured with great difficulty"), Sénard read the whole scene as Flaubert had written it, revealing that the dire "fall in the cab" to which his opponent had referred does not in fact take place, or at least is not described, in Flaubert's text. It was Flaubert who "lowered the curtains of the cab," a courtesy attributed by Pinard to the editors of the *Revue;* throughout the suppressed passage, as Emma and Léon rumble about the countryside, the curtains stay down, and the reader is left on his own to imagine what is going on behind them. Pinard's imagination had leapt directly to certainty, a mistake which gave his rival the chance to moralize: "What is unseen or suppressed comes to seem very strange indeed. People have imagined all sorts of things that did not exist, as you saw by the reading of the original passage [i.e., as the *Revue* had published it]. My God, do you know what people have imagined?"

The upshot of Sénard's argument was that lewdness resided not in Flaubert or his novel, but in the minds of the magazine's editors and the Public Prosecutor. Sénard neglected to point out, of course, that by keeping the cab curtains closed, Flaubert had set a precedent which his editors merely followed—hinting at horrors without displaying them, letting the reader imagine whatever he liked, including lewdness.[35] But even the dirtiest-minded reader, as Sénard went on to show, could have imagined nothing more lascivious than what was already to be found in *La Double Méprise* ("The Double Mistake") by the highly respected Prosper Mérimée. Mérimée's novel contained a scene in a post chaise compared to which Flaubert's curtained cab looked innocuous, and yet the book was widely admired and had never been indicted. That floodgate opened, Sénard was able to invoke a long roster of classic writers—mostly French, but also including Samuel Richardson—who had produced tableaux "lewder" than anything in *Madame Bovary*. Even the rite of extreme unction, quoted at length in the scene of Emma's death and particularly objected to by Pinard, turned out, when Sénard read it aloud from a missal, to be more physically explicit in its actual form than in Flaubert's version.

"It was marvelous," wrote Flaubert to his brother on the evening after the trial,[36] and he had good reason to gloat. Though the jury waited a week before delivering its decision, there was little doubt what it would be. Author, publisher, and printer were acquitted without costs; their guilt had been "insufficiently established." The jury took the opportunity, however, to express its literary opinions—thereby granting posterity a rare glimpse of what the mid-nineteenth-century common reader believed fiction should be and do. The beliefs are not startling: "the mission of literature should be to adorn and refresh the spirit by elevating the mind and refining morals, rather than to inspire disgust at vice by presenting portraits of the licentiousness which may exist in society." Flaubert and his co-defendants had failed to take into proper account "the boundaries which even the lightest literature must not cross." In a sense, Flaubert was guilty, but of a crime against which no laws had been passed: "he committed only the wrong of occasionally neglecting the rules which no self-respecting writer should transgress, and of forgetting that literature, like art, must be chaste and pure not only in its form but also in its expression, in order to accomplish the good effects it is called upon to produce." A few months later, *Madame Bovary* was published as a whole, with all cuts restored; it sold briskly from the first—thanks in part to the publicity of the trial—and was quickly recognized as a classic, a position it still holds.

If the problem of "pornography" could be solved at all, the trial of *Madame Bovary* would have done so in 1857. Every piece was already on the board, and the rules of the game were codified; even the outcome, the novel's vindication, occurred just as it would over and over again, with books as diverse as *Ulysses*, *Lolita*, and *Tropic of Cancer*. The interminability of the debate can also be seen in its first enactment. The exoneration of *Madame Bovary* made no impact whatever on either the law under which it was tried or the unwritten rules the law was intended to enforce. Bitterly as Flaubert opposed the hegemony of middle-class *bonnes moeurs*, much as all his work constitutes an extended polemic against conventional respectability, all the other parties in the trial—prosecution, defense, and jury alike—accepted the correctness of the status quo and saw no threat to it in the making of a single slight exception. Conducted on such grounds, and with such a result, the debate was bound to renew itself; even the question of the legitimacy of censorship had hardly been broached and would recur. The final lesson, that the indictment of a book remarkably improves its sales, might also have been learned and yet was not—except, perhaps, by publishers.

Flaubert's trial is customarily looked upon as an early skirmish in the century-long battle between selflessly committed artists and the hypocritical squeamishness of philistines. Yet it is by no means self-evident or natural that artists should stand in this relation to those who are not of their number. They had not done so in the past; the notion that the artistic life is a lonely vigil, that its products are admirable in direct proportion to their difficulty of manufacture and access, was new to Flaubert's time, though of course not invented by it. There had been precursors—Sade for one, but also doomed and self-doomed sufferers like Chénier in France, Chatterton, Byron, and Shelley in England—whom later artists venerated for having prepared the way. But the great success enjoyed by this vision of the artist, which goes on accruing interest even today, suggests by its very magnitude that it cannot have been the invention of a few individuals. It carries an air of historical inevitability; my first three chapters have attempted to outline some of the parallel developments that spawned, or ran in tandem with, the discovery of the otherness of art.

Not the least of these, acted out if not understood at the trial of *Madame Bovary*, was the widening gap between two concepts of representation. The Public Prosecutor thought of representations—words or pictures, it made no difference—as gaining value from the effect they produced. His hypersusceptible Young Person was a fiction, born from his own fears and desires; nevertheless, he granted her sovereignty over art because, for him, art existed first and foremost insofar as it touched an audience, even an imaginary one. Sénard was compelled to counter Pinard's argument by drawing attention away from the Young Person and toward the artist and his work. Sénard's case rested on a proposition that the United States Supreme Court would proclaim exactly a century later, as if it were new: that the tendency of a work is to be gauged according to the work taken as a whole, not from isolated naughty bits. And Sénard's emphasis on intention at least had the virtue of attributing integrity to the act of representing, whatever the response of its audience might be. It is provocative to see, before the word "pornography" was even in use, that the lines of argument had already been laid down, the unanswerable questions posed.

The year 1857 was indeed "critical," as Peter Gay has called it,[37] in the history of pornography and censorship. It is as if, like a boiler about to burst, the world of discourse was suffering such stresses that they could no longer be kept out of sight; the struggle had to go public, and it did so with a vengeance. A few months after *Madame Bovary* was vindicated, a second eventual classic, Baudelaire's *Les Fleurs du Mal*, came to trial on the same charge. Again, Pinard was the prosecutor; this time, probably thanks to a misguided defense strategy, he was more successful: Baudelaire was convicted of offenses against public morality and *bonnes moeurs* and fined three hundred francs (later reduced to fifty, at the intercession of the Empress Eugénie). Six of his poems were banned—the decision would not be officially reversed till 1949—and the court had the chance to express itself as it had been unable to do in Flaubert's case. *Les Fleurs du Mal* was an offensive book because "the intention of the poet, the goal he wished to attain and the route he took— whatever his efforts at style, whatever the condemnations preceding or following his portrayals—cannot mitigate the deadly effect of those portrayals which he offers the reader, and which, in the incriminated poems, are necessarily conducive to the arousal of the senses by virtue of a coarse realism offensive to modesty."[38] A note of vindictiveness is apparent in this judgment; the court seemed eager to demonstrate that *Madame Bovary* had been merely an exception to rules that had emerged stronger than ever from the test.

In England, 1857 saw the passage of the Obscene Publications Act, also called Lord Campbell's Act after John Campbell, the nobleman and magistrate who led the campaign for its adoption. Existing legislation authorized prosecutions for "obscene libel," but it did not permit the issuance of search warrants on grounds of obscenity. Lord Campbell sought to add these provisions to the law, because his judicial experience had shown him that, despite the efforts of private organizations like the Society for the Suppression of Vice, "a sale of poison more deadly than prussic acid, strychnine or arsenic—the sale of obscene publications and indecent books—was openly going on."[39] What a modern observer finds most remarkable in the debates over Lord Campbell's bill is that, though Victoria had been on the throne for twenty years, opposition to its enactment was vociferous and eloquent in both Houses of Parliament. Lord Lyndhurst, for example, won the distinction of becoming the first to state, in a public forum and for the public record, a problem that remains unsolved today, despite more than a century's argumentation. "My noble and learned Friend," he said, "is to put down the sale of obscene books and prints; but what is the interpretation which is to be put upon the word 'obscene'? I can easily conceive that two men will come to entirely different conclusions as to its meaning." He cited the example of Correggio's

Jupiter and Antiope, a much-revered painting displayed in the Louvre and gazed upon by "ladies of the first rank from all countries of Europe." Copies of this great work, and countless others like it, would be subject to seizure under Lord Campbell's bill. The poets, too, would be in jeopardy: not only Rochester, but Wycherley, Congreve, and even Dryden. "He has translated the worst parts of Ovid—his *Art of Love*—works for which Ovid was exiled, and died, I believe, on the shores of the Euxine. There is not a single volume of that great poet which would not come under the definition of my noble and learned Friend's bill."[40]

Lord Campbell (who was in fact as learned as Lyndhurst made out) insisted that "he had no intention whatever to make Horace, Juvenal, Voltaire or Lord Byron, seizable";[41] his bill was "intended to apply *exclusively to works written for the single purpose of corrupting the morals of youth*, and of a nature calculated to shock the common feelings of decency *in any well-regulated mind*. Bales of publications of that description were manufactured in Paris, and imported into this country."[42] Campbell brought with him into the House of Lords a copy of an English translation of the younger Dumas' *La Dame aux Camélias*—an up-to-the minute choice, since Verdi's *La Traviata*, based on Dumas' novel, was then playing in London and had aroused some controversy. Displaying the book, Campbell, as newspapers reported, made a double-edged declaration:

> He did not wish to create a category of offences in which this might be included although it was certainly of a polluting character. It was only from the force of public opinion and an improved taste that the circulation of such works could be put a stop to. . . . He was shocked to think that there should be so much circulation for works like the one in his hand—*The Lady of the Camellias*. In this work, the Lady described her red camellias and her white camellias; but he would not shock their Lordships by going further.[43]

It is doubtful whether that sophisticated audience would have been shocked by anything at all; but Campbell had staked out the entire terrain on which all battles over "pornography" would be waged.

Certain works, the acknowledged classics of all ages, countries, and genres, were sacrosanct, no matter what their nature might be. Certain others—these went unspecified—were automatically damned, thanks to their obvious and single intention to corrupt. Then there was a third class, a gray zone between light and shadow where *The Lady of the Camellias* lay. Works of this kind were "polluting," yet for some reason Campbell would not wish his bill to cover them. That reason was apparently the chimera of artistic value, the elusive, redemptive spirit that the twentieth century would struggle over and over again to define.

In England as well as France, the pornographic stage was fully set by 1857; there were, however, important differences between the two scenarios. The trials of *Madame Bovary* and *Les Fleurs du Mal* pitted self-conscious artistry against self-righteous conventionality. Both sides were aware that the encounter was taking place on the leading edge of literary innovation; there was no question of the rank, in either an artistic or a social sense, to which Flaubert, Baudelaire, and their writings belonged. These artists and their art were also indubitably French: the challenge they posed to prevailing values was of domestic origin, a product of the same society which resisted and censured it. In England, Lord Campbell's defense of his proposed Act made plain the class bias that structured it: works of known merit—works which gentlemanly consensus had canonized—should be exempt from prosecution, since they were encased in the various shields we have already examined. Articles without pedigree should be subject to seizure and destruction only when they were offered for public sale; Lord Campbell and his Act made no mention of privately circulated materials such as Ashbee and his cohorts collected, though Campbell must have known of their existence. Indeed, the possession of obscene materials has never been a crime in Britain, only their public display. No doubt, this is in part a symptom of traditional British—and American—respect for private property, but it also reflects the subtle prejudice at work in both countries in favor of those who have the means to obtain whatever they desire through private channels.

Lord Campbell relied on these features of the social order with a typically English confidence that the system would prevail indefinitely, and that laws were all the better for neglecting to specify the provisions that ought to govern their enforcement. Though Parliament may well have been persuaded to pass Lord Campbell's Act on the basis of such shared understanding, the text of the Act itself stated only, as Lord Chief Justice Cockburn would cite it in a momentous decision eleven years later, that "in respect of obscene books, &c., kept to be sold or distributed, magistrates may order the seizure and condemnation of such works, in case they are of opinion that the publication of them would have been the subject-matter of an indictment at law, and that such a prosecution ought to have been instituted."[44] Times would change, and the gentlemanly enclosure would suffer breaches beyond Lord Campbell's imagination; his Act, which remained in effect for a century, would give rise to innumerable useless confrontations, largely because the tacit agreement that was intended to temper it would break down.

Lord Campbell's Act also presupposed, without saying so explicitly, that obscenity came in from outside, mostly France, as *The Lady of the Camellias* had done. Xenophobia helps to account for this characteristically British attitude toward whatever was morally or politically suspect—an attitude adopted, with typical distortions and exaggerations, by the United States. But British and American insularity in this regard also depended upon a confidence that native art and literature, at least the respectable kind, would never transgress certain boundaries. So far, these boundaries had had no need of legislative formulation; by and large, Anglo-American artists felt content to operate within the limits of what their public found acceptable. This confidence was largely justified until the last quarter of the nineteenth century, when new influences—French, of course—began to inspire artistic rebelliousness in England and America. Trollope could express his placid trust in native art as late as 1875; seventeen years earlier—just a few months after Lord Campbell's Act was passed—George Eliot had expressed herself even more emphatically concerning her own fiction. Her publisher, John Blackwood, had written her to request an outline of *Adam Bede*, the novel on which she was then at work. She declined to provide one, for an appropriate reason:

> The mere skeleton of my story would probably give rise in your mind to objections which would be suggested by the treatment *other* writers have given to the same tragic incidents in the human lot—objections which would be far away from my treatment. The Heart of Midlothian would probably have been thought highly objectionable if a skeleton of the story had been given by a writer whose reputation did not place him above question, and the same story told by a Balzacian French writer would probably have made a book that no young person could read without injury. . . .[45]

The "subjects" of Scott's and Eliot's novels might have been baldly stated as "illicit sex and child murder"; in discreet British hands, however, even such potentially outrageous raw materials could be molded into inoffensive works of art.

In France, from a very early date, respectable artists took it upon themselves to slap society's face; in England, the adversary stance was much slower to develop. Lord Campbell had nothing to fear, for the moment, except from across the Channel and that other foreign country, the lower orders. The Obscene Publications Act had little effect for eleven years after its passage; prosecutions on charges of obscenity continued to be made much as they had been for decades, with the same hole-and-corner targets and the same high but unsatisfactory rate of success. Only in 1868 did the Act bite into history, by means of Lord Chief Justice Cockburn's clarification of it in the case posterity would know as *Regina* v. *Hicklin*. The hapless Benjamin Hicklin, whose name has been permanently enshrined as Queen Victoria's foe on the pornographic battleground, was in fact one of the lower-court magistrates who had judged obscene a pamphlet seized by the police under the authority of the Obscene Publications Act. Hicklin's decision had been reversed by Quarter Sessions; the higher-level Court of Queen's Bench, Cockburn presiding, would reinstate it, meanwhile reinterpreting—to no one's satisfaction but to far-reaching effect—the Act under which seizure had first been made.

The publication at issue was an old tract entitled *The Confessional Unmasked; Shewing the Depravity of the Romanish Priesthood, the Iniquity of the Confessional and the Questions Put to Females in Confession.*[46] It had evidently been written early in the nineteenth century and belonged to an ancient genre, dating at least from the Reformation. The current distributors were a righteous-sounding organization called the Protestant Electoral Union, whose avowed purpose, as Cockburn phrased it, was "to expose the errors and practices of the Roman Catholic Church in the matter of confession." Among those practices were "some of the most filthy and disgusting and unnatural description it is possible to imagine." Cockburn expressed no doubt as to the intentions of the Protestant Electoral Union or of Henry Scott, the Union member whose stock of *The Confessional Unmasked* had been seized. The Lord Chief Justice seemed to wish, as his French counterpart Pinard had done a decade before, that the question of intention might be shelved entirely. Cockburn's famous "test," which would vex the Western world for more than a century, dispensed with the intentions of author and publisher alike. "I think the test of obscenity is this," he said, "whether the tendency of the matter charged as obscenity is to deprave and corrupt those whose minds are open to such immoral influences, and into whose hands a publication of this sort may fall."

Cockburn found it "quite certain" that *The Confessional Unmasked* "would suggest to the minds of the young of either sex, or even to persons of more advanced years, thoughts of a most impure and libidinous character." This necessity was so apparent that he was willing (at the cost of some consistency on his own part) to deduce from it an intention that the Protestant Electoral Union might not even have been remotely conscious of:

although I quite concur in thinking that the motive of the parties who published this work, however mistaken, was an honest one, yet I cannot suppose but what they had that intention which constitutes the criminality of the act, at any rate that they knew

> perfectly well that this work must have the tendency which, in point of law, makes it an obscene publication, namely, the tendency to corrupt the minds and morals of those into whose hands it might come.

Cockburn's conclusion was positively breathtaking in its implications, though the statement of it seemed straightforward: "I hold that, where a man publishes a work manifestly obscene, he must be taken to have had the intention which is implied from that act."

Like Lord Campbell before him, Lord Chief Justice Cockburn relied with confidence upon a system of social organization whose eternal validity seemed unquestionable, though it was in fact already badly frayed and would soon disintegrate. Cockburn felt no anxiety that the classics might suffer immolation on account of his "test," though he went so far as to admit that "there are a great many publications of high repute in the literary productions of this country the tendency of which is immodest, and, if you please, immoral." Logically enough, Cockburn maintained that the law was unaffected by the admired status of these works: legally speaking, obscenity was obscenity, wherever it occurred. His tacit trust seemed to be, however, that the high repute in which the obscene classics were held would prevent indictments from ever being brought against them. No such honorable immunity protected *The Confessional Unmasked*, as was plain from the manner of its distribution: "This work, I am told, is sold at the corners of streets, and in all directions, and of course it falls into the hands of persons of all classes, young and old, and the minds of those hitherto pure are exposed to the danger of contamination and pollution from the impurity it contains."[47] Like Reynolds's penny dreadfuls and Dr. Sanger's overpriced dirty pictures, *The Confessional Unmasked* circulated not between gentlemen but on the streets, where promiscuous traffic foreshadowed the sexual promiscuity to which such books must naturally give rise.

It is impossible to overstress the significance of the "Hicklin test"; it became the basis of antiobscenity legislation in Britain and the United States throughout the subsequent century, was continually cited, paraphrased, and quibbled with, and still haunts discussions of pornography today. In its own time, it was hardly remarkable; Pinard had drawn on the same notions in prosecuting *Madame Bovary* in 1857, and in 1865 Dickens had held them up to ridicule as "Podsnappery." The impact of the Hicklin test derived principally from the fact that the Young Person was now no longer merely in the air but also in the law books. She had taken on what looked like a definite, objective existence—even a pseudoscientific one, as the word "test" implies. It would be convenient, henceforward, to appeal to Cockburn's brief, simple formula, instead of stumbling about in the murk of individual opinions and specific cases. In practice, the Hicklin test would prove itself no test at all; the extraordinary thing is that a century of argument was required to establish what should have been obvious at the beginning and was so to observers like Dickens—that the Young Person, in whose interest the test was devised, lived only in the nervous imagination of men inhabiting a particular class and historical moment. She was, indeed, as those men must have felt without recognizing it, a sign that the forces which had put them in their privileged place were constantly moving on and would not always keep them there. At the midpoint of the nineteenth century, shared understanding had to be buttressed by law: that in itself was a clear admission that the old consensus no longer seemed sturdy enough to endure without propping up.

The trial of *Madame Bovary* in France, and the case of *Regina* v. *Hicklin* in England, also mark the emergence of the obscenity problem into the full glare of public controversy. "Pornography," as the world would learn to understand it, is a public term, native to the courtroom, the pages of magazines and newspapers, and the promiscuous streetcorners where it goes on display. Its consumption and corruptive action occur in private, or at least in the minds of individuals; but if that were its only sphere of influence, no more concerted efforts would ever have been made against it than personal acts of censorship like Pepys's upon *L'Ecole des Filles*. The effects of "pornography" are presumed to be public—the debauching (or oppression) of womankind, the transformation of the whole culture into a brothel, the dismantling of society in general—and it is therefore appropriate that "pornography" should come into its own as a word not to be whispered but broadcast. The courtroom is the ideal forum for "pornography," since law cases usually have two sides, and charges of "pornography" have never been made without meeting resistance. The first significant obscenity trials were conducted in France and England, but the battle soon shifted to the United States, where it was waged with a fervor and ruthlessness that made the European experience look halfhearted. It is ironic, though fitting, that the land of the free should have occupied itself so obsessively with the menace of individual freedom.

CHAPTER FIVE

THE AMERICAN
OBSCENE

DURING THE DEBATE over Lord Campbell's bill, James White, M.P., came forward with a cogent objection to its enactment:

> In the United States [he said] there was a law which decreed the destruction of any obscene publications which might be imported thither. It happened curiously enough, not long ago, that an American traveller, returning home from Italy, brought with him a copy of that well-known work describing with figures, the principal statues, paintings, etc., of the Royal Museum of Naples. The name of this work is the *Museo Borbonico Reale;* its value some thirty or forty pounds; and we have it in the Library attached to this House. Now, this very work was by the Collector of the Customs at New York deemed obscene; and was then and there ruthlessly destroyed.

White challenged his colleagues to examine the famous catalogue for themselves; he added that it had been "published under royal authority"[1]—a fact which would guarantee its respectability, if not its wholesomeness. He had no need to point out that the price the unnamed American had paid—some 150 to 200 dollars in 1857, several times that amount in today's currency—made the same guarantee for the purchaser. White's concern was one he shared with Lord Campbell: that in the interest of decency, the distinction between art and trash would be lost sight of.

Condescension toward things American was and is a characteristically British attitude. In this case, the speaker was implying that rude American eyes saw no difference between the classic and the common. It ought to have seemed odd, however, though it evidently did not, that a nation founded on principles of individual freedom should have become exemplary of the havoc wrought when governmental authority intervenes in private affairs. The law under which the catalogue had been seized was the Customs Act of 1842, the first federal statute that so much as mentioned obscenity. In a sense, however, the official American attitude toward obscenity was almost identical to the British, at least in 1842. The Customs Act did not specify France as the most likely source of foreign filth, but America's first antiobscenity legislation was directed at imports, as if domestic manufacture were inconceivable.

Indecency, too, was a marginal matter for the framers of the Customs Act. Section 28 is wedged in between a regulation governing excess tariff duties and one specifying the meaning of the word "ton" as used throughout the Act—an undistinguished place for such a potentially far-reaching measure. Negligence is the most likely reason for the obscure debut of antiobscenity legislation in the United States: like their European counterparts, American lawmakers did not yet perceive a potent threat from obscene books and pictures. They were content, so far, to lump obscenity together with the other dangerous articles that might come in from abroad but were certainly not being produced at home. They made no attempt to define the words "indecent" and "obscene," surely knottier terms than "ton." And, of course, they had no occasion to grapple with "pornography," which had just been recognized by the Académie Française but would not enter English for another eight years.

The federal government was also able to take advantage of a peculiarly American option, one which continues to figure in debates over antipornography legislation. It could simply entrust the matter to the states, several of which already had relevant laws on their books. As early as 1711, the Massachusetts Bay Colony had prohibited the "Composing, Writing, Printing or Publishing, of any Filthy Obscene or Prophane Song, Pamphlet, Libel or Mock-Sermon, in Imitation or in Mimicking of Preaching, or any other part of Divine Worship"[2]—a typical eighteenth-century formulation making no distinction between obscenity and blasphemy. Other colonies adopted similar laws and carried them over into statehood, despite the fact that any such prohibition would seem to contradict the freedoms of speech and religion guaranteed in the Constitution. As in Europe, however, enforcement was so lax as to be virtually nonexistent, and the latent conflict was very slow to emerge. The first American conviction on a specific charge of obscenity did not take place until 1815, in Pennsylvania, and even then the case had to be decided on the basis of common law, since there was no explicit legislation to cover it. The State Supreme Court had, as it were, to make up a law as it went along, relying on an imaginary consensus that had not yet needed public expression because it had never been publicly breached.

Jesse Sharpless of Philadelphia and five of his cronies faced the charge that, on March 1, 1815, they

> unlawfully, wickedly, and scandalously *did exhibit, and show for money, . . . a certain lewd, wicked, scandalous, infamous, and obscene painting, representing a man in an obscene, impudent, and indecent posture with a woman*, to the manifest corruption and subversion of youth, and other citizens of this commonwealth, to the evil example of all others in like case offending, and against the peace and dignity of the commonwealth of *Pennsylvania*.[3]

There was, it appeared, no American (or at least Pennsylvanian) precedent for such a case. To find an approximation, Judge C. J. Tilghman had to go back to the London of 1663, when Sir Charles Sedley and Lord Buckhurst, chums of the infamous Rochester, had appeared naked on the balcony of a Covent Garden tavern and abused the plebeian crowd below. The parallel between Restoration noblemen and nineteenth-century Philadelphians was a bit strained, as Tilghman admitted:

> It is true that, besides this shameful exhibition, it is mentioned in some of the reports of that case, that he [Sedley] threw down bottles, containing offensive liquor, among the people; but we have the highest authority for saying, that the most criminal part of his conduct and that which principally drew upon him the vengeance of the law, was the *exposure of his person.*[4]

Even if we overlook the other differences between Sedley and Sharpless *et al.*, it seems that some distinction ought to have been drawn between displaying one's naked body in the street and inviting people in to see a picture. In the Sharpless case, however, as in innumerable others up to our own day, flesh and paint (or print or film) have been judged equivalent. The verdict was inconsequential—except for Sharpless and company—but it entered on dangerous ground: "Any offence which in its nature and by its example, tends to the corruption of morals, as the *exhibition of an obscene picture*, is indictable at common law."[5] This exhibition had taken place in a private house, before viewers who presumably had not been dragooned into attendance; their morals nevertheless had to be protected—by imprisonment.

The Sharpless case is also the first recorded instance of a dilemma that would recur at the trial of *Madame Bovary* and in scores of courtrooms throughout that century and the next. Given that the indictment was based on the supposed effects of seeing a picture, it would seem appropriate that the picture be displayed in court or at least minutely described. If the picture was "poison," however, as the judge declared (we may presume he had seen it), the jurors' morals would be jeopardized. Tilghman found a solution:

> As to the nature and manner in which the painting is represented to have been made, I hold it to be sufficient to state, that it represented a man in an obscene, impudent, and indecent posture with a woman, either clothed or unclothed, without wounding

our eyes or ears, with a particular description of their attitude or posture. Why should it be so described? If the jurors are satisfied on the proof, that the persons represented were painted in an impudent and indecent posture, will not this give the Court all the information they can require?[6]

The reasoning is perfectly circular and ought to have obviated a trial, yet it remains an endemic problem that trials of pornography cannot be fairly conducted without acting as new vehicles for the dissemination of the matter under indictment.[7]

Sharpless notwithstanding, only one state, Vermont, had enacted an antiobscenity statute prior to the Customs Act of 1842. In subsequent years, such legislation would beome ubiquitous; by 1900, thirty states had prohibited obscenity in some way or other, and by 1973 all fifty had done so.[8] Along the way, legislative action against pornography (and the trials that followed from it) would prove to offer better publicity than anything the pornographers could have afforded on their own. In the first half of the nineteenth century, however, despite a flare-up here and there, pornography appears to have been as much a nonissue in the United States as it was in England or France. The Customs Act bears testimony to the fact that European corruption (a long-standing American bugaboo) was starting to be perceived in new forms. Indeed, if Henry Spencer Ashbee is to be trusted, obscenity did not become a native American industry until the Act had been in effect for four years. As Ashbee wrote in 1877:

America, as in other branches of industry, has made of late years great progress in the production of books, and not the least of those of an improper character. Until 1846 the Americans produced nothing, but merely imported such books; when an Irishman, W. Haines, began to publish, and soon became a rich man. Up to 1871 he had published not less than 320 different works, and we are told that the number of such books sold annually in New York amounts to 100,000.

But just as the United States seemed about to enter the modern pornographic age, a nemesis appeared: "Mr. A. J. Comstock . . . 'has succeeded, in the course of a few years, in confiscating and destroying over thirteen tons of this class of publications.' The American laws respecting this traffic have lately been rendered more stringent, and such publications are now as difficult to procure there as they are here."[9]

The source of Ashbee's quotation on the extent of Comstock's plunder has not been traced, but it seems to be a gross underestimate. In January 1874, Comstock himself had reported the seizure and destruction of 134,000 pounds of "books of improper character," along with 194,000 pictures and sundries like 60,300 "rubber articles" and 5,500 "indecent" playing cards—this in less than two years.[10] The pioneering Haines (or Haynes) had been among the crusader's first victims. In 1871, the surgeon-turned-publisher died, supposedly by suicide. The night before, he had received this message: "Get out of the way. Comstock is after you. Damn fool won't look at money."[11] Later, Comstock supervised the burning of Haines's stock and bilked his widow out of the stereotype plates, which were also destroyed.[12] And the increased stringency of American laws, wistfully lamented by Ashbee, had been engineered almost single-handedly by the same man, Anthony Comstock.

The most bizarre feature of the history of the American obscene is that its early days were virtually dominated by an obsessed individual. In previous chapters, it was possible to consider this figure or that one as symptomatic of his age; the *Zeitgeist* prevailed, and it was neither embodied nor challenged by any particular person. Official policy might have lagged behind public mood and at times chafed against it; there was no indication, however, that governmental action, erratic and tyrannical though it often was, ran completely counter to the feelings of the public or else was totally irrelevant to them. Perhaps this is because "the public," in England and France, was never conceived of as the entirety of the populace, but only as the sphere of citizens who mattered—principally the *haute bourgeoisie* in both countries, confident of agreement on all essential issues of morality and ethics, equally confident that it possessed the power to enforce obedience if agreement was not forthcoming. The breakdown of that consensus was a major origin of "pornography"; in the United States, consensus seems never to have existed, or to have established such a tenuous grip that it could be challenged almost inadvertently, as the Sharpless case illustrates. The kind of moral hegemony that dominated England and France failed in the United States for peculiarly American reasons. And the failure had an even more peculiar byproduct—the empowerment of an unelected official to operate by covert and unconstitutional means in the interest of a cause that practically no one but the official himself believed in.

Anthony Comstock was born in 1844 in New Canaan, Connecticut, then a farming community. His parents were of Puritan descent, but a century had passed since Puritanism was carried into practice with anything like young Anthony's gusto. In 1862, aged eighteen, he broke into a saloon-cum-general store in nearby Winnipauk and, anticipating Carrie Nation by some years (though apparently without an ax), spilled the proprietor's liquor upon the floor. After a stint in the Union army, Anthony settled in New Haven, where he entered the profession that would engage him until his cause was found and even for a while afterward—clerk and bookkeeper in a dry-goods store. A year or so later he moved to New York City, continuing at his old trade and eventually marrying Margaret Hamilton, ten years his senior. This was January 1871; there was so far nothing to suggest that, before three years were out, Anthony would become the recipient of a singular honor—a federal statute that, in unofficial parlance, bore his name.

Not long after the Comstocks had set up housekeeping in Brooklyn, a revelation came to Anthony. As a sympathetic commentator described it in 1893:

During this time Mr. Comstock became aware, through information gathered from his associates, of the demoralizing influence of the obscene literature, pictures, etc., of the day, and from various sources gathered some idea of the enormous traffic in this stuff. Indeed, a number of his associates, bright and intelligent young men, were ruined before his eyes in this manner. In the early part of 1872 one or two sad cases came to his attention, of young men who had been ruined; one of them was turned out of his home. . . .

Comstock sprang into action, and his own enlightenment followed:

On March 2, 1872, at the instance of Mr. Comstock, seven persons were arrested for alleged dealing in obscene literature. These were the first arrests. Shortly after the appalling fact was revealed to him that there was a business, regularly organized and backed by large capital, systematically carried on through the mails.[13]

The strange blend of vigilantism and naiveté in Comstock's first large-scale campaign would characterize America's greatest antismut crusader throughout his long career. It is hard to conceive of a mind tactically ruthless and emotionally virginal, able to move without a jolt from bragging over a wrongdoer's suicide to blushing at a risqué photograph. But Anthony Comstock possessed such a mind.

Nearly a year later, though he had already destroyed William Haines and avenged his ruined associates, Comstock was still an employee of Cochran, McLean & Co., at the corner of Grand Street and Broadway, in Manhattan; he was still a dry-goods clerk. He had, however, found his métier. All that remained was to obtain official recognition of his activities, some sanction or espousal that would make him more powerful than a mere individual. There was clearly no use in appealing to government, since it was government's failure to enforce its own laws that had compelled Comstock's private action in the first place. In the spring of 1872, however, Comstock acquired his first institutional backing, from an unlikely seeming agency—the Young Men's Christian Association. The Y.M.C.A. had lobbied for several years in favor of a New York State antiobscenity law; it had been instrumental in pushing through the 1868 statute under which Comstock made his early arrests. By 1872, it had become as clear to the Association's board of directors as it was to Comstock himself that the ordinary authorities were either disinclined or impotent to halt the traffic in obscenity. The Board knew of no one willing to expend the time and effort demanded by such a cause, until Secretary Robert R. McBurney received a letter from a young man in Brooklyn, offering his services. McBurney passed the letter along to the president of the Association, Morris K. Jesup, who invited Comstock to meet with both men and explain his intentions. "At that meeting," Comstock later wrote, "I disclosed the facts that I had discovered. I said I thought if I had a little money I could get at the stock of the publishers."[14]

Something in Comstock's self-presentation must have been convincing, because a little money soon arrived, in the form of a $650 check from Jesup. Further contributions followed; by 1874, the Y.M.C.A. had donated $8,498.14 to finance Comstock's labors.[15] In later years, the crusader's opponents would often accuse him of mercenary motives, but it seems clear that Haines's anonymous informant had been right: "Damn fool won't look at money"—at least, not beyond the minimum necessary to carry on his work and support his family in modest comfort. The enormous publicity Comstock received—most of it negative, but publicity nonetheless—along with the arbitrary power he was authorized to wield over anyone who offended him, might suggest that megalomania was his ruling passion. Yet the most curious thing about this extremely curious figure is that, so far as his conscious mind went, nothing moved him but a pure, altruistic desire to save his country.

Shortly after Comstock's interview with Jesup and McBurney, the Y.M.C.A. established a Committee for the Suppression of Vice, modeled in name and program on the British Society. Under the auspices of the Committee, Comstock continued his local crusade for a few more months, but he and his superiors had already set their sights higher. The Customs Act of 1842 had been strengthened in 1857, and in 1865, a federal statute had prohibited the shipment of obscene books and pictures through the mails; this statute had been toughened in 1872. Just as in New York State, however, the existence of laws meant nothing without their strict enforcement; from the point of view of the Committee, the law was inadequate and its enforcement negligible. Late in 1872, Comstock made his second trip to Washington (the first had been his honeymoon, the previous year), to begin lobbying for a new antiobscenity law drafted by the Committee's legal advisors. After much discouraging delay, on March 3, 1873, President Grant signed into law "An Act for the Suppression of Trade in, and Circulation of, obscene Literature and Articles of immoral Use," which had already been unofficially dubbed the "Comstock Law."

The new Act was far more specific and wide-ranging than any of its precursors. It read in part:

> That no obscene, lewd, or lascivious book, pamphlet, picture, paper, print, or other publication of an indecent character, or any article or thing designed or intended for the prevention of conception or procuring of abortion, nor any article or thing intended or adapted for any indecent or immoral use or nature, nor any written or printed card, circular, book, pamphlet, advertisement or notice of any kind giving information, directly or indirectly, where, or how, or of whom, or by what means either of the things before mentioned may be obtained or made, nor any letter upon the envelope of which, or postal-card upon which indecent or scurrilous epithets may be written or printed, shall be carried in the mail. . . .[16]

Comprehensive as the Act was intended to be, its most effective provision did not appear on the books but was arranged privately, outside of ordinary legal channels. Weeks before the Act came to a vote, Senator William Windom had persuaded the Committee on Appropriations to earmark $3,425 for the use of a "special agent." The sum had been approved, but only with the Postmaster General's promise that, if the Act was passed, Comstock would receive the appointment.[17]

Comstock retained this unique commission until the end of his life, and until 1907 his pay was not considered a salary, merely the defrayment of expenses. He occupied a position both inside and outside the law: it was the law he was charged to enforce, and he was issued a badge to signal his official status; but he was on no one's payroll, had no immediate superior, and was free to interpret the law as he saw fit. There were also no restrictions on the means he might employ to catch the people he had defined as criminals. It is one of the most striking oddities of American history that for more than forty years, from Comstock's appointment in 1873 till his death in 1915, problems of public morality were entrusted almost wholly to the discretion of one man, an agent of the Post Office Department. The anomaly is partly due to the peculiar role the Post Office had played in American life ever since its founding in 1792. It was the only federal agency that touched the individual citizen on a regular, daily basis; no matter how jealously states and localities might guard their sovereignty, it was compromised from the start by their acceptance of this federal service. The Constitution, furthermore, guarantees no right to use the mails. It merely provides, in Article I, Section 8, for congressional power to establish post offices and post roads. As Comstock was fond of pointing out to his detractors, a number of Supreme Court decisions had determined that mail service "is not a duty, but a *power;* and like all the other powers enumerated in the eighth section of the first article, the extent and mode of its exercise depend entirely on the discretion of Congress."[18]

Before Comstock, this power had seldom been used restrictively, though mail had been censored during the Civil War and the antiobscenity statutes of 1865 and 1872 had been sporadically enforced. In Comstock's hands, the power to short-circuit the ordinary route of governmental action suffered a new twist: Comstock, a private citizen, employed the authority of Congress in campaigns against other private citizens, many of whom he knew well enough to grab them by the coat collar, some of whom took the intimate liberty of kicking him downstairs. In these tawdry scuffles, innumerably repeated throughout Comstock's energetic career, the Post Office, Congress, and the Constitution itself vanished between two brawlers, each bent on knocking the other out. There is something quintessentially American in this absurd topsy-turviness. Perhaps its most American feature is that it all came into existence because too few people cared about either what the laws said or whether anyone enforced them.

In the spring of 1873, just turned twenty-nine, Comstock embarked on his life's mission; in the autumn of that year, he resigned from the dry-goods trade and devoted himself full-time to the policing of American morals. He brought almost incredible stamina to the task, along with the clerkly habit of keeping running totals. In his first ten months on the job, for example, Comstock calculated that he had traveled 23,500 rail miles chasing smut;[19] it was at this point that he made the tally of plunder so much underestimated by Henry Spencer Ashbee. One could not expect him to maintain that pace, and indeed the yearly mass of seized obscenity did drop off as time went on, partly on account of Comstock's very success, partly because he had taken on many other causes as well. Nevertheless, in a 1913 interview with the New York *Evening World*, he was able to brag that he had destroyed 160 tons of "obscene literature" and convicted "persons enough to fill a passenger train of sixty-one coaches, sixty coaches containing sixty passengers each and the sixty-first almost full."[20]

Comstock exhibited a blithe disregard for all other laws than the one he was commissioned to enforce. He commonly answered advertisements under false names, and he often put on disguises in order to examine suspicious wares in person. He employed henchmen, including one Joseph A. Britton, said to be even more unscrupulous than his chief. Comstock's targets were numerous and by no means restricted to obscenity; at one time or another (sometimes simultaneously), he also combated lotteries, pool parlors, saloons, and quack medicines. His greatest ingenuity and enthusiasm, however, went into the pursuit of pornography—though he never, so far as I have been able to discover, used that newfangled term. He called his favorite prey "smut," "obscenity," "lewdness," "filth," and the full roster of other traditional names. His unarticulated definition of these words was breathtakingly broad, and a modern observer cannot help finding in Comstock the archetype of the Victorian prurient prude, able to see lewdness everywhere because he was always eager for lewdness. It is in this guise that Comstock entered American popular history; the process was already well underway in his lifetime, when scores of newspaper caricatures lampooned him for possessing just this kind of perverted imagination. A close look at Comstockian "obscenity" reveals that, whatever else it might have been, it was consistent—unrelentingly and perhaps insanely so.

A picturesque illustration of both Comstock's tactics and his notion of the obscene is provided by the case of A. Prosch, stereopticon maker, with premises at the corner of Catherine and Division streets, Manhattan. In the spring of 1877, Prosch was invited by a patron of his shop to put on a show before a local temperance society. At first, Prosch was unwilling; he was a manufacturer, not a showman. To please a customer, however, he obliged. "The pictures used were chaste and moral, a portion of which were of statuary and ancient paintings, embracing, of course, some nude figures; none were from life. Many gentlemen and their wives were present, and everybody was pleased, and none were in the least shocked by the exhibition."[21] Evidently this opinion fell short of unanimity, because one of the company reported the proceedings to Britton, who promptly informed Comstock. Receiving instructions "to work up a case," Britton approached the stereopticon maker and proposed a similar show, for payment, at a "political club" to which Britton claimed to belong. The only provision was that the pictures shown to the temperance society had not been spicy enough. "Now, you see," Britton is supposed to have told Prosch, "our club is composed mostly of young men, and we are fond of something rich and a little gay. Those pictures you have exhibited are well enough, but can't you get something for us a little 'stronger' or more fancy?"[22] The unlucky Prosch, having succumbed to one temptation, fell easy victim to another. He agreed to obtain gayer pictures; and when, a few days later, Comstock appeared at Catherine and Division streets claiming to be a member of the "political club," Prosch freely showed him samples. The result was immediate arrest. Comstock dragged Prosch out of his shop to the sidewalk, refusing to let him put on his coat, though the April day was raw and Prosch was sixty-four years old. Shortly thereafter, members of the temperance society to which Prosch had first displayed his wares appealed on his behalf to Samuel Colgate, president of the Y.M.C.A.'s Committee for the Suppression of Vice. Informed of his one-time subordinate's dealings, Colgate was "appalled"; thanks to his intervention, the Prosch case was never called up.[23]

The underhandedness of Comstock's operations was typical; the most remarkable fact about this little episode, however, is the extreme vigilance Comstock exercised, his willingness to spend time and sweat on the most trivial case—even when, as here, it had nothing to do with the mails. After only five years on the job, Comstock had transformed himself into the sole guardian of an entire nation's morals, with special attention to his home city, where the bulk of domestic filth was thought (with justice) to originate. Only a man of Comstock's extravagant physical energy could have played such a part; only a man fired by absolute conviction would have cast himself in it. The question remains, however, exactly what the conviction was that drove Comstock so hard for so many years. To a large extent, his understanding of the threat posed by obscene books and pictures strongly resembled the European view, but there were provocative differences that marked him as distinctively if almost parodically American.

In his 1883 jeremiad, *Traps for the Young*, Comstock painted a portrait of American life that, if it had been accurate, would have revealed a country teetering on the brink of total moral and physical collapse. The landscape was so thickly littered with "traps" of all descriptions that only by miracle or the most improbable self-restraint could a child reach adulthood free from corruption. Newspapers, "half-dime" novels, advertisements, theatres, saloons, lotteries, pool halls, postcards, photographs, even painting and sculpture—wherever the poor child turned, in Comstock's nightmarish America, something lurked, ready to debauch him. Methodist minister James Monroe Buckley, who supplied an introduction to *Traps for the Young*, was quite right in admitting that "this work does not claim high literary merit";[24] Comstock's style plods, and his occasional attempts at cleverness fall flat. But he had enough literary skill to devise a governing metaphor and stick with it—the trap. No doubt recalling his own rural youth, Comstock begins with a list of animal traps, varying in subtlety and violence, each holding its appropriate bait. The ghastliest is the bear-trap—"a huge piece of tempting meat must be fastened in the bear-trap to entice bruin from his cave in the rocks and secure him as the trapper's prey"—but even the lowly box-trap, with its "sweet apple to tempt the rabbit or squirrel," is a ruthless instrument of mutilation and death. The analogy with human traps is plain:

> After more than eleven years' experience contending for the moral purity of the children of the land, and seeking to prevent certain evils from being brought in contact with this ever-susceptible class, I have one clear conviction, viz., that *Satan lays the snare, and children are his victims.* His traps, like all others, are baited to allure the human soul.[25]

Human traps possess no sawteeth for piercing flesh, but their moral effect remains a brutally physical one.

Comstock draws no clear line between the mental and the physical; for him, the two often appear to be the same—or, rather, mental phenomena exist and can be known only through their physical side effects. The wages of sin, as the Bible says, is death; and in Comstock's view that death has no metaphoric dimension. It is the death of the body, blunt and simple, without a hint that the fate of a child reading a half-dime novel might differ in any significant way from that of a bear mauling planted meat. Like many of his contemporaries, Comstock waxed hysterical about masturbation, which he took to be both the cause and the consequence of falling into one or another "trap":

> Fathers and mothers, look into your child's face, and when you see the vigor of youth failing, the cheek growing pale, the eye lustreless and sunken, the step listless and faltering, the body enervated, and the desire to be much alone coming over your offspring; when close application to work or study becomes irk-

some, and the buoyancy of youth gives place to peevishness and irritability, then seriously look for a cause. It may not always be the case, but in many instances it will be found to come from secret practices, which have early in life sapped the health of mind and body.

The results, potential and actual, are horrific:

Is not this awful curse to the young prevalent enough to command a remedy? to call for attention from parents? Go to the insane asylums and epileptic hospitals for a reply. Our youth are falling on every side. Lives that otherwise might shine as the stars in the firmament are shrouded with a veil of darkness, with horrors to the victim's mind which no pen can describe.

The fear is conventional and conventionally expressed, but it comes in tandem with testimony from an "eminent professor in a Southern college" that "seventy-five if not ninety per cent of our young men are victims of self-abuse."[26] For Comstock, all other traps bring on masturbation, and masturbation leads to death: if almost all of America's young men are addicted to this lethal practice, what hope remains for America?

None, it seems. *Traps for the Young*, like Comstock's other writings and the course of his extraliterary career, bears witness to an apocalyptic vision. He sometimes implies that the present generation will be the nation's last; the sins of the fathers will simply annihilate their children. Comstock expended his life's energies endeavoring to assure that his own grim prophecy would not be fulfilled. It was in the name of America's children that he carried on his work, and he never tired of invoking the terrible plight in which these innocents found themselves. Yet Comstock's peculiar rhetoric, with its relentless blurring of the mental into the physical, produces some queasy effects of which the children's champion must have been unconscious. Warning parents against the fatal consequences of letting various "traps" invade the home, he favored blunt physical analogies:

Is any parent so heartless and cruel that he would take either of his beloved children and hold him as a victim while a stranger should, with still greater barbarity, inflict torture or cut off a limb? Surely no. Will any parent dismember his offspring, or even inflict needless pain? . . . Would it pay to shut your children up, and then open a cage of wild beasts in the room with them? or to bring in adders, centipedes, and scorpions for them to play with?[27]

The context here is the bodily devastation wrought by "rum traps"; images of mutilation might therefore be justified. But they creep in everywhere, with an insistence that a modern reader cannot help but find unnerving. "Story-papers," for example, "speak to many youthful minds like the piercings of a sword—a *poisoned* sword!"[28] And lust, *"the constant companion of all other crimes,"* drags its helpless prey through "a succession of sickening, offensive, and disgusting scenes . . . until life, to such a one, must be made up of disease, wounds, and putrefying sores."[29]

The unspecified reference here is to venereal infection; typically, Comstock would rather enumerate the loathsome symptoms than write the taboo words "gonorrhea" and "syphilis." In European tracts on prostitution, the consequences of venereal disease were portrayed just as graphically and with equal verve. The difference is that Comstock's very delicacy lends a grotesque vividness to images that would be placed in proper perspective, at least, if their proper sequence were made clear. By omitting the intermediate steps—alcoholism in the case of rum traps, venereal disease in the case of lust—Comstock makes it seem that liquor and obscenity generate instantaneous physical corruption, without the possibility of variation from one case to another. No doubt the abruptness was intentional, but it also allowed Comstock to dwell with morbid enthusiasm on the imagined spectacle of maimed, pierced, and blistered children. It is difficult to avoid the conclusion that this spectacle possessed a certain charm in its own right.

This was not Comstock's private quirk. In the United States, where the Young Person exercised a power unknown in Europe, solicitude for the child was habitually paired with evocations of the child's destruction. Henry James's short novel *Daisy Miller* (1878) is the most famous literary example: coddled to the point of stupefaction in her American upbringing, Daisy blunders through corrupt Europe with an insouciance that leads inevitably to defamation and death. James returned to the theme again and again, ringing changes: in *The Turn of the Screw* (1898), the ruined children are said to be English, and in *The Golden Bowl* (1904), the spoiled American girl has grown up. In both cases, however, as in many others, James exhibits a characteristically American fascination with the corruption of youthful innocence, often accompanied by images of cruelty and pain. Comstock's imagination was infinitely cruder than James's; that very crudity, however, gave him a special rapport with those who supported his efforts. Fantasies of violence against children came to their lips, as to his, with unself-conscious ease. A certain Mrs. Barker, one of the "Lady Managers" of the 1893 Chicago Columbian Exposition, unwittingly proved this imaginative affinity in a letter to the Director-General complaining about the hoochie-coochie dancers at the Midway Plaisance. Comstock had attended a performance and urged Mrs. Barker to do likewise; predictably scandalized by the display, she wrote bluntly: "I object to the vile, licentious foreign dances. I would sooner lay my two boys in their graves than that they should look at the sights I saw yesterday." Gruesome as Mrs. Barker's alternative was, it fell short of Comstock's own, at least in scope. "The whole World's Fair must be razed to the ground," he told a reporter for the New York *World*, "or these three shows must stop."[30]

Mrs. Barker also shared with Comstock the habit of imagining the threatened Young Person as male, in contrast to the European fantasy of imperiled girls or young women. In the European case, the scenario of a maiden corrupted by pornography verged itself on the pornographic; in the United States, where visions of violence predominated, woeful dreams were more likely to feature maimed boys. Comstock was highly consistent in this regard: from the start of his career (when the ruination of some "bright and intelligent young men" enlightened him), his fables of disaster almost always had male protagonists. His nonpornographic "traps," like gambling and liquor, were in fact more likely to ensnare boys than girls, on account of boys' greater freedom; but even when he discussed the domestic perils of novels and newspapers, his imagination still focused on the corruption of the male. Again, Comstock's exaggerated squeamishness might explain this oddity: his reverence for the female might simply have prevented his even dreaming of her susceptibility to temptation. Comstock's obsession with blighted manhood was also a symptom of his belief that America was hurtling toward damnation. Men, the bearers of the future, would be a more significant loss than women, who were expendable. Like many of his contemporaries, Comstock understood the world in fundamentally economic terms; what alarmed him most was waste and dispersal. Male sexual constitution suited itself more readily to economic metaphors than its female counterpart did. Corrupted men ran dry: corrupted women did something quite different, something that apparently eluded Comstock's imaginative grasp.

Profound as Comstock's rapport may have been with a certain segment of the American population, he was drastically out of touch, it seems, with most of it. Without the indifference of the public at large, he would have died a dry-goods clerk. Only because he and his few cohorts persisted, and because the majority hardly cared which way the fight turned out, was Comstock able to push through the Act that bore his name and to sustain the official-unofficial position that legitimized his illegalities. From Comstock's own point of view, his worst enemy was neither saloon keepers nor newspaper publishers nor even those who peddled smut; it was the utter indifference the nation at large continued to display, amazingly, in the face of impending disaster. For more than forty years, Comstock strove to rouse alarm, but the perverse outcome was that, as time went on, apathy grew. From a nemesis, Comstock turned into a figure of fun; in his last decade particularly, he became a greater annoyance to his supporters than to his opponents. He never ceased campaigning to make the public aware of dangers that seemed to him frightful and obvious; gradually, however, even his foes gave up fighting and took to mocking him.

In Comstock's early days, by contrast, some observers perceived him as a far greater menace than the illegal goods he hunted down. His underhanded methods were repeatedly denounced in the press—not a wholly altruistic gesture, since Comstock's actions against false advertising had cut deeply into the revenues of many magazines and newspapers. The peak of public opposition to Comstock was a petition, said to bear 70,000 signatures, presented to the House of Representatives in February 1878, with the aim of repealing the Comstock Law. The names were headed up by that of Colonel Robert G. Ingersoll, one of Comstock's principal *bêtes noires*, whose outspoken agnosticism he would later proclaim mere "scoffings, sneers, and blasphemies."[31] The petition maintained that the Comstock laws, "executed ostensibly to prevent the passage of *so-called* obscene literature through the mails of the United States," in fact "*have been and are being enforced to destroy the liberty of conscience in matters of religion, against the freedom of the press, and to the great hurt of the learned professions. . . .*"[32] Fervent though the petitioners were (and greatly though they outnumbered Comstock's forces), the House Committee blandly ruled that there had been no violation of the Constitution, and the petition was denied.

In the view of Comstock's biographers, his declining credibility after about 1900 was a symptom of progress: "To his youthful countrymen, he had become a great tradition, a joke, a scapegoat."[33] The passage of time did discredit Comstock, and in 1927, when Heywood Broun and Margaret Leech published their biography, that change seemed unmistakably progressive. With a longer perspective, however, it is possible to be more specific. His numerous foibles aside, Comstock represented an impulse that we have seen before in European contexts—the urge to limit dissemination of all kinds, to control the availability of representations almost irrespective of their subjects. Like his more sophisticated contemporaries in France and England, Comstock at bottom feared nothing so much as the universal distribution of information. The prospect called up nightmarish images of a world without structure, where all barriers had been breached and all differences leveled. It was appropriate that sex should become the focus of such nightmares, since long before the modern threat arose, sex already stood for loss of control and the scattering of substance. Comstock found in the postal system a perfect metaphor for this ancient terror: spread throughout the country, indiscriminately accessible, public and private at once, the postal system had (odd as it may sound) something sexy about it. Left unpoliced, sex bred chaos; uninspected, the mails might do the same. It is absolutely fitting that America's foremost antisex crusader was an agent for the Post Office Department. It is also fitting that his job took him so many miles by rail: the railroad network strongly resembled and often coincided with the postal system, and the sexiness of railroads is generally acknowledged.

The decline of Comstock's impact in his later years may have been due in part to the normalization of technology, and to its rapid advance. Before he died, Comstock witnessed the advent of telephone, wireless, motion pictures, automobiles, and airplanes—all of which contributed to a geometrical rise in the rate at which representations, even things themselves, could be disseminated. Until the end, Comstock resisted these developments; though he took full advantage of their power, his goal was always the damming up of the very channels he employed. There was a profoundly pastoral quality about his efforts, a plaintive yearning for a time (his New Canaan childhood, no doubt, but Wordsworth had had the same dream long before) when each household had constituted a world unto itself. Later generations, for whom the charmed circle of the family was growing less and less sacrosanct, who were coming to value technology as a self-evident boon, found Comstock's Puritan pastoralism both retrograde and laughable. They called the change progress; a couple of generations later yet, we may wish to reconsider.

The majority of the books Comstock burned were of the lowest quality; they fell squarely into the underground regions mapped by Ashbee and his friends.[34] Now and then, however, Comstock locked horns with art, inevitably arousing much more derision than came from his subterranean endeavors. In *Traps for the Young*, under the rubric "Artistic and Classical Traps," he felt obliged to express his outrage at the poisonous effects that even art might produce if it were too widely distributed. Some "men," he declared, had made a full-time job of degrading the public by artistic means: "Accordingly Pompeii, the art galleries, and the museums of Europe are explored to find some new work of an obscene character or tendency which they can reproduce, which shall possess the quality to satisfy this low taste, and yet shall be labelled 'art' for their protection."

Having asserted that much, Comstock tumbled into a familiar trap. Not all art was bad, only some of it:

> Because some foul-minded man places his filthy conceptions upon canvas is no reason why such a daub should be protected under the name of *art*. Art is high and exalted. Its worth commands respect. Its intrinsic value is derived from its perfection.

Perhaps it would have been well if Comstock had backed off at this point, leaving aesthetic questions alone. But, relentlessly explaining and justifying himself, he forged ahead, making it clear that he had no real objection to obscene art, so long as it stayed where it belonged:

> These things, until recently, were so restricted that their power for evil was confined to a narrow limit. But of late, since the grosser-worded publications cannot be obtained generally as before, men calling themselves respectable citizens, and holding prominent positions in society, have popularized these works by getting out low-priced editions and extensively advertising them.

It seems unlikely that a reader deprived of *The Lustful Turk* would flee to Boccaccio instead, but the point is plain: "Again, let the rights of all artists be protected, if we must have 'works of art' that are shocking to modesty, or offensive to decency, by public sentiment's restricting these products to the galleries of art, and not permitting counterfeits of the vile in them to be disseminated indiscriminately before the public."[35]

Indiscriminate dissemination—the same villain on both sides of the Atlantic. When Comstock set his sights, however, on objects to which any articulate group attributed artistic value, an outcry went up and was gleefully publicized in the press. Meanwhile, hole-and-corner productions were being burned by the ton with hardly a protest. Comstock always lost when he encountered high-toned opposition. In his last years, though his nose for filth seems to have sharpened, he occasionally restrained himself when filth was also art. In 1913, for example, he took no official action against Paul Chabas' classic piece of kitsch *September Morn*, merely demanding that a copy be removed from a Manhattan shop window (it was soon put back, but Comstock let it stay).[36] And in the following year, when the *Chautauquan* printed on its cover a photograph of a naked Roman faun—not Pompeiian, but similar in spirit—he contented himself with a protest.[37]

By the time of Comstock's death in 1915, he had already been immortal for a decade, though hardly in a way that would have pleased him. Modern dictionaries all contain "comstockery," sometimes capitalized but more often not, and variously defined as "overzealous censorship of the fine arts and literature, often mistaking outspokenly honest works for salacious ones" (*American College Dictionary*, 1963), or "overzealous censorship of literature and the other arts because of alleged immorality" (*American Heritage Dictionary*, 1975). Even the impartial authority of the English language condemns Comstock for overzealousness, immortalizing not his campaigns against gambling or quack medicines but the one set of attitudes that made him ridiculous. Ironically, "comstockery" was born in a contretemps with which Comstock had nothing personally to do. In September 1905, an official of the New York Public Library ordered that the circulation of *Man and Superman* and other of George Bernard Shaw's works be restricted. Shaw was not yet a world-famous figure, but he was enjoying some notoriety in New York just then, because *Man and Superman* had recently opened at the Hudson Theatre. Robert W. Welch, London correspondent for the *New York Times*, was informed of the Library's action and wrote to Shaw for his opinion, which the *Times* published in the last week of September. With his typical grandiose egotism, Shaw blew a trifling local incident up to international proportions; in the process, he coined a word.

"Nobody outside of America," Shaw wrote, "is likely to be in the least surprised. Comstockery is the world's standing joke at the expense of the United States. Europe likes to hear of such things. It confirms the deep-seated conviction of the Old World that America is a provincial place, a second-rate country-town civilization after all." He went on to develop his favorite theme of the moment, denouncing marriage as "the most licentious of human institutions" and proudly proclaiming that *Man and Superman* was an "explicit attack" on it. Seen from this standpoint, the restriction of Shaw's play shone forth as "a symptom of what is really a moral horror both in America and elsewhere, and that is the secret and intense resolve of the petty domesticity of the world to tolerate no criticism and suffer no invasion." Self-aggrandizement naturally followed:

> I am an artist, and, it is inevitable, a public moralist. . . . I have honor and humanity on my side, wit in my head, skill in my hand, and a higher life for my aim. Let those who put me on their restricted lists so that they may read me themselves while keeping their children in the dark, acknowledge their allies, state their qualifications, and avow their aim, if they dare.

After various other threats to "the Comstockers" in their "corrupt and sensual . . . bigoted connubiality," Shaw concluded with a warning that, oddly, put him in agreement with Comstock: "I do not say that my books and plays cannot do harm to weak or dishonest people. They can, and probably do. But if the American character cannot stand that fire even at the earliest age at which it is readable or intelligible, there is no future for America."[38]

Comstock apparently had never heard of Shaw before this brouhaha flared up. "Never saw one of his books," he told the *Times* reporters who found him in his garden and showed him Shaw's published letter, "so he can't be much." But Comstock made a spirited reply:

I see this man Shaw says down here that he knows that his works can probably do harm to weak and dishonest people. Well, that lays him, his works, his publishers, the people who present his plays and all who or which has anything to do with the production or disseminating of them liable to the law which was made primarily to protect the weak. He convicts himself.[39]

It may have been a desire for retribution that led Comstock, less than a month later, to endeavor to prevent a New York production of the even more outrageous *Mrs. Warren's Profession*, to which the British Lord Chamberlain's office had repeatedly refused a license. Comstock took no legal steps, but merely wrote to Arnold Daly, the would-be producer, informing him of the nature of the law, with the clear implication that *Mrs. Warren's Profession* would be actionable under it. As innumerable entrepreneurs would do after him, Daly took advantage of this veiled threat from the hit man of institutional morality. He summoned reporters, read them Comstock's letter, challenged him to attend a rehearsal (he did not), and awaited the opening-night crowds. Police had to be called in to restrain them.[40]

It is in some ways unfortunate that Comstock's name should have entered the language by means of such minor, even silly clashes as those with Shaw and Daly. Comstock's full attention seldom went to the rooting out of "artistic and classical traps," and his greatest impact, for both good and ill, was felt in other areas. His enshrinement as America's archprude was related to his participation in the development of a cultural myth that enjoyed great popularity in Comstock's own day and has become canonical since—that of the visionary, self-denying artist, who works in splendid isolation and constant jeopardy of suppression by the philistine public. "I am an artist," Shaw got the chance to say, as if the profession of writing plays possessed an aura that exempted its practitioner from ordinary civility. The development of "pornography" is closely bound up with the triumph of this scheme, but it is a distortion to remember Comstock only for the role he played in it. As one who would hang crinolines on the Venus de Milo, Comstock can be laughed at and dismissed; his actions against other "obscenities," however, brought less-amusing results. The most lamentable of them was his lifelong war against contraception.

From the first, Comstock saw no difference between smutty playing cards and serious tracts on birth control; the perennial muddle over a writer's intentions, so worrisome to early European "pornographers," troubled him not at all. He and his Y.M.C.A. associates wrote this nondistinction into the Comstock Law; it squeezed articles "intended for the prevention of conception or procuring of abortion" between publications "of an indecent character" and things "adapted for any indecent or immoral use." With an indiscriminate law behind him, Comstock proceeded indiscriminately for decades, but he concentrated with special vigor and cruelty on those who performed or even advocated birth control by any means. His most notorious prosecution of this kind occurred in 1878 and was directed against the shadowy, ambiguous Ann Lohman, known as "Madame Restell," New York City's foremost abortionist—or "female physician and professor of midwifery," as she styled herself. Since about 1836, when she married Charles R. Lohman (already in the trade), Madame Restell had been selling contraceptive devices, performing abortions, and delivering unwanted babies. She began in a modest establishment on disreputable Greenwich Street, but healthy profits and a burgeoning clientele soon enabled her to move uptown to a Fifth Avenue mansion which she decorated, as a contemporary put it, "with unexceptionable taste."[41]

In their public utterances, Madame Restell's fellow citizens regarded her with unalloyed horror: she was nicknamed "Madame Killer," and her home was dubbed "the house built on babies' skulls."[42] Privately, however, a sizable number of New Yorkers must have felt differently, since for more than forty years, Madame Restell carried on her business fairly openly and with great profit. Though polite society shunned her—except when her clandestine services were required—she planted herself in its midst and unabashedly flaunted her wealth; at her death in 1878, despite decades of heavy bribes to the police, she was said to be worth one and a half million dollars.[43] And she filled a pressing need in a culture dominated by views of which this 1872 outcry is typical:

Men and women tell their friends every day that they do not mean to increase their families. They do mean, however, to enjoy the blessings of the married state, and to avoid its responsibilities. There is scarcely a physician in the city who is not applied to almost daily by persons of good position for advice as to the best means of preventing conception. The physicians of New York are men of honor, and they not only refuse to comply with the request, but warn the applicants for advice as to the true moral and physical nature of the course they are seeking to adopt. Yet this warning does not turn them from their purpose. Failing to secure the assistance of scientific men, they seek the advice, and purchase the drugs, of the wretches whose trade is child murder.[44]

According to a pattern that time has not altered much, Restell and her colleagues were sustained by a moral code that tolerated their activities so long as they remained underground and therefore as dangerous as possible. Most observers confined their outrage to words; Comstock was ready to take action.

His tactics were at least as shady as any ever employed by Madame Restell. According to Restell herself, testifying in court after Comstock and a police escort had apprehended her in her Fifth Avenue "palace," Comstock had presented himself as a desperately poor father, facing bankruptcy if he and his wife should have another child. Only after hearing this "sad tale" had Restell "timidly produced her remedies"—a doubtful assertion, because her defense was apparently going to be the manifest lie that she had been a swindler all along, peddling only placebos.[45] But that defense was never presented. Having tried in vain to bribe her pursuer, Restell despaired and cut her throat with a carving knife—leaving Comstock to boast that she was the fifteenth malefactor he had driven to suicide, in less than five years on the job.[46]

There were those even in 1878 who deplored the outcome of the Restell affair, though less because a woman had been hounded to death than because such underhanded means had been employed to entrap her. A modern observer can hardly help pitying Madame Restell, however vulgar and venal she may have been; she and Comstock were equally typical of their time, and no one should have died in such a purblind battle. Restell's fate looks even more poignant when it is contrasted to that of another advocate of birth control who ran afoul of Comstock nearly four decades later, at the very end of Comstock's career. Margaret Sanger operated no abortion parlor and dispensed no drugs; she did, however, distribute what in Comstock's view might have been worse—information on birth control to those who desired it and encouragement to those who were unsure. And she did so with a self-righteous fervor that matched Comstock's own.

Born in Corning, New York, the sixth of eleven children, Sanger, *née* Higgins (1883–1966), showed few signs in her early life of the qualities that would later propel her into worldwide notoriety. She trained as a schoolteacher, then as a nurse; she married architect William Sanger in 1904 and bore him three children. The breakthrough came one night early in 1912, when, returning from a futile nursing visit to a woman already dead at the hands of "a five-dollar professional abortionist," Sanger had a vision:

> As I stood at the window and looked out, the miseries and problems of that sleeping city arose before me in a clear vision like a panorama: crowded homes, too many children; babies dying in infancy; mothers overworked; baby nurseries; children neglected and hungry—mothers so nervously wrought they could not give the little things the comfort nor care they needed; mothers half sick most of their lives—'always ailing, never failing'; women made into drudges; children working in cellars; children aged six and seven pushed into the labor market to help earn a living; another baby on the way; still another; yet another; a baby born dead—great relief; an older child dies—sorrow, but nevertheless relief—insurance helps; a mother's death—children scattered into institutions; the father, desperate, drunken; he slinks away to become an outcast in a society which has trapped him.[47]

This virtuoso passage, written twenty years after the event, captures the hallucinatory vividness of a vision hardly less apocalyptic than Comstock's own. Sanger's apocalypse was present, not waiting in some lurid future like Comstock's; she conjured up just as many pictures of battered children, but hers were derived from eyewitness experience, not morbid fantasy.

Inspired, Sanger resolved to give up nursing and devote herself to eradicating the root of the evil, but everyone around her issued a time-honored warning: "Comstock'll get you if you don't watch out."[48] She soon discovered the truth of it. Early in 1913, Anita Block invited her to contribute a series of articles on health to the radical newspaper *The Call*, under the title "What Every Woman Should Know." Sanger's aim was oddly reminiscent of Comstock's—to defend children against negligent and ignorant adults—though her means were very different: "I attempted . . . to introduce the impersonality of nature in order to break through the rigid consciousness of sex on the part of parents, who were inclined to be too intensely personal about it."[49] The series was a success and met no opposition; it was followed, however, by "What Every Girl Should Know," a project with a much riskier goal: "If the mother can impress the child with the beauty and wonder and sacredness of the sex function, she has taught it the first lesson." After only three or four issues, the column was suppressed by the Post Office Department.

In pamphlet form, however, *What Every Girl Should Know* circulated unmolested; Comstock's influence was fading, and his aged energy was no match for Sanger and her youthful comrades. He and Sanger nevertheless did battle more than once again, in the two years that remained of Comstock's life. In the autumn of 1913, the Sanger family made a brief, eccentric tour of Glasgow and Paris, where the contrast between British and French methods of planning progeny impressed itself forcibly on Margaret. Back in New York (William remained in Paris till the following summer), further inspired by her experience of Glaswegian squalor and Parisian prudence, she set out deliberately to bait her adversary with a monthly magazine called *The Woman Rebel*. "Its message," she later wrote, "was a scathing denunciation of all organized conventionalities. It went as far as was necessary to arouse the Comstockians to bite."[50] They did. The first issue of *The Woman Rebel*, March

1914, was declared unmailable under the Comstock Law; the same juryless verdict was passed on the issues of May and July. But Sanger, forewarned, acted as too few before her had done: she read the statutes.

"Many times I studied Section 211 of the Federal Statutes, under which the Post Office was acting," she recalled in her *Autobiography*. "This penal clause of the Comstock Law had been left hanging in Washington like the dried shell of a tortoise. . . . To me it was outrageous that information regarding motherhood, which was so generally called sacred, should be classed with pornography." Actually, of course, it had not been; "pornography" was not in general use in 1873, and the word appeared nowhere in the Comstock Law. Sanger also apparently never delved far into the meaning of "sacred," which in its oldest sense refers to forbidden things, precisely those about which information ought not to be distributed. But she did understand the statute correctly ("I had not broken the law, because it did not prohibit discussion—merely giving advice"), and she acted briskly, gathering her friends together to deposit a few copies of *The Woman Rebel* in each of hundreds of mailboxes all over New York City, so that no significant number could be seized at once.[51] For the first time, Comstock and his allies had run up against opponents who not only shared their self-righteousness, but who were also willing to creep about the streets at midnight for the sake of their cause.

In August 1914, Sanger was indicted on nine counts of violating federal statutes; conviction on them all would have brought a prison sentence of forty-five years.[52] In October, the night before her trial was to convene, she fled via Canada to England, where she met prominent birth-control advocates like Havelock Ellis, Edward Carpenter, and Marie Stopes; she also heard, surprisingly for the first time, about the 1877 trial of Annie Besant and Charles Bradlaugh, a celebrated case that prefigured Sanger's own.[53] In September 1915, she was summoned back to the United States: her husband had been arrested by no less a personage than Comstock himself. Though the Sangers had in effect suspended their marriage nearly two years before, when Margaret left William behind in Paris, they remained on amicable terms, and William gave full support to Margaret's birth-control campaign. A few months before, a Mr. Heller had presented himself in William's New York studio, claiming to be an acquaintance of Margaret's and interested in her work. The gullible William handed over a copy of Margaret's pamphlet *Family Limitation*, which she had had secretly printed before her flight to Europe but never formally published.

Heller turned out to be a Comstock flunky: William fell for a very old trick, one which had hardly changed since the days of the unfortunate Prosch, nearly four decades earlier. A few days after Heller's visit, in William's words, "a grey-haired, side-whiskered, six-foot creature presented himself and said: 'I am Mr. Comstock. I have a warrant for your arrest.' " Gruff as ever, Comstock was still not above cajoling his victim. He tried to persuade William to plead guilty (a suspended sentence was promised); he fished for details on the Sangers' unconventional marital arrangements; he sought to elicit Margaret's whereabouts, assuring acquittal for William if he squealed. But for once in his long career, Comstock had misjudged his opponents. William would divulge nothing; and when he asked Comstock "what he would do to the author of a pamphlet like 'Family Limitation,' " the old man's brimstone flared up again: *"He said he would recommend that such a party be given the limit of five years' hard labor for every one printed."*[54]

In Comstock's imagination, this would be Margaret's fate should she be so foolhardy as to return to her native land—despite the fact that no such extravagant sentence had ever been pronounced against any of his trainload of victims. He succeeded in obtaining William's conviction, a typical one of $150 or thirty days in jail; William defiantly chose the latter. But Margaret, who arrived in New York in mid-October 1915, would eventually triumph, though Comstock would not live to suffer that humiliation. She could do nothing to help her husband, who served his time; but she, who bore the much more serious charge of having fled the country under indictment, never stood trial. Her case was dismissed on February 18, 1916. In both of Sanger's memoirs, she attributes the government's nolle prosequi to the popular sentiment in favor of birth control that had burgeoned during her exile and rose to a crescendo upon her bold return. Her claim is valid to some extent, but she neglects to mention that the primary instigator of both Sangers' prosecution, Anthony Comstock, had died on September 21, 1915, about the time she set out from Bordeaux on her risky homeward journey. From his start in Winnipauk, Connecticut, Comstock had endeavored to instill his own enthusiasm into lackadaisical law officers and magistrates; bereft of his invigorating presence, they sank back into somnolence. Sanger went on to fight many more battles against Comstockery and won most of them; she and her arch enemy never met head-on, but she would spar for another half century with his ghost.

In *My Fight for Birth Control*, Sanger announces that "Anthony Comstock had taken a chill at the Sanger trial, was taken to his home in a taxicab, and a few weeks later died."[55] Actually, neither Sanger had anything directly to do with Comstock's death. He had been President Wilson's delegate to the International Purity Congress at the Golden Gate Exposition; he traveled cross-country by train, lectured repeatedly, and trained home again—the exertion overtaxed him, and he succumbed to pneumonia. An era, and the peculiar tangle of fear, buoyancy, and ruthlessness that characterized it, died with him. "Comstockery," as Shaw defined it, would endure and is lively still, but the peculiarly American social conditions that spawned it had already changed during Comstock's lifetime. In the future, no individual would be able to hold on for long to the virtually autocratic power that Comstock wielded for forty-two years. The very development Comstock feared most—the increasingly widespread distribution of information—would only accelerate, as if of its own accord, compelling those who would restrict it to combine in ever-larger organizations or else to content themselves with merely local jurisdiction.

In many ways, Comstock and Sanger were twin products of nineteenth-century America. Separated in time by two generations, they nevertheless shared a crusader's conviction that great and praiseworthy things had to be done, along with a cynic's belief that regularly constituted authority would never do the job. Neither was a revolutionary; they wanted to improve the given order, not overthrow it. But both were unscrupulous in the interest of causes that, in their eyes, transcended mere scrupulousness. And both envisioned a grim apocalypse, though Sanger's was present and real, while Comstock's lurked in a future fueled by overheated dreams. On one point, however, they differed absolutely. Sanger put her faith in the beneficial effects of knowledge; she was willing to take whatever risk might accompany the dissemination of frank talk about sex, trusting that the good done would enormously outweigh any incidental evils. Comstock inhabited a world thick with demons; he could conceive of no good arising from sex talk, frank or otherwise, and he spent his life in dubious battle against an entire culture that *would* talk about sex. That insistence has only grown in the decades since Comstock's death; the triumph of campaigners like Sanger, along with the pervasive influence of Freud and his followers, has resulted in a prevailing anti-Comstockery almost as oppressive as its defeated counterpart. Yet the old injunction not to see and not to know has never passed away; it flourishes still, in new guises that make Comstock's rough-and-ready deviousness look straightforward.

As in the case of the trials of *Madame Bovary* and the Sangers, "pornography" obtained its complete definition only on a battleground where prosecution met defense; neither side ever won full sway. Whether in the courtroom or the less formal forum of books, newspapers, and placards, the struggle to obliterate "pornography" always met resistance, and the almost universal twentieth-century experience has been that resistance wins. It is far from obvious why this should be so. Even if one identifies the opposition with enlightenment and freedom, it would be naive to suppose that the opposition triumphs because good is stronger than evil. In recent years, this apparently sure dichotomy has shown a disconcerting aptitude for reversing itself: exponents of freedom can demand the burning of books and pictures, while those who would preserve them can be labeled oppressors. The two sides are inseparable and deeply implicated in one another.

CHAPTER SIX

GOOD INTENTIONS

ANTHONY COMSTOCK has been called everything from a "perverted genius"[1] to an "obvious psychopath,"[2] and he merits the abuse. He possessed, however, a certain advantage over his detractors—simplicity. For him, anything that remotely smacked of sex ought to be burned, regardless of its point of view or manner of presentation. Few of Comstock's opponents were willing to match this stance with its equally simple opposite, to declare that nothing deserved burning, no matter how lewd or disgusting it was. Instead, the anti-Comstockers felt the need to make fine distinctions. For them, representations of sex were not forbidden a priori; all depended on style, attitude, audience, and most of all, intention. Certain books and pictures should suffer a. Comstockian fate; others had to be preserved, because some value redeemed them. The history of "pornography" in the twentieth century has been a vast, frustrating endeavor to separate the valuable from the worthless—a struggle with which Comstock, genius or psychopath or both, never troubled himself.

When Margaret Sanger visited England in 1915 and first heard about the Besant-Bradlaugh trial of 1877, she must have reflected that, in regard to birth control, America deserved its reputation as what Shaw had called "a second-rate country-town civilization." Sanger, if she returned home, faced prosecution and possible imprisonment for having distributed birth-control information; a federal statute forbade what she had done. In Britain, by contrast, though practice lagged far behind the enlightened example of the French and Dutch, there was no interdict against such knowledge. Lord Campbell's Act was less sweeping than the Comstock Law; it made no mention of "any article or thing designed or intended for the prevention of conception." And almost forty years earlier, when the Comstock Law was in its infancy, a celebrated English case had ended in the acquittal of two crusaders whose goal was not very different from Sanger's own.

Annie Besant (1847–1933) and Charles Bradlaugh (1833–91) were arrested in April 1877 for publishing and selling *Fruits of Philosophy, or The Private Companion of Young Married Couples* by the American physician Charles Knowlton, a pamphlet continuously available on both sides of the Atlantic since its first appearance in 1832. No prosecution had ever been launched against it in the United States, and nothing had been done in England until December 1876, when a Bristol bookseller, Henry Cook, was sentenced to two years' imprisonment under Lord Campbell's Act for having published a new edition with a title page and illustrations of his own devising. Cook, whom a modern historian has called the conductor of "an undercounter trade in pornography and an on-counter sale of secular literature,"[3] had already served a similar sentence on a similar charge. Nothing might have come of his recidivism, but on January 8, 1877, the London police also arrested George Watts, whose earlier edition of the old pamphlet Cook had embellished. Watts ultimately pleaded guilty and had to pay £25 court costs, but in the meantime Besant and Bradlaugh, who had urged resistance upon the reluctant Watts, had begun publication of their own edition of *Fruits of Philosophy*, price sixpence. Like Sanger a generation later, they were inspired by a cause; they courted arrest and eagerly submitted to trial, which began on June 18 before Lord Chief Justice Alexander Cockburn, then seventy-five years old and famous as the inventor of the Hicklin test.

The charge, read in court by Solicitor-General Sir Hardinge Giffard, was ferocious enough despite its quaint phraseology. Besant and Bradlaugh, "unlawfully and wickedly devising, contriving, and intending, as much as in them lay, to vitiate and corrupt the morals as well of youth as of divers other liege subjects of our said lady the Queen, and to incite and encourage the said liege subjects to indecent, obscene, unnatural and immoral practices, and bring them to a state of wickedness, lewdness and debauchery," had printed and sold "a certain indecent, lewd, filthy, bawdy, and obscene book, called *Fruits of Philosophy*, thereby contaminating, vitiating, and corrupting the morals."[4] The prosecution's redundancy was extravagant even by the standards of governmental prose, but it typified the desperate synonym-mongering that was characteristic of such topics and that seemed to get more severe as the nineteenth century advanced. Much antiobscenity legislation reflects the same busy concern with plugging up all possible loopholes—although, as several critics have pointed out, such words as "indecent," "lewd," and "obscene" can be defined only in terms of one another, producing a closed system that thwarts even the most assiduous inquiry into what any part of it might mean.

In this case, however, redundancy was the least of the government's problems. Besant and Bradlaugh spoke in their own defense, taking advantage of the opportunity to inform judge and jury—and the general public, by means of the newspapers that extensively covered the trial—of their freethinking views on several subjects, not all of them relevant to the issue at hand. Besant, for example, was able to take a few digs at the court's special solicitude for the young women who might be debauched by their book: "young men," she remarked, "do not seem to be taken into consideration on matters of this kind; it is apparently allowed that they may be as fast or objectionable as they choose."[5] Bradlaugh waxed eloquent on the implicit class bias in the indictment, finding numerous parallels to *Fruits of Philosophy* in Sir William Acton's respected, expensive *Functions and Disorders of the Reproductive Organs* (1857), which had never been charged with obscenity. "I say it is a horrible thing," he intoned, "to put us in danger of imprisonment for giving that information to the poor, which may with impunity be given to the rich."[6] The most embarrassing fact the defendants brought forward was that the sale of Knowlton's pamphlet had been enormously boosted by legal action against it. According to Besant, 700 copies had been sold during the year before the prosecution; in the last three months, the total had soared to 125,000.[7] The trial of *Madame Bovary* had long ago set a precedent for this classic side effect of antiobscenity proceedings, but it was still unfamiliar enough in 1877 to have a discouraging influence on the prosecution.[8]

The case against Besant and Bradlaugh, however, fell into confusion less through their efforts than on account of a flaw in the indictment itself. The charge was twofold: *Fruits of Philosophy* was obscene, and the defendants had intended to corrupt the nation by publishing it. In framing the Hicklin test, Cockburn had been at great pains to exclude the author's or publisher's intentions from consideration: the Protestant Electoral Union might have been sincere in distributing *The Confessional Unmasked* as a warning against the horrors of Catholicism, but the book itself, objectively examined, would nevertheless tend to deprave and corrupt. Even the relatively straightforward Hicklin case had compelled some devious reasoning on the Lord Chief Justice's part; now, nine years later, the problem of intention rose up once more. Throughout the Besant-Bradlaugh trial, Cockburn endeavored to deflect the jury's minds from the admirable character and noble aims of the defendants, in the teeth of the defendants' efforts to focus attention exactly there. In the end, the jury returned a double verdict: the book was obscene, but the defendants' intentions were pure. This would not do. Cockburn explained himself once more, calling on the same nonlogic he had employed in the Hicklin case: "If you find that the book is calculated to corrupt and deprave public morals, you must, although you did not think they had a motive to corrupt public morality, yet as their intention to publish was deliberate, you must find that as it is calculated to do so they had a corrupt motive in publishing it." Understandably, the jury could make no reply; when the clerk of the court asked if they all thought the defendants guilty, the foreman nodded, no one dissented, and in this ludicrous manner, a guilty verdict was arrived at.[9]

It did not last long. The following February, the Court of Appeals threw it out, on the grounds that the prosecution had been insufficiently clear in establishing its case—surely an understatement. This precedent, murky though it was, had the effect of permitting a relatively free circulation of sex information in England, but that freedom was far from unlimited. It failed, for example, to encompass yet another "lewd, wicked, bawdy, scandalous, and obscene" book, Havelock Ellis's *Sexual Inversion*, the first volume of his *Studies in the Psychology of Sex*.[10] In 1898, a London bookseller, George Bedborough, was arrested for selling a copy of *Sexual Inversion* to John Sweeney, a Comstockish policeman who had made friends with Bedborough in order to entrap him.[11] Ellis defended his work in terms that the long-dead Parent-Duchâtelet would have recognized: "The said book was written by me as the result of many years of scientific study, investigation and observation and was written purely in the interests of science and scientific investigation and to the best of my ability in a scientific spirit." He also obtained letters of support from, among others, George Bernard Shaw, who called the prosecution "a masterpiece of police stupidity and magisterial ignorance."[12] Despite these defenses, the court concluded by treating Bedborough like a naughty child. Sir Charles Hall, Recorder of London, dismissed him:

> I am willing to believe that in acting as you did, you might at the first outset perhaps have been gulled into the belief that somebody might say that this was a scientific work. But it is impossible for anybody with a head on his shoulders to open the book without seeing that it is a pretence and a sham, and that it is merely entered into for the purpose of selling this obscene publication.[13]

Bedborough was released on personal recognizance of £100, and the history of British obscenity grew still murkier.

The appeal to the "scientific spirit," the oldest rebuttal to charges of obscenity, had helped vindicate Besant and Bradlaugh's personal motives, but it was no help to Bedborough and Ellis twenty years later. Of course, Besant and Bradlaugh had disseminated information concerned only with the intercourse between husband and wife, while Ellis provided case histories of homosexuals, treating them in a reasonably sympathetic manner. Ellis's book probably also suffered from the fact that the trial of Oscar Wilde, held in April 1895, was still fresh in public memory; Wilde had been released from prison just a few months before *Sexual Inversion* was published.

In the twentieth century, the claim to scientific detachment would be surpassed in popularity by the assertion of artistic value; a long series of court decisions would establish "art" as the antithesis of "pornography" and something like its antidote. As early as 1857, artistic integrity had been called upon, with success, to defend both Flaubert and *Madame Bovary;* in the same year, however, a similar defense failed to vindicate Baudelaire and *Les Fleurs du Mal.* Probably the most disgraceful obscenity trial in English history also hinged on the question of art, and French art at that. The case did not instigate a trend, though it proved how vicious the guardians of the status quo could be when they felt themselves confronted with a challenge that seemed both morally subversive and foreign. It also illustrated, long before the end of the nineteenth century, how far the literary intelligentsia had diverged from the official canons of public taste—a disparity that would widen in the twentieth century and become the central issue in innumerable court battles.

Like Balzac before him, Emile Zola was very slow to reach an English-speaking audience. Zola's first novel was published in 1864, but nothing of his appeared in English until Frank Turner's translation of *Au Bonheur des Dames* (*Ladies' Delight*) in 1883.[14] The following year, the respected publishing house of Henry Vizetelly & Co. began issuing a series of Zola translations, which had grown to eighteen in number by 1888. Vizetelly (1820–94) made a specialty of works that possessed literary merit but that prudes might find objectionable. Not long after embarking on the Zola project, he founded the Mermaid Series of Elizabethan and Jacobean dramatists, all unexpurgated, under the general editorship of Havelock Ellis and with contributions by John Addington Symonds, Algernon Charles Swinburne, and Edmund Gosse. According to Vizetelly's son Ernest, even these recognized native classics were found by "some young anonymous scribes" to be " 'pornographic' in that hour when cant and hypocrisy poured venom on virtually every form of literature that had not received the *imprimatur* of Pecksniff & Co."[15] But such complaints were as nothing compared to the furor that arose over Ernest's translation of the eighteenth Zola novel on the Vizetelly list—*The Soil* (*La Terre*).

In Chapter 3, I quoted the hysterical response to this book by an anonymous writer for the *London Sentinel*: two pages had been displayed in the window of a London bookshop, and the writer, passing by, had seen a fourteen-year-old boy reading them. Horrified, the writer barged into the shop and demanded that the offending volume be removed. "The matter was of such a leprous character that it would be impossible for any young man who had not learned the Divine secret of self-control to have read it without committing some form of outward sin within twenty-four hours after." The outcry is ridiculous—though it is only the reductio ad absurdum of a monkey-see-monkey-do notion of human response still current a century later—and it would have been quickly forgotten had action not been taken by the National Vigilance Association. This appropriately named group was founded in 1886 to replace the Society for the Suppression of Vice, which had ceased operations a few years before. Thanks to the Association, Zola's alleged debauchery of the Young Person became the topic of a debate in the House of Commons on May 8, 1888, when Samuel Smith of Flintshire read the article from the *London Sentinel* before a sparse gathering of his colleagues. Smith launched into xenophobic rhapsodies. "Now, he asked, were they to stand still while the country was wholly corrupted by literature of this kind? Were they to wait until the moral fibre of the English race was eaten out, as that of the French was almost? It overspread that country like a torrent, and its poison was destroying the whole national life. France, to-day, was rapidly approaching the condition of Rome in the time of the Caesars."[16]

Smith also adduced some picturesque anecdotes that carried him rather far from Zola:

Only to-day he was told of a case in which a gentleman in the country received an advertisement of boots and shoes from a house in London, and inside that was a small notice that on application photographs would be sent. He made an application, and a parcel of most indelicate photographs of nude females was sent to him. He (Mr. Smith) asserted that in England we suffered from mistaken ideas of liberty.[17]

The immediate result of Smith's tirade was the adoption of a resolution: "That this House deplores the rapid spread of demoralizing literature in this country, and is of opinion that the Law against obscene publications and indecent pictures and prints should be vigorously enforced, and if necessary strengthened."[18] Again the matter might have stopped there, but the National Vigilance Association pushed on, and in August 1888, it obtained the issuance of a summons to Vizetelly naming three of Zola's novels, *The Soil*, *Nana*, and *Piping-Hot* (*Pot-Bouille*). The issuing magistrate, John Bridge, called them "the three most immoral books ever published";[19] a sort of self-fueling mania seems to have seized the authorities in what Ernest Vizetelly would later term "that hour of frenzied cant and unscrupulous injustice."[20] At the end of October, father and son appeared in Central Criminal Court before Solicitor-General Sir Edward Clarke and a largely hostile jury; among the prosecutors was the young Herbert Henry Asquith, who would render his country worthier service as Prime Minister during the first years of World War I.

The prosecution chose a familiar tactic: twenty-five objectionable passages had been selected and were read to the jury, which finally balked when it was asked to listen to the most infamous of all, an episode in the first chapter of *The Soil* depicting the peasant girl Françoise's plucky assistance at the insemination of her cow, while Jean Macquart looks on. In a modern translation, the most outrageous part of the episode reads: "Carefully, as though undertaking something of great importance, she [Françoise] stepped quickly forward with pursed lips and set face; concentration made her eyes seem even darker. She had to reach right across with her arm as she grasped the bull's penis firmly in her hand and lifted it up. And when the bull felt that he was near the edge, he gathered his strength and, with one single thrust of his loins, pushed his penis right in. Then it came out again. It was all over; the dibble had planted the seed." This no doubt was too much for the unwilling auditors to hear; it is questionable whether their shock would have been soothed by the narrator's mitigating comment a few lines later: "It never entered his [Jean's] head to make the sort of bawdy jokes which the farmhands indulged in when girls used to bring their cows to be covered. This young girl seemed to find it so completely normal and necessary that, in all decency, there was really nothing to laugh about. It was just natural."[21]

Facing unanimous resistance, the defense hurriedly changed its plea to guilty, and Vizetelly received a fine of £250. The National Vigilance Association was not done with him yet, however. In the spring of 1889, it haled him into court again, this time on account of thirteen translations from the French, including eight Zola novels and a version of *Madame Bovary* by Karl Marx's daughter Eleanor Marx Aveling. Sixty-nine years old, ill, and nearly bankrupt, Vizetelly could put up no fight when his defense attorney, the "fat, unwieldy" Mr. Cock, advised another guilty plea.[22] Because he was unable to pay a fine, Vizetelly was sentenced to three months in prison—a term which, incredibly, he served in full. He was released in August and survived another four and a half years, but he never regained his health, his spirits, or his fortune.

The ferocity of the Vizetelly prosecution is difficult to explain. It was far from typical; no other case in the history of Anglo-American obscenity trials offers a comparable example of determined hostility and ruthlessness toward an individual. One can only suppose that a foreign-sounding name (though the family, originally Italian, had resided in England for centuries), combined with high intellectual pretensions and a record of sailing close to the wind in matters of obscenity, made Vizetelly the unwitting focus of several animosities, no one of which would alone have ruined him. The case was surrounded by bitter ironies. Ernest's translation of *La Terre* was, as he asserted, "undoubtedly an expurgated one"; on reading the French, his father had advised that it definitely needed " 'toning' for the English reader."[23] Three weeks before the prosecution began, the French government had awarded Zola the Legion of Honor, citing *La Terre* as among his greatest achievements. And even in England the furor was quickly forgotten. Two years after Henry Vizetelly's death, Zola visited London for the first time, to great acclaim; and in 1898, in trouble at home for his stand in the Dreyfus case, he sought asylum in friendly England, where he remained for a year.

The inconsistencies brought on by an almost instantaneous public memory span are endemic features of the history of obscenity trials. But the Vizetelly case is a landmark because it articulated, in unusually clear and brutal form, some issues that would dominate the discussion of "pornography" for the next fifty years. During Vizetelly's first prosecution, when he still had the strength and money to offer resistance, he took vigorous action. He imitated Annie Besant by publishing a pamphlet with the sonorous title *Extracts Principally from the English Classics, showing that the Legal Suppression of M. Zola's novels would logically involve the Bowdlerising of some of the greatest works in English literature;* his list includes scenes from twelve Shakespeare plays, the entirety of *Venus and Adonis*, a wide sampling of Restoration drama, and works by Fielding, Smollett, Sterne, Byron, and D. G. Rossetti.[24] He also sent an open letter to Solicitor of the Treasury Sir J. F. Stephen, official conductor of the prosecution (and Virginia Woolf's uncle). Like the pamphlet, Vizetelly's letter seems to have had little effect, but it posed a question that had often been heard before and would wait seventy years for an unequivocal answer: "Is *actual* life to be no longer described in fiction, simply because the withdrawal of the veil that shrouds it displays a state of things unadapted to the contemplation—not of grown-up men and women, but of 'the young person of fifteen,' who has the works of all Mr. Mudie's novelists to feast on?"[25]

Vizetelly's small voice joined a chorus of protest that had been slowly rising for more than a generation, as the aims of artists carried them ever further from the desires and expectations of their audience. Dickens's merciless portrait of Mr. Podsnap is a prime example of the disdain that novelists, as early as 1865, were beginning to feel toward a certain segment of the public—though Dickens never seriously affronted even Mr. Podsnap's appalling squeamishness. In the following year, however, Algernon Charles Swinburne took that step with a vengeance in *Poems and Ballads*, a volume attacked by reviewers as, among many other things, "prurient trash"[26] and "an attempt to glorify all the bestial delights that the subtleness of Greek depravity was able to contrive."[27] Outrage was not universal, and it focused more on Swinburne's anti-Christian attitude than on his clammy sexuality, but his respectable publisher, Moxon & Co., was inspired to withdraw *Poems and Ballads* from circulation and transfer publication rights to the shadier John Camden Hotten, whom Ashbee would later list as the publisher of such specialties as *The Romance of Chastisement* (1870).[28]

Swinburne was not about to take such exile lightly. Late in 1866, he published, with Hotten's imprint, a pamphlet entitled *Notes on Poems and Reviews*, in which he lavished polysyllabic invective on the "animalcules and infusoria" of the periodical press, accused his attackers of incompetence in Latin and Greek pronunciation, and came at length to the really important point:

> Literature, to be worthy of men, must be large, liberal, sincere; and cannot be chaste if it be prudish. Purity and prudery cannot keep house together. Where free speech and fair play are interdicted, foul hints and vile suggestions are hatched into fetid life. And if literature indeed is not to deal with the full life of man and the whole nature of things, let it be cast aside with the rods and rattles of childhood. Whether it affect to teach or to amuse, it is equally trivial and contemptible to us; only less so than the charge of immorality.[29]

Since the dawn of Western culture, artists have been regarded as exceptional beings, whether divinely inspired, as the epic poets were said to be, or merely gifted with the mysterious faculty called "genius." Not until the turn of the nineteenth century, however, did the specialness of artists come to entail a necessary alienation as well as difference from ordinary mortals. Increasingly grandiose claims for the value and power of art were yoked together with a growing sense that the public failed to appreciate that value and did little more than lip-service to that power. "Poets," announced Percy Bysshe Shelley in 1820, "are the unacknowledged legislators of the world"[30]—a famous phrase in which the emphasis should probably fall on "unacknowledged." In the same essay, Shelley also called the poet "a nightingale, who sits in darkness and sings to cheer its own solitude with sweet sounds."[31] It is difficult to see how these two roles, that of a lawgiver and that of a solitary singer, could be reconciled.

Indeed, they never were. As the nineteenth century advanced, the burgeoning reading public came to regard poetry, and the arts in general, less with dread than with mildly skittish hopefulness. For the common reader—well represented by the jurors who chastised Flaubert, Baudelaire, and Vizetelly—the proper function of art was to soothe and elevate, not to shock in any way. When, in 1828, the young John Stuart Mill sought relief from abysmal depression, he found it in Wordsworth's poetry—"medicine for my state of mind," he said.[32] Generations of Victorians would follow this lead, not because they thought poetry or the other arts trivial, but because they were unwilling to grant art the extravagant power that artists insisted on claiming for it. The popular attitude was an early, rudimentary form of consumerism; poets and painters naturally found it insulting. There were, however, to be more drastic side effects.

If good art is medicine, then bad art is poison; like drugs, books and pictures must possess at least the potential to kill, if they have the power to heal. With the possible exception of sewage (which, of course, can also be poisonous), the analogy between obscenity and poison is the most common rhetorical device in the limited repertoire of the pornography debate. The analogies have solidified into clichés, prepackaged units of meaning that need not be analyzed, because their truth goes without saying. In the case of pornography-as-poison, it has often been forgotten that to damn certain representations as lethal implies that all representations *ought* to do good in an equally visceral way: they should act like medicine, as Wordsworth's poetry did for Mill. Art's power to injure or benefit real-life behavior had already been a subject of disagreement between Plato and Aristotle; it took on special urgency in the nineteenth century, however, as artists began rebelling against the injunction that they, like a league of spiritual pharmacists, were obliged to dole out remedies to their customers.

A potent rallying cry was "art for art's sake," a catchy phrase of apparently French origin that neatly fuses integrity with exclusionism. The attitude for which it stood as shorthand came eventually to be known as aestheticism, the prevailing doctrine of the avant-garde around the turn of the twentieth century. Aestheticism never issued anything so official as a manifesto, but its tenets were asserted innumerable times, with a tendency to grow more intractable in each new formulation. Among the earliest examples is Théophile Gautier's preface to *Mademoiselle de Maupin* (1835); along with fierce assaults on the hypocritical moralism of popular journalists, he asserted that art is beauty, and beauty is the opposite of usefulness: "Nothing truly beautiful serves any purpose; all useful things are ugly, because they are the expression of some need, and human needs are vile and nasty, like man's poor, weak nature. The most useful place in a house is the toilet."[33] If art is useless, no artwork can be judged according to any external standard—religious, political, or moral. Introducing the phrase "art for art's sake" into England, Swinburne laid special stress on art's immunity, indeed antagonism, to moral prescriptions: "Art for art's sake first of all, and afterwards we may suppose all the rest shall be added to her (or if not she need hardly be overmuch concerned); but from the man who falls to artistic work with a moral purpose, shall be taken away even that which he has—whatever of capacity for doing well in either way he may have at starting."[34]

Though the term is anachronistic, nineteenth-century advocates of art for art's sake gradually formed themselves into something resembling a "technocracy." If art could be judged only on its own terms, irrespective of its effects on those who read or saw it, then no one but a poet had the right to an opinion about poems, no one

but a sculptor about statues, and so on. The nonartistic public—
which nevertheless was expected to honor art and even, on occasion,
to buy it—was degraded in this view to the level of infants or
barbarians, qualified only to gape. In a sense, of course, the late-
nineteenth-century public was indeed infantile and barbaric; it included a vast number of people who, in prior generations, would
have had no access to art and hence no opportunity for forming
opinions on it. The self-made aristocracy of fin-de-siècle artists was,
in part, a means of defense against the vulgarization that the arrival
of mass culture seemed to threaten. Art preserved its integrity, but
it lost the rapport with its audience that had been Dickens's pride
and that other mid-century artists like Tennyson, Thackeray, and
Trollope also gloried in.

The nonartistic public had understandable difficulty accepting
the idea that art, a human product intended to be read, seen, or
heard by other human beings, was exempt from the rules that
applied to all other areas of social intercourse. Nonartists persisted
in finding ethical and moral precepts where there were supposed
to be none, or in misinterpreting the subtleties of aestheticism when
it did preach morals. A famous instance is Walter Pater's *Studies in
the History of the Renaissance*. In a less nervous intellectual climate,
this collection of essays on relatively arcane subjects might have
attracted little notice, but in late-nineteenth-century England it
became the object of extravagant advocacy and bitter condemnation, wholly for moral reasons. The center of controversy was
Pater's "Conclusion," which is in fact a design for living, not merely
for looking at art. In its first edition (1873), the Conclusion seems,
if carelessly read, to recommend a life of no-holds-barred hedonism.
Physically and mentally, Pater says, we are in constant flux— "that
strange perpetual weaving and unweaving of ourselves." To form
habits is failure, "for habit is relative to a stereotyped world":

> While all melts under our feet, we may well catch at any exquisite
> passion, or any contribution to knowledge that seems, by a lifted
> horizon, to set the spirit free for a moment, or any stirring of the
> senses, strange dyes, strange flowers, and curious odours, or work

of the artist's hands, or the face of one's friend. Not to discriminate every moment some passionate attitude in those about us, and in the brilliance of their gifts some tragic dividing of forces on their ways is, on this short day of frost and sun, to sleep before evening. With this sense of the splendour of our experience and of its awful brevity, gathering all we are into one desperate effort to see and touch, we shall hardly have time to make theories about the things we see and touch.

Instead of making theories, Pater recommended a suppler stance; memorably phrased, his advice at once became a slogan and eventually a cliché: "To burn always with this hard gem-like flame, to maintain this ecstasy, is success in life."[35]

Pater's influence was slow to make itself felt; not until 1890 would Oscar Wilde express the avant-garde consensus by calling him, "on the whole, the most perfect master of English prose now creating amongst us."[36] But the Conclusion to the *Renaissance* had raised such a furor that Pater removed it from the second edition (1877); he restored it, slightly revised, in the third edition (1888), with a footnote: "This brief 'Conclusion' was omitted in the second edition of this book, as I conceived it might possibly mislead some of those young men into whose hands it might fall."[37] To be so misled (or "depraved and corrupted," as the courts phrased it) those young men would have had to misread Pater rather strongly, especially his final warning: "Only, be sure it is passion, that it does yield you this fruit of a quickened, multiplied consciousness. Of this wisdom, the poetic passion, the desire of beauty, the love of art for art's sake has most; for art comes to you professing frankly to give nothing but the highest quality to your moments as they pass, and simply for those moments' sake."[38] Nevertheless, Pater's consistent emphasis on the exotic ("strange dyes, strange flowers, and curious odours"), along with his insidious homoeroticism ("the face of one's friend"), made him more than an exponent of art's high, pure pleasures. He invited the kind of misreading that made him an advocate of strangeness for strangeness' sake, a prophet of what would come to be known as "decadence."

Pater's cleverest misreader was Oscar Wilde, who condensed Paterian sonorities into witty, perverse epigrams designed to shock conventional expectations. The Preface to *The Picture of Dorian Gray* (1891), for example, is a string of hyperaesthetic one-liners: "There is no such thing as a moral or an immoral Book. Books are well written, or badly written. That is all. . . . No artist has ethical sympathies. An ethical sympathy in an artist is an unpardonable mannerism of style. . . . All art is quite useless."[39] The last remark brings us back to Gautier half-a-century earlier, but Gautier's feistiness has been transformed into a cool sneer. In obedience to his principles, Wilde maintained that sneer in life as well as art; like his mouthpiece Vivian in "The Decay of Lying" (1889), he believed that "Life imitates Art far more than Art imitates Life,"[40] and he seemed determined to enact in reality the unspecified debaucheries indulged in by his fictional Dorian Gray. In March 1895, he was arrested under Britain's harsh Criminal Law Amendment Act, which made it a misdemeanor for "any male person" to solicit or commit "any act of gross indecency with another male person."[41] Convicted in May, he was sentenced to two years' hard labor; like Vizetelly before him, Wilde served his full term and emerged a broken man. He died in Paris on November 30, 1900, aged forty-six.

Several species of hysteria collaborated to bring about Wilde's downfall; fear of his artistic creed counted, no doubt, among the least of them. But one effect of his disgrace was, as Cyril Connolly puts it, "a flight from aestheticism" that lasted well into the succeeding generation.[42] The British public had never trusted the exemption of art from the laws that governed life; the popular prejudice continued to be (and the Wilde exposé seemed to prove it correct) that if art glorified the forbidden, life would learn to seek the forbidden out. None of Wilde's own writings was obscene,[43] but there never had been any room for the notion of obscenity in the program of "art for art's sake," and Wilde's critical essays lampooned the whole idea. The discrediting of aestheticism that resulted from Wilde's imprisonment contributed to a curious twist in the history of "pornography." James White, M.P., found it easy to ridicule American provincialism in the debate over Lord Campbell's Bill in

1857, and in 1915 Margaret Sanger might have thought it self-evident that Britain would be decades ahead of the United States in its attitude toward the distribution of information on birth control; but in a long series of court decisions, the American authorities were showing themselves steadily more tolerant of alleged obscenity, so long as a fair case could be made that the supposedly obscene material was redeemed by art.

The process began in 1894, when the New York State Supreme Court heard a case involving the bankruptcy of the Worthington Book Publishing Company. The company was in receivership, and the receiver had taken the unusual step of asking the court for instructions on the proper way to dispose of its stock. Worthington's inventory contained a number of titles that the Society for the Suppression of Vice (represented by Anthony Comstock) found objectionable. The publications at issue were the *Arabian Nights*, Ovid's *Art of Love*, Boccaccio's *Decameron*, the *Heptameron* of Margaret of Navarre, *Gargantua and Pantagruel*, *Tom Jones*, Rousseau's *Confessions*, and two unpedigreed items called *Tales from the Arabic* and *Alladin* (sic). Physically, as Judge Morgan J. O'Brien said in his decision, these volumes were "choice"; they were unlikely to be "generally sold or purchased, except by those who would desire them for their literary merit, or for their worth as specimens of fine book-making."

It is very difficult to see upon what theory these world-renowned classics can be regarded as specimens of that pornographic literature which it is the office of the Society for the Suppression of Vice to suppress, or how they can come under any stronger condemnation than that high standard of literature which consists of the works of Shakespeare, of Chaucer, of Laurence Sterne, and of other great English writers, without making reference to many parts of the Old Testament Scriptures, which are to be found in almost every household in the land. The very artistic character, the high qualities of style, the absence of those glaring and crude pictures, scenes, and descriptions which affect the common and vulgar mind, make a place for books of the character in question, entirely apart from such gross and obscene writings as it is the duty of the public authorities to suppress.

Because these books were "rare and costly," O'Brien concluded that they "would not be bought nor appreciated by the class of people from whom unclean publications ought to be withheld. They are not corrupting in their influence upon the young, for they are not likely to reach them."[44]

O'Brien's decision in the Worthington case, despite its thorough conventionality, is novel in one respect: it represents the emergence of the term "pornographic" into American judicial discourse, already with the rudiments of a definition that the courts would spend the next six decades refining. According to O'Brien, "pornographic literature" was not the classics and did not come expensively bound; it lacked "artistic character" and "high qualities of style," but it did offer "glaring and crude pictures, scenes, and descriptions which affect the common and vulgar mind." Beyond this, O'Brien felt no need to go; like many of his successors, he acted as if he knew perfectly well what pornography was and could recognize it instantly, along with its effects on minds very different from his own. In the case at hand, however, no such recognition was called for. Whatever nerve it was in Judge O'Brien that twitched when pornography came near failed to respond to the Worthington Company's publications.

The next few years saw American high courts grappling with various ancillary issues and arriving at decisions little more precise than O'Brien's. In 1896, the United States Supreme Court reviewed two lower-court convictions on obscenity charges. The first involved Lew Rosen, publisher of *Broadway*, an illustrated paper with no pretensions to classic stature. The special "Tenderloin Issue" had contained patches of lampblack which could be rubbed off with a piece of bread to reveal "females in different attitudes of indecency." A jury in New York had sentenced Rosen to thirteen months' hard labor on the grounds that these pictures "would suggest or convey lewd and lascivious thoughts to the young and inexperienced," a standard derived from the Hicklin test. The Supreme

Court upheld Rosen's conviction, holding that, as Associate Justice John M. Harlan said, "in view of the character of the paper, the test prescribed was quite as liberal as the defendant had any right to demand."[45] The second decision, handed down six weeks later, concerned the September 21, 1894, issue of the Burlington, Kansas, *Courier*, which had contained a wildly vituperative assault on a local politician: "He is lower, meaner, filthier, rottener than the rottenest strumpet that prowls the streets by night," and so on. The Court overturned the conviction of Dan K. Swearingen, editor of the *Courier*, on the grounds that though the language was "exceedingly coarse and vulgar," the article held nothing "of a lewd, lascivious and obscene tendency, calculated to corrupt and debauch the mind and morals of those into whose hands it might fall."[46] So far, the Hicklin test, nearing its thirtieth birthday, seemed adequate to the purposes for which it had been devised.

Not until 1913, in one of the last proceedings instigated by Comstock, did the test (forty-five years old by then) encounter a significant challenge. Later commentators customarily date the erosion of the Hicklin test from District Court Judge Learned Hand's decision in the case of Mitchell Kennerley, publisher, whom a grand jury had indicted for mailing copies of Daniel Carson Goodman's novel *Hagar Revelly*. Hand upheld the indictment, but he grew so eloquent in expressing his doubts that he seemed to invite reversal by a higher court—which occurred a few months later. Hand was the first high-court official to suggest that the Hicklin test might be growing a bit moldy:

I hope it is not improper for me to say that the rule as laid down, however consonant it may be with mid-Victorian morals, does not seem to me to answer to the understanding and morality of the present time, as conveyed by the words, 'obscene, lewd, or lascivious.' . . . Indeed, it seems hardly likely that we are even today so lukewarm to our interest in letters or serious discussion as to be content to reduce our treatment of sex to the standard of a child's library in the supposed interest of a salacious few, or that shame will for long prevent us from adequate portrayal of some of the most serious and beautiful sides of human nature.

Hand's comments contain a good deal of the post-Victorian self-congratulation popular in the early decades of the twentieth century, but they are noteworthy because, in addition to questioning the adequacy of the Hicklin test, Hand also challenged the tyranny of Comstock's darling, the Young Person: "to put thought in leash to the average conscience of the time is perhaps tolerable, but to fetter it by the necessities of the lowest and least capable seems a fatal policy."[47]

These remarks were phrased with great caution and carried no official weight; the Supreme Court would not finally junk the Hicklin test and oust the Young Person until 1957. Nevertheless, Hand's misgivings testify to the growing twentieth-century sense—popular as well as judicial—that morality is a relative matter, for which no eternal rules can be laid down. They also reflect a desire, tentative in 1913 but gaining strength, to extend to modern works of fiction the same latitude already established for the classics. *Hagar Revelly* is a novel in the naturalistic vein, directly descended from Zola, and the objections raised against it hardly differed from those that had brought Henry Vizetelly to grief a quarter-century earlier. Hand's response suggests that American legal opinion (and perhaps that of American culture at large) was coming to agree with points made by the literary avant-garde of the 1880s. Hand echoed, for example, judgments like this one by Henry James in an otherwise very unfavorable review of *Nana* (1880): it may be said that our English system is a good thing for virgins and boys, and a bad thing for the novel itself, when the novel is regarded as something more than a simple *jeu d'esprit*, and considered as a composition that treats of life at large and helps us to *know*.[48]

Vizetelly's jury thought differently, but much had changed between 1888 and 1913.

Among other things, the English and American novel had changed, absorbing the French-spawned notion that no subject, in and of itself, should be prohibited from fictional treatment. It would take until the 1960s for the courts to grant total freedom in this regard; the process has generally been looked upon as a regrettably slow liberation. It is by no means certain, however, that the gradual unfettering of the printed word has been an unmitigated boon. Laws, as we know, are not made against things no one wants to do. The liberation of writing from the shackles of moral censorship has proceeded apace with loss of the belief, all-powerful in the nineteenth century, that writing wields immediate force upon its reader. That belief remains as strong as ever when it comes to pictures, still or moving; but the peril of print has nearly vanished, perhaps because the Western world no longer attributes to words the quasi-magical aura that once invested them. One reason why the century-long debate over "pornography" looks quaint in retrospect is that most of it was a war about words. The post-pornographic era has returned to a distant origin: the first pornographers did not write, they drew pictures.

Of equal importance is the emergence of "art" as nonpornographic by definition, in all media. Despite Lord Chief Justice Cockburn's valiant (if muddled) efforts to separate intention from obscenity, intention invaded even his judgments, and it has figured centrally in every significant obscenity trial of the twentieth century. Thanks to Zola and his followers, it became established early that the meticulous representation of reality's muckiest byways was not merely compatible but identical with the aim of producing pure art. Vizetelly's jurors might well be forgiven for failing to comprehend why a description of a peasant girl's grasping a bull's pizzle was fit to be read aloud; they had too little sense of "art" to understand that art made all things wholesome. Eventually, however, the public would learn that lesson. By 1933, American courts had established—the British would slowly follow—that art, by nature, was unable to arouse anyone to sexual activity. Art might make you vomit, but that gesture has never been widely thought of as seductive.

The next significant step in the redemption of art took place in 1922, when the New York State Court of Appeals vindicated *Mademoiselle de Maupin*, one of the earliest texts to proclaim art's uselessness. In 1917, a New York City bookstore clerk, Raymond D. Halsey, had sold a copy of Gautier's old novel to John S. Sumner, whose unenviable task it was to follow in Comstock's footsteps as hit man of the Society for the Suppression of Vice. Halsey was acquitted in the Court of Special Sessions; he retaliated by suing the Society for malicious prosecution; finally, the Court of Appeals found in Halsey's (and Gautier's) favor and awarded the clerk $2,500 damages. The case is often cited for Judge William S. Andrews's comment that, though "taken by themselves" some passages of *Mademoiselle de Maupin* were "vulgar and indecent," the book "must be considered broadly, as a whole."[49] Andrews made a contribution to what has been called the "whole-book concept," generally thought of as an advance in legal sophistication. So it was, but only in the sense that official discourse had once again absorbed tenets proclaimed by the artistic avant-garde of prior generations.

The culling of "flowers" and "beauties" from the works of literary artists had been a favorite pastime of nineteenth-century critics and editors—the reverse, as it were, of bowdlerization. Few well-to-do drawing rooms lacked their "Keepsakes" or "Annuals," fancy volumes padded with excerpts from the great poets. Though the practice of taking snippets applied poorly to painting and sculpture, it flourished where writing was concerned; Matthew Arnold even made a pseudoscience of it in essays like "The Study of Poetry" (1880), which asserted that a mind festooned with classic tag lines was the only sort qualified to pass judgment on any literature. Carried to Arnold's extreme, the idea becomes silly; the succeeding generation reacted violently against it, elevating to perhaps equally silly eminence the concept of "form." Mid-nineteenth-century readers, accustomed to receiving their fiction piecemeal in pamphlets or magazine installments, were insensitive to the appeal of "form," which, as twentieth-century courts would belatedly affirm, can be perceived only when the fiction is viewed all at once, as a whole. And "form," like most other ideas kicked back and forth in the pornography debate, is also a function of intention, the blameless desire to make art.

In the second decade of the twentieth century, the frequency of obscenity trials accelerated geometrically, a pace they would keep up until just after the centenary of Lord Campbell's Act, when it slowed down, as if exhausted. In almost every case, the article that someone had once called pornographic was declared not to be so. Eventually, the courts would turn their attention to material for which even its manufacturers made no artistic claims, the sort of stuff Comstock and his progeny had been routinely immolating since 1873. In the meantime, however, would-be censors continued to attack books with at least some pretension to art, losing routinely. In 1926, H. L. Mencken found it "impotent and absurd" of the book burners to ignore "books that are frankly pornographic and have no other excuse for being" in favor of "books that have obvious literary merit, and are thus rather easily defended." Among such futile prosecutions he listed those of *Mademoiselle de Maupin*, Theodore Dreiser's *The "Genius"*, and James Branch Cabell's *Jurgen*— three of the many similar cases he might have mentioned. [50] To Mencken, it seemed foolish to embark on doomed crusades, but the antipornographers were following a certain inevitable logic. The prevailing assumption was that there existed a sort of spectrum of moral acceptability in books, ranging from the pristine at one end to the "frankly pornographic" at the other. It was also believed— by Mencken as well as the book burners—that both extremes were equally obvious. If the morally unacceptable was to be banned— again, everyone agreed that it should be—controversy could occur nowhere but in the middle range, where doubt was possible.

The vindication of *Mademoiselle de Maupin* in 1922 virtually completed the exemption of the respectable classics from large-scale prosecution. Old villains like Aristophanes, Petronius, Shakespeare, Fielding, and Sterne would come under local attack from time to time—they still do—but such skirmishes have been minor. [51] Modern fiction, not yet endowed with the patina of years, remained vulnerable, though it, too, gradually won immunity, if at least a modicum of artistic value could be found in it. On both sides of the Atlantic, the case of Radclyffe Hall's *The Well of Loneliness* (1928) is especially noteworthy for establishing the suitability to art of a subject that even Havelock Ellis's science had been forbidden to handle thirty years earlier, "sexual inversion." Hall (1886–1943) was a figure of some literary stature, having won the British Femina Prize in 1927 for her novel *Adam's Breed*. *The Well of Loneliness*, however, dealt directly—though without explicit descriptions and in a distraught manner—with lesbianism. Jonathan Cape published it in the summer of 1928, eliciting from James Douglas in the *Sunday Express* an old-fashioned shriek that a late observer called "the most fatuous saying of the decade."[52] "I would rather," wrote Douglas, "put a phial of prussic acid in the hand of a healthy boy or girl than the book in question."[53]

Others felt similarly, including Home Secretary Sir William Joynson-Hicks (known popularly as "Jix"), Britain's closest approximation, though a pale one, to Anthony Comstock. At Jix's instigation, the novel was prosecuted under Lord Campbell's Act; it came to trial at Bow Street before Chief Magistrate Sir Chartres Biron and a roomful of people willing to testify for the defense. Among them was Virginia Woolf, who recorded her impressions in her diary:

> What is obscenity? What is literature? What is the difference between the subject & the treatment? In what cases is evidence allowable? This last, to my relief, was decided against us: we could not be called as experts in obscenity, only in art.[54]

Desmond MacCarthy was the sole expert in art allowed to take the stand on behalf of *The Well of Loneliness*, but when Norman Birkett, K.C., posed his first question—"In your view is it obscene?"—Biron broke in:

> No I shall disallow that. It is quite clear that the evidence is not admissible. A book may be a fine piece of literature and yet obscene. Art and Obscenity are not disassociated at all. There is a room at Naples to which visitors are not admitted as a rule, which contains fine bronzes and statues, all admirable works of art, but all grossly obscene. It does not follow that because a book is a work of art it is not obscene. I shall not admit the evidence.[55]

In his decision, ordering Hall's novel destroyed, Biron came back to this point: "It must appear to anyone of intelligence that the better an obscene book is written the greater the public to whom it is likely to appeal."[56]

Biron must have been aware that he was taking a distinctly unfashionable stance; by 1928, the popular prejudice was already well established that the surest antidote to sexual arousal was a stiff dose of art. He also exhibited a rather touching confidence (and an outmoded one) in the power of fine writing to reach a wide audience; a crowd of experts, if they had been allowed to speak, would have assured him that things ran just the opposite way. From time to time in later years, a magistrate would return to Biron's position—like Jerome Frank, who observed in 1948 that if "a book is dominantly obscene, the greater the art, the greater the harmful impact on its 'average' reader."[57] But these were rare protests against a conviction that grew as the century advanced, until its truth came to seem self-evident. The most famous and widely cited decision of this kind, which put the United States decisively ahead of Britain in the race to prove art innocuous, came on December 6, 1933, when Judge John M. Woolsey of the United States District Court, Southern District of New York, exonerated a work far more artfully obscene than any that had come to trial before—James Joyce's *Ulysses*.

"The New Deal in the law of letters is here," crowed Morris L. Ernst, who had defended publisher Bennett Cerf in court. "The *Ulysses* case marks a turning point. It is a body-blow for the censors. The necessity for hypocrisy and circumlocution in literature has been eliminated. Writers need no longer seek refuge in euphemisms. They may now describe basic human functions without fear of the law."[58] Ernst's glee was overstated but understandable: *Ulysses* had been the prime target of censors in both Britain and the United States for more than thirteen years, since a time even before the novel was finished. Joyce's novel began serial publication in March 1918 in the *Little Review*, an avant-garde American literary magazine operated by Margaret Anderson and Jane Heap. Installments appeared regularly, with grumbles but no action from the censors, until September 1920, when John S. Sumner filed an official complaint against the July-August number, which contained the second half of the thirteenth chapter, known as the *Nausicaa* episode. It is not difficult to see why, having restrained himself for two and a half years, Sumner felt compelled to move. Indeed, he might have objected just as strongly to Book Six of the *Odyssey*, which Joyce's episode is designed to recall. Homer's middle-aged hero, covering his nakedness with only an olive branch, begs aid from the young princess Nausicaa, on the coast of whose father's kingdom he has been shipwrecked. Joyce's modern counterpart, Leopold Bloom, never speaks to Gerty MacDowell, a fatuous adolescent he observes on the Sandymount shore. Gerty, her head full of pulp-fiction fantasies, catches Bloom staring at her and casts him in a romance:

> She was a womanly woman not like other flighty girls, unfemi-nine, he had known, those cyclists showing off what they hadn't got and she just yearned to know all, to forgive all if she could make him fall in love with her, make him forget the memory of the past. Then maybe he would embrace her gently, like a real man, crushing her soft body to him, and love her, his ownest girlie, for herself alone.[59]

As a reward for Bloom's attention, Gerty leans as far back as she can, exposing her stockings and garters. Bloom, meanwhile, has been masturbating: "Mr Bloom with careful hand recomposed his wet shirt. O Lord, that little limping devil. Begins to feel cold and clammy. Aftereffect not pleasant. Still you have to get rid of it someway. They don't care. Complimented perhaps."[60]

Joyce must have been aware that he had gone too far this time. The mildly graphic physical details would have been enough to rile the censors, but Gerty is also a classic Young Person, acting as if she had already been debauched by reading *Nausicaa*. The *Little Review* ceased serialization of *Ulysses* after December 1920, and in February of the following year Anderson and Heap were fined fifty dollars each, on the understanding that they would print no more; nearly half the novel remained unpublished.[61] From her Paris book-store, Shakespeare and Company, Sylvia Beach would ultimately publish the complete *Ulysses* in February 1922; as early as April

1918, however, Harriet Weaver had written to Virginia Woolf with the suggestion that the Hogarth Press might publish it in England. The first episode, *Telemachus*, had just appeared in the United States, but Weaver had been unable to find an English printer willing to take it on. In her official reply, Woolf begged off on the grounds that the Press—founded just the previous year—was too small to handle anything so large as Joyce's novel. To other correspondents, however, she expressed different feelings. "The directness of the language," she wrote to Nicholas Bagenal, "and the choice of incidents, if there *is* any choice, but as far as I can see there's a certain sameness—have raised a blush even upon such a cheek as mine."[62] Woolf's doubts would persist, though later they came to center on the still open question whether her own work was not "being better done by Mr. Joyce."[63] But it is interesting to see a charter member of liberated Bloomsbury transformed, even briefly, into a Young Person.

Ulysses went into its second printing in October 1922; a German translation followed in 1927 and a French in 1929. Literary figures of all persuasions read and argued about it: in May 1922, James Douglas (the would-be dispenser of prussic acid) denounced it as "the most infamously obscene book in ancient or in modern literature";[64] for Virginia Woolf in December 1923, it had become simply boring;[65] and in August 1924, William Butler Yeats evenhandedly called it "as obscene as Rabelais" but also "indubitably a work of genius."[66] None of these critics thought it appropriate to mention that their opinions, published or unpublished, positive or negative, concerned a book which could not be legally imported into the countries where they had presumably been reading it. During its contraband years, *Ulysses* figured as the star exhibit (and one of the last) in the Secret Museum.

The process that would lead to the breaking of the lock was begun in March 1932, when Joyce signed a contract with Bennett Cerf of Random House, New York, for an American edition of *Ulysses*. Cerf engineered the seizure of a copy at customs, and Judge Woolsey spent most of the summer reading the book. On both sides, the litigants were determined to be erudite: Ernst's brief was packed with the names of weighty authorities, and Woolsey's decision looks as if it had been written by a professor of English. Unlike Judge Biron in the *Well of Loneliness* case only five years before, Woolsey gladly admitted the testimony of literary experts; he also seemed eager to prove that he himself was one. Perhaps recalling his strenuous summer, he began with the declaration that *Ulysses* "is not an easy book to read or to understand"; he went on to provide a short—and, in the event, influential—definition of "pornography": "in any case where a book is claimed to be obscene it must first be determined, whether the intent with which it was written was what is called, according to the usual phrase, pornographic,—that is, written for the purpose of exploiting obscenity."[67] His conclusion was equally memorable: "But in 'Ulysses,' in spite of its unusual frankness, I do not detect anywhere the leer of the sensualist. I hold, therefore, that it is not pornographic."

But the law said nothing about the "pornographic"; it was concerned only with the "obscene," which it defined, in Woolsey's words, as matter "tending to stir the sex impulses or to lead to sexually impure and lustful thoughts." On this aspect of the case—which, strictly speaking, ought to have been the only one—Woolsey had consulted two of his friends, who had already read *Ulysses* and who, he said, belonged to the class of "what the French would call *l'homme moyen sensuel*"—"a person [actually, "man"] with average sex instincts." These "literary assessors" agreed that *Ulysses* "did not tend to excite sexual impulses or lustful thoughts but that its net effect . . . was only that of a somewhat tragic and very powerful commentary on the inner lives of men and women." *Ulysses* was both nonpornographic and nonobscene:

I am quite aware that owing to some of its scenes "Ulysses" is a rather strong draught to ask some sensitive, though normal, persons to take. But my considered opinion, after long reflection, is that whilst in many places the effect of "Ulysses" on the reader undoubtedly is somewhat emetic, nowhere does it tend to be an aphrodisiac.

"Ulysses" may, therefore, be admitted into the United States.

The Circuit Court of Appeals upheld Woolsey's decision in August 1934; the government elected not to press the case further. A British edition belatedly followed in October 1936, and *Ulysses* rapidly became the above-ground classic it remains today.

The *Ulysses* decision was momentous for several reasons, not the least of which being the slap it delivered to the Young Person, whose century-long hegemony had been in steady decline since Learned Hand's comments in the *Hagar Revelly* case twenty years earlier. Woolsey also produced the most eloquent judicial assertion so far of the tonic effects of art. The bulk of his decision was couched in a kind of literary-critical language that had rarely been heard in the courtroom:

> Joyce has attempted—it seems to me, with astonishing success—to show how the screen of consciousness with its ever-shifting kaleidoscopic impressions carries, as it were on a plastic palimpsest, not only what is in the focus of each man's observations of the actual things about him, but also in a penumbral zone residua of past impressions, some recent and some drawn up by association from the domain of the subconscious.

The "screen of consciousness" recalls Henry James; the kaleidoscope of "impressions" recalls Pater and late-nineteenth-century painting; the "subconscious" recalls Virginia Woolf, with overtones of Freud. Woolsey also laid great stress on Joyce's "sincerity," how "loyal to his technique" he had been. Indeed, Woolsey went so far as to say that if Joyce had "funked" the implications of that method, the result would have been "artistically inexcusable." To complete his legalization of aestheticism, he offered a memorable twist on a familiar old phrase: "I have not found anything that I consider to be dirt for dirt's sake."

Despite the efforts of Justice Cockburn and a few of his successors, the concept of intention refused to go away; it kept recurring, ever more insistently, and it won a resounding victory in the *Ulysses* case. At the same time, a distinction was beginning to emerge, in all forms of public discourse, between old-fashioned "obscenity" and something now called "pornography." The latter, though in 1933 Woolsey described it as "the usual phrase," had still something newfangled about it; some writers continued to enclose it in quotation marks, suggesting that they thought of it as a neologism. Just as "art," in Woolsey's view, was redeemed by good intentions, so "pornography" was damned by the "leer of the sensualist." At that time, however, "pornography" remained a curiosity, understood almost wholly in terms of what it was not—though commentators were already saying, as they have not ceased to do, that they might not be able to define it, but they knew it when they saw it. For the next half century and more, an odd backward process would ensue, in which one authority after another attempted to find meanings for a word almost universally used as if everyone of course knew what it meant.

CHAPTER SEVEN

HARD AT THE CORE

THE LEGALIZATION OF *Ulysses* did not, of course, end the censorship of literary obscenity in the United States or Britain. High courts in both countries would go on grappling with the issue for another three decades, and only in 1966 would the United States Supreme Court effectively resolve the debate by setting free the oldest pornographic classic in English, *Fanny Hill*. Judges and lay people alike would continue to make the plausible counterargument that obscenity and literary merit are unrelated—that, indeed, artful obscenity, because it has more power, should be all the more forcibly suppressed. Woolsey's comments on *Ulysses*, however, clearly indicated the trend of public opinion in 1933, a trend that would accelerate. Whatever "pornography" might be, it was not "art": whatever "art" might be, it was not "pornography." It is appropriate that two indefinable abstractions should ultimately cancel each other out.

To mention "public opinion" is to invoke a third abstraction, one not yet indefinable in the United States of 1933 but well on its way to becoming so. The concept of a public remained relatively stable and coherent until the early nineteenth century; it meant an extreme minority—well-to-do, educated, and predominantly male—that shared an inherited system of values. "Pornography" arose (and "art" with it) as cheaper printing methods, rising literacy rates, and dissolving social arrangements made it less and less certain into whose hands a book or picture might fall. In the regionally diverse

United States, "the public" was a shaky idea even at the start; vastly expanded territory, along with ethnic and religious multiplicity, had emptied the phrase of its old meaning long before Woolsey spoke. Yet he did speak for a public, and not an inconsiderable one. It was represented by himself, Bennett Cerf, Morris L. Ernst, and the *hommes moyen sensuels* whose opinions Woolsey had solicited. Men like these could properly appreciate *Ulysses*; since most of those responsible for the novel's initial publication were female, some women might also fill the bill. Length, difficulty, and "emetic" qualities would serve as gatekeepers to repel the rest.

Similar internal defenses remained in force, as they had for a century, in scientific and hygienic works. The pioneering "pornographers," students of prostitution for the sake of public health, had been eager to assure their readers that even the most infectious matter could be safely handled, if "scientific" detachment was maintained. This tactic worked for Annie Besant and Charles Bradlaugh in 1877 and for Margaret Sanger thirty years later. It failed Havelock Ellis in 1898, though "science" itself went unscathed: the prosecutor did not impugn the validity of science in general, he merely declared that Ellis had not really been "scientific." With the popularization of psychoanalysis and the development of disciplines like sexology (a term first recorded in English in 1920), the English-speaking world gradually accustomed itself to free talk about penises and vaginas, so long as the tone remained clinical and the lexicon polysyllabic.[1] The influence of Freud and "Freudianism"—another new word, dating from 1923—cannot be overestimated. Scientific and accessible at once, Freud's thought allowed educated men and women to speak in public about subjects that, a generation earlier, had been reserved for Latin treatises and bedroom whispers. Such talk was completely respectable now, because it was always serious, never tainted with jocularity or low-class innuendo. Whatever its role in psychoanalytic theory, Freud's relentless focus on sex struck his early followers as a brave and wholesome righting of the balance. Sex talk was more than a privilege; it became something like a duty. Freud's profound and pervasive influence on twentieth-century culture is impossible to gauge, but within the context of the obscenity debate, his most significant effect may have had less to do with psychology than with vocabulary.

Freud also contributed to the ennobling of sex, its elevation from a mean reminder that men are animals to a solemn rite verging on the sacramental. Prior to the nineteenth century sex had been problematic in various ways, but it had not been of definitive importance. The Victorians began the apotheosis of sex by moving it from the periphery of human concerns to the center; in the first third of the twentieth century, the post-Victorians—obsessively conscious of the immediate past—rebelled against a din they took for silence. Early-twentieth-century sex talk, in order to be legitimate, had to obey rules that were different from the nineteenth-century variety though just as restrictive. It affirmed the centrality of sex, though in a newly positive sense; it insisted upon the righteousness, cleanliness, and utility of sex—all of which (except the last) had been denied by preceding generations. As a topic of public discourse, sex was no longer hemmed in by euphemism and circumlocution, but it still had to be spoken of in a certain manner. Otherwise—if, for example, the "leer of the sensualist" showed up—sex remained as obscene as ever.

In 1930 and 1931, a pair of celebrated court decisions gave official approval to this modified view of talking about sex. The first involved Mary Ware Dennett's *The Sex Side of Life: An Explanation for Young People,* which Dennett had composed in 1919 for the education of her two adolescent sons. It was published in the *Medical Review of Reviews* and later as a pamphlet, price twenty-five cents; 25,000 had been sold, most by mail, before legal proceedings began. These were initiated by a Mrs. Carl A. Miles of Grottoes, Virginia—described as "an entrapper for the Post Office Department"[2]—to whom a copy was mailed in 1926. Indicted in a Brooklyn court under the Comstock Law, Dennett was convicted and sentenced to pay a fine of $300; appeal was made to the Second Circuit Court, which reversed the conviction on March 5, 1930. Admitting that the pamphlet might contain some "unnecessary details," Augustus N. Hand and his two fellow judges were nevertheless in full accord with Dennett's intentions:

. . . we hold that an accurate exposition of the relevant facts of the sex side of life in decent language and in manifestly serious and disinterested spirit cannot ordinarily be regarded as obscene. Any incidental tendency to arouse sex impulses which such a pamphlet may perhaps have, is apart from and subordinate to its main effect.[3]

The following year, in a case beguilingly called *United States* v. *"Married Love,"* John M. Woolsey cited the Dennett case and laid the groundwork for his own later judgment on *Ulysses*. Marie Stopes's *Married Love*, first published in 1918, was a firmly established European bestseller, offering hygienic advice to young married couples. Intending to produce an American edition, the New York publisher G. P. Putnam's Sons had attempted to import several copies, which were seized under the Smoot-Hawley Tariff Act of 1930.[4] Ironically, this "obscene" book had already been expurgated for American readers: all information on birth control (for which Stopes was chiefly famous in Europe) had been removed from the imported copies. As many others would do after him, Woolsey went to the *Oxford English Dictionary* for the definition of "obscene," coming back with the familiar disagreeable tangle—"offensive, disgusting, repulsive, filthy, foul, abominable, loathsome, unchaste, lustful, impure, indecent, lewd." None of these adjectives, in Woolsey's opinion, could be attached to *Married Love*. In fact, he archly remarked, Stopes's book "may fairly be said to do for adults what Mrs. Dennett's book does for adolescents."

To one who has read Havelock Ellis, as I have, the subject-matter of Dr. Stope's [*sic*] book is not wholly new, but it emphasizes the woman's side of sex questions. It makes also some apparently justified criticisms of the inopportune exercise of the man in the marriage relation of what are often referred to as his conjugal or marital rights, and it pleads with seriousness, and not without some eloquence, for a better understanding by husbands of the physical and emotional side of the sex life of their wives.[5]

Woolsey got a chance to rehearse his erudition, and Anthony Comstock took another turn in the grave.

The Dennett, Stopes, and *Ulysses* cases confirmed the twin standards of literary and scientific value that had already operated, clumsily enough, in the nineteenth century. For the next three decades, the whittling process would continue, as "value" was discovered in more and more places and the true province of "pornography" steadily shrank. Most often, obscenity trials followed the pattern H. L. Mencken had observed in 1926: lower-court convictions would be overturned in higher courts, because the condemned material was so manifestly worthwhile that only the most Comstockian fanatic would wish to burn it. Now and then, however, the courts drew close to the dark zone where real pornography resided. In 1936, for example, the Second Circuit Court—the same panel of judges which had upheld the legality of *Ulysses* two years before—heard the case of Esar Levine, convicted under the Comstock Law for mailing obscene advertisements. Levine's credentials were nothing like Joyce's; neither were his wares. Three were at issue: *Secret Museum of Anthropology*, *Crossways of Sex*, and *Black Lust*. The first, according to Learned Hand in his majority opinion, had an "extremely tenuous" claim to consideration as a work of "serious anthropology"; it consisted mostly of pictures of "nude female savages of different parts of the world." *Crossways of Sex* proclaimed itself "a scientific treatise on sexual pathology," but this was "more than questionable," since its supposedly authoritative author had chosen to remain anonymous. And *Black Lust*, a fictional "study in sadism and masochism," possessed "considerable merit" but was also "patently erotic," capable of arousing "libidinous feelings in almost any reader."

One might suppose that nothing could salvage Levine's merchandise: its scientific pretensions were patently spurious, and its literary merit was tainted with eroticism. Yet the lower-court judgment was reversed, on the grounds that the judge had failed to consider the modification of the Hicklin test introduced by the *Ulysses* decision. Hand had been uncomfortable with the test even in 1913, when he was called upon to apply it in the case of *Hagar Revelly*. Then, he had confined himself to questioning whether modern readers should still be bound by the strictures of "mid-Victorian morals" as Justice Cockburn had codified them. Two decades later, with several significant court decisions (including his own on *Ulysses*) to support him, Hand was able to reject the sixty-eight-year-old test absolutely. The lower-court judge had interpreted the New York State obscenity statute as designed to protect "the young and immature, the ignorant and those who are sensually inclined." These, said Hand, might indeed have been the people Cockburn had in mind, but the standard was no longer applicable:

> This earlier doctrine necessarily presupposed that the devil against which the statute is directed so much outweighs all interests of art, letters or science, that they must yield to the mere possibility that some prurient person may get a sensual gratification from reading or seeing what to most people is innocent and may be delightful or enlightening. No civilized community not fanatically puritanical would tolerate such an imposition, and we do not believe that the courts that have declared it, would ever have applied it consistently.[6]

Hand was willing to concede the possible obscenity of all three books—his cousin and fellow judge, Augustus N. Hand, disagreed with the majority opinion on account of *Crossways of Sex*—but this consideration became irrelevant next to the obsolescence of the Hicklin test.

The Levine case was a harbinger, but it was unusual in its own time because it concerned material for whose "value" no persuasive argument could be made. On the whole, though the volume of obscenity trials swelled alarmingly during the next thirty years, they tended to follow the old pattern: value was in there somewhere and fairly easily teased out. Gradually, the testimony of "experts"— rejected out of hand in such earlier trials as that of *The Well of Loneliness*—came to be a standard feature of the proceedings. Scientific works were less frequently indicted than literary ones, perhaps because built-in safeguards of difficulty and price continued to limit their circulation. But even when literature was on trial, it grew to seem obvious that, as Leo M. Alpert wrote in 1938, "the task of judging literature [is] beyond the average judge's capacity and ability."[7] Erudite men like Woolsey and Hand would no doubt have disagreed; if a judge was incompetent to evaluate literature, the job was certainly too much for the normal reader, although his susceptibilities were supposed to be the rationale of the updated Hicklin test. Theoretically, experts were not consulted on "obscenity," a matter of law; they testified only to the "value" of the work on trial. In practice, however, the two concepts could hardly be separated, since each was thought of as the opposite, and in some sense the determinant, of the other. The result was a steadily thickening muddle.

Experts figured prominently in the 1938 trial of *Life* magazine publisher Roy Larsen. The April 11 issue of *Life* had featured an article called "The Birth of a Baby," including numerous photographs and diagrams, all in the declared interest of enlightenment and hygiene. Newsdealers in at least two States had been arrested for selling the issue; in an unusual move (publishers were seldom so brave), Larsen chose to take personal responsibility for what he had published. The case came before the New York City Criminal Court, where a panel of three judges unanimously acquitted Larsen, after having listened to "responsible public health authorities, welfare workers and educators who testified to the sincerity, honesty and educational value of the picture story complained of." The prosecution had objected to the admission of this testimony—correctly, as Judge Nathan D. Perlman acknowledged. But, he added, evidence of this kind is "rationally helpful and in recent years Courts have considered the opinions of qualified persons."[8] They had done so, for example, in the 1933 trial of The Viking Press, publisher of Erskine Caldwell's novel *God's Little Acre*. Viking summoned a battalion of experts, including John Mason Brown, Carl Van Doren, Malcolm Cowley, and Sinclair Lewis, all of whom found notable merit in the book. Despite the objections of the tireless John S. Sumner, Magistrate Benjamin Greenspan concluded that "so large and representative a group of people" was better qualified "to judge the value of a literary production than one who is more apt to search for obscene passages in a book than to regard the book as a whole."[9]

In his written opinion, Greenspan made a significant distinction: "The Courts have strictly limited the applicability of the statute to works of pornography and they have consistently declined to apply it to books of genuine literary value."[10] As Judge Perlman would say in the Larsen case, "the jury or the triers of the facts must declare what the standard shall be"—not, that is, the experts. But the line between assessment of value and determination of fact is a wavering one, and soon it would become blurred beyond identification.

From one widely held point of view, it was an unalloyed benefit to serious literature that so many books were tried as obscene during the first half of the twentieth century. Not every case ended in acquittal, and very often a book found obscene in one jurisdiction was set free in another, creating persistent confusion; but the unmistakable trend was toward widening the definition of the nonobscene and narrowing that of its opposite, which increasingly took on the label "pornography." This apparent progress, however, entailed some regrettable side effects, notably the relegation of "literary value" to the province of experts—critics, reviewers, and artists. By the middle of the twentieth century, in the United States at least, literature was firmly enclosed within the fortresses of academic authority, where experts were employed purveying it to ignorant children who had paid for the privilege. It is understandable that this professionalizing and academicizing of literature should be carried over into the courtroom, where even judges were prepared to receive instruction. The legal process may have gained in wisdom as a result, but as the freedom of literature grew, its power diminished, until it seemed that "literary value" was a synonym for impotence.

In actuality, the judicial system was no closer to a definition of "obscenity" than it had been in Lord Campbell's day. Indeed, generations of attempts to locate the obscene had resulted only in its transformation into a nonidea, indefinable by definition. Justice Cockburn made no effort to explain what "obscenity" meant; he merely devised a standard by which to recognize its effects. There has been a long tradition of opinion that words like "obscenity"

and "pornography" require no definitions, in fact are better off
without them. This point of view was neatly expressed by Virginia
Woolf in 1929:

> There can be no doubt that books fall in respect of indecency
> into two classes. There are books written, published and sold
> with the object of causing pleasure or corruption by means of
> their indecency. . . . There are others whose indecency is not the
> object of the book but incidental to some other purpose—scien-
> tific, social, aesthetic, on the writer's part. The police magistrate's
> power should be definitely limited to the suppression of books
> which are sold as pornography to people who seek out and enjoy
> pornography. The others should be left alone. Any man or woman
> of average intelligence and culture knows the difference between
> the two kinds of book and has no difficulty in distinguishing one
> from the other.[11]

Supreme Court Justice Potter Stewart phrased the same viewpoint
more succinctly in 1964: "I know it when I see it."[12] The upshot
of all such formulations was the same. Just as the response of the
average person (whom no one had ever met) provided the modern
legal test for pornography, so pornography itself could be identified
without evidence or prior experience.

The paternalistic elitism of this attitude is obvious; perhaps the
courts are to be commended for working, however blunderingly,
in the opposite direction—toward some objective definition of either
what obscenity is or what it does. No clear statement has ever been
enunciated, but over a period of decades the omnium gatherum
called "obscenity" was steadily pared down, like some fleshy fruit
with an indigestible stone at its heart, to lay bare what came to be
known as the "hard core." This popular phrase was first given
prominence in judicial discourse by acting Solicitor General J. Lee
Rankin, who used it as the basis of the government's argument in
two important Supreme Court cases of 1957. In *United States* v.
Roth, the federal antiobscenity statute was challenged as unconstitutional, for the first time in its ninety-two-year history; *Alberts* v.

California, decided on the same day, made a similar claim against a state law. The *Roth-Alberts* decision (or *Roth*, as it is usually called) became famous as marking the end of the Hicklin test in the United States; within less than ten years, the old debate over value would also be closed, and "pornography" would acquire its ultimate meaning. " 'Hard-core' pornography," Rankin explained to the Justices, was both the "main objective" and the "major catch" of the federal statute, constituting ninety percent of the material seized under its authority. This stuff—photographs and movies as well as books—represented men and women engaged in "every conceivable kind of normal and abnormal sexual relations"; the only "idea" it expressed was "that there is pleasure in sexual gratification, whatever that means." The "social value" of this idea was, "of course, nil."[13] In fact, value had never been an issue for either Roth or Alberts; neither maintained the pretense that his merchandise possessed worth of any kind—social, scientific, or literary. It is just as well that they did not.

The sixty-five-year-old Samuel Roth was a familiar figure on the obscenity circuit. As far back as 1925, he had won some notoriety for publishing unauthorized excerpts from Joyce's *Work in Progress* (eventually to become *Finnegans Wake*) in his magazine *Two Worlds*. Roth belatedly paid the irate author $200 for the privilege, and Joyce was appeased. But in 1927, in another magazine called *Two Worlds Monthly*, Roth published a "slightly expurgated" version of the first three episodes of *Ulysses*. Taking advantage of the fact that the United States had not signed the 1885 Berne Convention on copyrights, he paid Joyce nothing. Outraged by both the expurgation and the nonpayment, Joyce circulated a letter of protest bearing the signatures of virtually every distinguished intellectual figure in the world, among them Albert Einstein, Benedetto Croce, Hugo von Hofmannsthal, and Paul Valéry. At the end of 1928, Roth was enjoined by a New York State court from further use of Joyce's name;[14] two years later, though not at Joyce's instigation, he served sixty days in a Philadelphia jail for selling copies of *Ulysses*.[15] In subsequent years, Roth was arrested on obscenity charges seven more times and convicted five times,[16] occasionally compelling the courts to strenuous efforts of reasoning. In 1948, he came before the United States District Court for the Southern District of New York on the charge of having mailed copies of a translation of Balzac's *Contes Drolatiques (Droll Stories)* and an item called *Waggish Tales from the Czechs*, described by the Postmaster General as "in fact American-made or shared smoking room jests and stories, obscene by any refined standard."[17] The District Court convicted Roth; on appeal, he was heard by Circuit Court Judges Jerome Frank and Augustus N. Hand, who upheld the conviction.

In an appendix to his concurring opinion, however, Frank—a newcomer to the obscenity game—expressed some serious doubts. Writing in the literarily allusive manner that was becoming de rigueur on such occasions, he cited Tolstoy, Goethe, Macaulay, Aristophanes, and Juvenal; he also questioned the power of obscenity to act as legislators assumed it did:

> I think that no sane man thinks socially dangerous the arousing of normal sexual desires. Consequently, if reading obscene books has merely that consequence, Congress, it would seem, can constitutionally no more suppress such books than it can prevent the mailing of many other objects, such as perfumes, for example, which notoriously produce that result. . . . Perhaps further research will disclose that, for most men, such reading diverts from, rather than stimulates to, anti-social conduct. . . .

Frank even challenged the notion of "literary distinction" as an antidote to obscenity, pointing out that, strictly applied, it would transform the Postmaster General into a literary critic and reviewing judges into "super-critics." "I cannot believe," he concluded, "Congress had anything so grotesque in mind."[18]

When Roth next encountered Frank, eight years later, the Judge's opinions had considerably ripened. They had benefited, as Frank declared at the outset, from the most learned judicial statement on the subject so far, Curtis Bok's long, thoughtful opinion in a 1949 Pennsylvania prosecution of nine novels, including James T. Farrell's *Studs Lonigan* trilogy, *Sanctuary* and *Wild Palms* by William

Faulkner, and Harold Robbins's *Never Love a Stranger*. Bok vindicated all the books; in the process, he provided a survey of English
and American obscenity cases, from Wilkes's *Essay on Woman* in
1770 and Sharpless's impudent painting of 1815, through a score
of others, up to *Forever Amber* in 1948. He summarized the "modern
test of obscenity":

> the modern rule is that obscenity is measured by the erotic al-
> lurement upon the average modern reader; that the erotic allure-
> ment of a book is measured by whether it is sexually impure—
> i.e., pornographic, 'dirt for dirt's sake,' a calculated incitement
> to sexual desire—or whether it reveals an effort to reflect life,
> including its dirt, with reasonable accuracy and balance; and that
> mere coarseness or vulgarity is not obscenity.

In the end, Bok expressed dissatisfaction with even this streamlined
version of Justice Cockburn's eighty-one-year-old formula. Borrow-
ing a famous phrase from Oliver Wendell Holmes, he proposed
that obscenity statutes be subjected to the same standard as other
laws regulating public utterance: a "clear and present danger" had
to be demonstrated in the material at hand, not merely a suppo-
sitious "tendency" to deprave and corrupt. Though Bok remained
skeptical that any such danger could be shown, he did not preclude
it in the case of books that were "sexually impure and pornographic"
according to the modern test.[19]

Praising Bok's "brilliant decision," Frank again attached a long
appendix to his concurrence in Roth's conviction; his argument
culminated in the declaration that "no sane person can believe it
socially harmful if sexual desire leads to normal, and not anti-social,
sexual behavior since, without such behavior, the human race would
soon disappear."

Like Bok, Frank pointed to the paucity of "competent studies"
of the link between obscenity and anti-social conduct; the whole
rationale for legislation in this area rested on the connection, yet it
had never been objectively established. He quoted as representative
a survey by the New York City Bureau of Social Hygiene, con-

ducted more than thirty years earlier under a grant from the Rock-efeller Foundation. Ten thousand women, all unmarried college graduates, had been sent a twelve-page questionnaire delving into every aspect of their sexual knowledge, feelings, and activities. Of the 1,200 who filled it out, only 72 (six percent) reported that their earliest sex information had come from reading. The books men-tioned included everything from the Bible (especially Genesis) to John Lothrop Motley's three-volume *Rise of the Dutch Republic* (1856); no one mentioned *The Mysteries of Verbena House* or anything like it. Asked what they found most sexually stimulating, 95 women said "books," 40 "drama," and 218 simply "man." Surveying these flimsy statistics, Frank concluded, with Bok, that the requisite bond be-tween obscenity and sexual action had not been proven—though he, too, stopped short of asserting its nonexistence.[20]

Freighted with this baggage, appealed to the legal limit, Roth's last case arrived before the United States Supreme Court in April 1957. Along with it came the case of David Alberts, on appeal from the California Superior Court. The material at issue in both cases was tawdry: Roth had been convicted of mailing such articles as *Good Times* (a magazine containing nude pictures and erotic stories), a book entitled *American Aphrodite*, and provocative advertisements for these and other products. Alberts, with his wife, Violet, had operated a mail-order business called Male Merchandise Mart, spe-cializing in "filthy books, bondage pictures, and prurient photo-graphs."[21] One can hardly imagine a wider discrepancy than that between these low-grade objects and the portentous legal issue they brought forth—the constitutionality of the federal and California antiobscenity statutes, and by implication all such laws throughout the nation. The Supreme Court had never before been presented with this question in clear-cut form; it was fitting that it came up in the centenary year of Lord Campbell's Act.

Both convictions were upheld, by majorities of six to three for Roth and seven to two for Alberts; as before, the Court affirmed the constitutionality of antiobscenity legislation on all levels of gov-ernment.[22] In Justice William J. Brennan's majority opinion, cov-ering both cases, the point was made in what looks like an unequivocal manner:

implicit in the history of the First Amendment is the rejection of obscenity as utterly without redeeming social importance. This rejection for that reason is mirrored in the universal judgment that obscenity should be restrained, reflected in the international agreement of over fifty nations, in the obscenity laws of all the forty-eight states, and in the twenty obscenity laws enacted by the Congress from 1842 to 1956. . . . We hold that obscenity is not within the area of constitutionally protected speech or press.

"Obscenity," however, needed a new definition, because "sex and obscenity are not synonymous":

Obscene material is material which deals with sex in a manner appealing to prurient interest. The portrayal of sex, e.g., in art, literature and scientific works, is not itself sufficient reason to deny material the constitutional protection of freedom of speech and press. Sex, a great and mysterious motive force in human life, has indisputably been a subject of absorbing interest to mankind through the ages; it is one of the vital problems of human interest and public concern.

Consequently, eighty-nine years after *Regina* v. *Hicklin*, a new test was born: "Obscene material is material which deals with sex in a manner appealing to prurient interest, and the test of obscenity is whether to the average person, applying contemporary community standards, the dominant theme of the material appeals to prurient interest."[23]

The decisive-sounding language of Brennan's opinion might have conveyed the impression that, at last, after decades of fruitless haggling, the obscenity debate had been settled. In fact, however, confusion was only growing denser, as the next few years would show. The exclusion of obscenity from protection by the First Amendment had been confirmed by the nation's highest court, but this boon to the censors had been accompanied by the bothersome phrase "utterly without redeeming social importance." "Utterly" was the worst culprit, since it seemed to suggest that if the tiniest nugget of "social importance" could be dug out of a book, it would neutralize a mountain of prurience. In later decisions, the Supreme Court would modify this perhaps inadvertently radical stance; but the decade following *Roth* saw the opening of floodgates, as books that no one had dared bring to trial before were discovered not to be "utterly" worthless. This is a paradoxical outcome, since the 1957 decision upheld two lower-court obscenity convictions, but not a surprising one, given the convoluted history of the subject.

Roth cleared nothing up, but it did reflect a new maturity in public discourse on "the obscene." Until then, no matter how much learning judges had displayed, decisions in such matters customarily bore an air of groping in the dark. For decades, however, a body of work had been accumulating that treated obscenity as a subject worthy of study in its own right, from a social and not merely a legal point of view. Starting with a scattering of books and essays around the turn of the twentieth century, the volume of production gradually swelled; the decade or so after 1957 saw an all-time peak in the volume of writing about obscenity, most of it focusing on *Roth* as either the end of the argument or the inauguration of a new era of disorder. By 1970, though perhaps nothing else was settled, obscenity had firmly established itself as a research topic, with a hefty bibliography all its own.[24]

In a sense, Anthony Comstock wrote books about obscenity, as did Swinburne, George Moore, and other opponents of literary censorship. But, on both sides, these early polemicists tended to treat the problem in terms of eternal verities, not as the subject of investigation and analysis. Among the earliest book-length studies to take a historical point of view was *"Obscene" Literature and Constitutional Law* (1911) by free-speech advocate Theodore Schroeder—a well-documented survey, full of entertaining absurdities, but hardly distinguished for its detachment.[25] Heywood Broun and Margaret Leech's 1927 biography of Comstock represented a notable step in that direction, and both of these studies served as sources, in 1928, for the book that established the pattern followed by all subsequent studies of obscenity, *To the Pure* by Morris L. Ernst and William Seagle. Ernst was just embarking on a distinguished legal career that would feature the defense of *Ulysses;* he would also write a long series of books related to censorship, including the best of the post-*Roth* crop, *Censorship: The Search for the Obscene* (with Alan U. Schwartz, 1964). Significant as his role in the courtroom was, his books probably had greater impact, since they educated a wide public in the history of the debate, the knottiness of the problems involved, and most of all the dangers inherent in any form of censorship.

Like Broun and Leech the year before, Ernst and Seagle had an obvious bias in regard to their subject; yet they, too, were able to refrain from rant and offer a judicious assessment of a history that condemns itself without editorializing. And they did not fall into the trap that would catch most of their successors—attempting to define "obscenity" or propose model legislation for its control. In their view, it was already apparent that "obscenity" (or its newfangled variant, "pornography") was such a vague abstraction that to offer yet another definition would only muddy the issue further. They were aware that the core of the problem lay not in the nature of "obscenity," however it might be defined, but in the psychology of those who would seek it out and suppress it.[26] They pointed to the "paternalistic concern" that censors had traditionally expressed toward groups other than themselves—women and the poor first of all, and, more recently and locally, "Negroes."[27] And they concluded with a statement that later generations should have listened to more closely: "The final refutation of the criminal obscenity laws lies in their futility."[28]

Subsequent studies of pornography and censorship modeled themselves on *To the Pure,* but Ernst and Seagle's argument was seldom followed to its inseparable pair of conclusions: "obscenity" cannot be adequately defined, and legislation against it is both impracticable and undesirable. Instead, later essays and books seemed to have taken their cue from a rather surprising source—D. H. Lawrence. It might be supposed that Lawrence (1885–1930) had enough experience of censorship to wish it abolished across the board, his novel *The Rainbow* having been seized at his London publisher's and ordered burned, on the grounds that the book was "a mass of obscenity,"[29] and his *Lady Chatterley's Lover* having been banned in Britain and the United States. A few months after its publication, Lawrence wrote to Morris L. Ernst (who had sent him a copy of *To the Pure*), railing against "the censor-moron": "It is our developing and extending consciousness that he threatens—and our consciousness in its newest, most sensitive activity, its vital growth."[30] But despite his authorship of one of the twentieth century's most notorious "pornographic" novels, Lawrence was by no means immune to blushes. Molly Bloom's soliloquy at the end of *Ulysses*, for example, shocked him powerfully: "it is the dirtiest, most indecent, obscene thing ever written," he told his wife, Frieda. "It is filthy."[31] Nor was he averse to censorship as such; in fact, toward the end of his short life, he came out strongly in favor of it.

Lawrence's essay "Pornography and Obscenity" (1929) has become a classic declaration of what is generally taken to be the enlightened, even libertarian view of the subject. His reservations, however, have probably been more influential than his assertions. The essay begins with a plausible demonstration that neither "pornography" nor "obscenity" can be defined. "But," Lawrence adds, "even I would censor genuine pornography, rigorously," as the Supreme Court would also do: "It would not be very difficult. In the first place, genuine pornography is almost always underworld, it doesn't come into the open. In the second, you can recognise it by the insult it offers, invariably, to sex, and to the human spirit." Lawrence defined pornography for the twentieth century, cloaking in specious frankness a self-righteous fervor indistinguishable at bottom from Cockburn's or Comstock's:

> Pornography is the attempt to insult sex, to do dirt on it. This is unpardonable. Take the very lowest instance, the picture postcards sold underhand, by the underworld, in most cities. What I have seen of them have been of an ugliness to make you cry. The insult to the human body, the insult to a vital human relationship! Ugly and cheap they make the human nudity, ugly and degraded they make the sexual act, trivial and cheap and nasty. It is the same with the books they sell in the underworld. They

are either so ugly they make you ill, or so fatuous you can't imagine
anybody but a cretin or a moron reading them, or writing them.

Like all of his predecessors and most of his followers, Lawrence
identified the scene of pornographic distribution with the scene of
pornographic portrayal. He might have felt more at ease with the
modern, industrialized society he so fervently damned if he had
reflected that, by pushing pornography "underground," culture had
already gone halfway toward his own goal of getting it out of sight.
It might also have occurred to him that there were other than
aesthetic connections between the cheapness of pornographic pictures and the cheapness of the paper they were printed on. He had
no need, of course, to consider any of this; he was (we may be
thankful) an artist, not a legislator. But his worst failure was not
to see that his definition of "unpardonable" pornography, if it became law, would turn out just as oppressive as the other definitions
that had plagued his literary career.

Directly or indirectly, Lawrence's notion of pornography as "the
attempt to insult sex, to do dirt on it," was of decisive influence on
all redefinitions of the elusive word for the next half century. Judge
Woolsey's famous phrase "dirt for dirt's sake" recalls Lawrence as
well as Pater, and scores of later authorities, literary and judicial
alike, made the same point in slightly differing language. Eventually, in 1957, the United States Supreme Court adopted a version
of it; by then, however, it was already axiomatic that, as John
Courtney Murray wrote in 1956, "pornography, . . . the kind of
obscenity that is a perverse and vicious profanation of the sacredness
of sex, seems to hold a permanent attraction for a portion of hu-
manity. That it is a corruptive social influence is not to be denied;
consequently, few would deny that its repression is necessary."[32]
In the years after *Roth*, the flourishing cottage industry of books
about pornography brought forth a repetitive chorus of agreement.
Walter Allen in 1962:

> It is fantasy writing, wish-fulfilment writing, differing from other
> forms of fantasy writing, such as romantic fiction, by being ex-

plicitly sexual. . . . Pornography is transcribed masturbation fantasy.[33]

George P. Elliott in 1965: *"Pornography is the representation of directly or indirectly erotic acts with an intrusive vividness which offends decency without esthetic justification."*[34] Richard Kuh in 1967: "It tends to depersonalize sex, to exalt it for its own sake."[35] Harry Clor in 1969: "Pornography, then, is a certain kind of obscenity—it is sexual obscenity in which the debasement of the human element is heavily accentuated, is depicted in great physiological detail, and is carried very far toward its utmost logical conclusion."[36]

The list could be indefinitely extended; over and over again, especially in the decade after *Roth*, writers made the same few points with slight variations in emphasis. It seems odd that if everyone knew pornography when he saw it, these obvious truths would have to be hammered home so often; all studies of the subject in this period betray nervousness that, plain as the facts were said to be, their phrasing might not be exactly right, some necessary qualifier might have been omitted. Hence, perhaps, the continuing need—and presumably also public taste—for an avalanche of books that told the same story and arrived at the same conclusions. Not all such studies, of course, were equal in quality or influence; they ranged from hack work like Richard Kyle-Keith's *The High Price of Pornography* (1961) to significant works of literary and historical scholarship like Steven Marcus's *The Other Victorians* (1964). Whatever their individual value, however, they converged with remarkable unanimity on a Lawrentian definition of "pornography," best formulated by psychologists Eberhard and Phyllis Kronhausen in 1959:

In pornography (hard core obscenity) *the main purpose is to stimulate erotic response* in the reader. And that is all. *In erotic realism, truthful description of the basic realities of life, as the individual experiences it, is of the essence*, even if such portrayals (whether by reason of humor, or revulsion, or any other cause) have a decidedly anti-erotic effect.[37]

The "hard core" had at last been brought to light: it was single-minded, fantastic, and, as Justice Brennan said, "utterly without redeeming social importance."

It was also, everyone agreed, infantile. The sexual response it aimed to elicit could come, perhaps, only from mature organs, but the minds attached to those organs were distinctly retarded. It is curious that, after more than a century of campaigns to protect the immature from ruination by obscenity, obscenity itself should turn out to be not quite grown up. "Inside every pornographer," wrote Steven Marcus, "there is an infant screaming for the breast from which he has been torn."[38] The popular pathology of pornography, its association with stunted mental states, also owed something to the influence of Sigmund Freud. Freud traced sexual deviance, in all its forms, to arrested development. His *Three Essays on the Theory of Sexuality*, first published in 1905 and repeatedly expanded through 1925, proposed that all individuals experience homosexual, oral, and anal phases on their way to the achievement of genitally centered heterosexuality. Every variation from this norm—either in the object of desire or in the means of satisfying it—should be seen not as perversion or corruption but as a failure to mature. "Every pathological disorder of sexual life," he wrote, "is rightly to be regarded as an inhibition in development."[39] In Freud's own work, there is no disdain toward homosexuality, masturbation, anal erotism, or any other variant of desire on the grounds that it is childish or warped. Indeed, by suggesting that we all were perverts—and every kind of pervert—at some point in our lives, Freud may have contributed to lessening the stigma attached to sexual deviance. He did, however, set up monogamous, genital heterosexuality as the universal goal of human development; when popular culture took over his ideas, it welcomed this familiar notion. Popular culture was also able to add a sneer to the scheme. Masturbation might no longer be a snare of the devil, as it had been for Comstock, but it was a retarded activity, indicating mental enfeeblement on the part of the masturbator and those who catered to him. Since "hard-core" pornography did exactly that, it earned grimaces of patronizing distaste from practically everyone who commented on it.

Again the counters had shifted, but the game remained the same. The Young Person, supposedly dead, rose again in a new shape. She was no longer the girl or boy about to be debauched by a book; now she was the more sinister figure of a mentally defective adult—probably male, probably also of lower-class origin—who wallowed in infantile idiocy and wished to make others do the same. This mid-twentieth-century Young Person had no taste for art, literature, or anything of "social importance." Reality itself had no charm for him; he preferred to dwell in the never-never land that Marcus dubbed "pornotopia." He was dangerous, however, even more dangerous than his predecessors, because he was inclined to bend reality to suit his dreams. He had to be restrained, therefore—and the best way to restrain him was still, as it had always been, to control his access to representations. Public attitudes toward the representation of sex became steadily laxer as the twentieth century went on, but they continued to reserve a special zone—now called the "hard core"—where the burning of books and pictures was as necessary as ever. The explosion of pornography studies after *Roth* lent a measure of intellectual authority to this apparently indestructible idea.

These studies also gave pornography a burst of publicity it could hardly have obtained without their aid. Thanks to the Kronhausens, the ordinary reader of 1959 could peruse excerpts from *The Autobiography of a Flea*, *The Memoirs of a Russian Princess*, and other Ashbeeish curiosities.[40] Marcus provided a detailed discussion, with long, unexpurgated quotations, of *My Secret Life* and *The Lustful Turk*, a durable classic of 1828. Whether or not they offered quotations, all these books were at pains to characterize their subject exactly, including the means by which it was produced and disseminated. In the process, as the prosecutors of *Madame Bovary* had discovered a century before, they thrust into public prominence the very material they wished to keep in shadow. By 1970, "hard-core" pornography had grown from the secretive, underworld stuff that made Lawrence ill into the subject of scores of books and almost daily articles in the popular press. In that year, it won the honor of a report by a Presidential Commission, filling several volumes and itself the center of acrimonious controversy. That ludicrous incident will be discussed in the next chapter; for now, we may take 1970 as a convenient date at which to end the pornographic era that began with the excavations at Pompeii more than two centuries before. The argument did not cease; it had, in fact, a few surprising twists in store. But the classic age of pornography was over, and the post-pornographic era had begun.

Already by 1966, in the United States, the printed word had won immunity from large-scale suppression on charges of obscenity. Local prosecutions of various kinds would continue, and school libraries would remain a favorite hunting ground for censors; but in 1966, the Supreme Court ruled in favor of the "redeeming social importance" of a book that for more than two hundred years had served as a handy synonym for "obscenity," John Cleland's *Memoirs of a Woman of Pleasure*, universally known as *Fanny Hill*. In earlier chapters, we encountered this underground novel in various contexts—repudiated by its author in 1750, prosecuted as obscene in Massachusetts in 1821, packed up like a sure-fire drug by the author of *My Secret Life*. Widely reprinted and circulated though it was, *Fanny Hill* remained disreputable long after far more explicit books had stood trial and been acquitted. Its prohibition had come to have an almost sentimental quality; the weight of tradition was overwhelmingly on the side of Justice Tom Clark, who dissented from the majority opinion: "Though I am not known to be a purist—or a shrinking violet—this book is too much even for me."[41] Only the march of inevitability, it would seem, could disperse the time-honored belief that *Fanny Hill* was unfit to be sold above the counter. Inevitability, however, was on the move, thanks to the Roth "test" and the efforts of lawyer Charles Rembar.

Rembar had defended *Lady Chatterley's Lover* in 1959 and played an important role in the approximately sixty trials of Henry Miller's *Tropic of Cancer* during the next few years. His presentation of both books, and of *Fanny Hill*, was grounded in the Supreme Court's 1957 definition of obscenity as "utterly without redeeming social importance"—emphasizing the "utterly" and changing "importance" to "value." The change might seem a mere matter of semantics, but from Rembar's point of view it was crucial. As he later explained:

> In the *Lady Chatterley* case, . . . I referred to the suggested criterion as the "social-value test." That is, I was reading the word "importance" in the sense of "value." "Importance," however, has other meanings—not synonymous with value—that would impose a higher standard. "Some value" might not be too hard to show; "some importance" could be something else again.[42]

Even lawyers might not wish to argue long over the difference between value and importance, whether *Fanny Hill* possessed any of either, and to what degree. In any case, the Supreme Court did not; in a six-to-three decision handed down March 21, 1966, Justice Brennan accepted Rembar's "social-value test" and redeemed Cleland's novel:

> a book cannot be proscribed unless it is found to be *utterly* without redeeming social value. This is so even though the book is found to possess the requisite prurient appeal and to be patently offensive. Each of the thee federal constitutional criteria is to be applied independently; the social value of the book can neither be weighed against nor canceled by its prurient appeal or patent offensiveness. . . .[43]

This slight modification of the "three-pronged" test promulgated in *Roth* remains the Supreme Court's last significant statement on the obscenity of the printed word. "So far as writing is concerned," Rembar gloated a year later, "there is no longer any law of obscenity."[44]

Literally speaking, *Fanny Hill* is unquestionably pornographic; it is the story of a prostitute, told as if in her own words. But it also has undeniable value, the same value possessed by the obscene bric-a-brac that troubled the early excavators of Pompeii and Herculaneum. Some of those artifacts were fine examples of painting or sculpture, but many were crudely done and could lay no claim to artistic stature. Their primary value, however, did not depend on art; indeed, it might be said that they were most worth saving simply because they were crude. They were the sort of thing that time would never have preserved if Vesuvius had not safely buried them. They bore unwitting testimony to the nature of daily life two thousand years ago—a value that had nothing to do with artistic intention or value. Similarly, Cleland's novel, though reasonably well written, rises in no way above the ordinary standard of its time. Its plot is schematic, its characters sketchy, its euphemistically graphic sex scenes repetitive and dull. Yet it is, unmistakably, an eighteenth-century novel; without in the least intending to do so, it provides information on the customs and attitudes of its time that a latter-day reader might well find valuable. These trappings are minimal, but they prevent *Fanny Hill* from being classed with the "pornotopian" fantasies that Marcus described. Ironically, it is in its minimal trappings that the novel's whole twentieth-century value resides.[45]

In the aftermath of the *Fanny Hill* decision, a great number of other pornographic "classics" were published in modern editions, many by Grove Press, which had also published *Lady Chatterley's Lover* and *Tropic of Cancer* and steered them through the courts. Grove's list soon included the works of the Marquis de Sade, the monumental anonymous memoir *My Secret Life*, and Frank Harris's *My Life and Loves*, along with more dubious items like *Venus School-Mistress or Birchen Sports* and *The Pearl, a Journal of Facetiae and Voluptuous Reading*, which even Ashbee had found "crapulous."[46] By 1970, any enterprising reader could amass a library rivaling Ashbee's, and at a tiny fraction of the cost, since most modern reprints appeared as inexpensive paperbacks. In some cases, "social value" could be found in these books only by painfully stretching the term; nevertheless it was found, and they were freely circulated. As at Pompeii, once excavation was begun it had to continue, no matter what horrors the past might yield up. The same impulse seemed to operate in modern fiction, as novels like Hubert Selby's *Last Exit to Brooklyn* and Pauline Réage's *Story of O* pushed hard against the outer limits of community tolerance. Whatever one might think of these books, old or new, they were no longer "obscenity"; that had been pared down to the hard core—"worthless trash," as Rembar called it at the *Fanny Hill* trial.[47]

Sewage, garbage, trash—the oldest metaphors for obscene representations continued to circulate, long after Comstock's poisoned swords and Douglas's prussic acid had fallen out of use. "Pornography" had come as close to a final definition as it would ever get: utterly loathsome stuff with no redeeming qualities of any kind. Comstock would have approved of this definition, though he would have applied it more widely than his late-twentieth-century successors did. Most of his booty, after all, had consisted neither of Boccaccio nor even the Marquis de Sade, but of lewd playing cards, cheap lithographs, and risqué stereopticon slides. The courts and the public at large had seldom paid much heed to this sort of thing; the argument about "value" had held center stage for more than a century. After 1970, however, with that issue apparently settled, there was nowhere else to turn but toward the hard core. Like the ancient detritus of Pompeii, modern trash had been lurking in darkness all along, waiting for a chance at the light.

CHAPTER EIGHT

THE POST-PORNOGRAPHIC ERA

IN OCTOBER 1967, the United States Congress authorized the establishment of a Commission on Pornography and Obscenity, boosting the subject to the highest level of publicity it had yet attained. There had been Congressional hearings before—three sets of them during the past fifteen years, all yielding inconclusive results—but the Commission, with its ample budget, large support staff, and two-year working span, was evidently intended to say the last word, to settle for once and all an argument that had been sputtering ineffectually for more than a century. Public Law 90-100 assigned the Commission four tasks: "to evaluate and recommend definitions of obscenity and pornography"; "to explore the nature and volume of traffic in such materials"; "to study the effect of obscenity and pornography upon the public"; and "to recommend such legislative, administrative, or other advisable and appropriate action as the Commission deems necessary to regulate effectively the flow of such traffic, without in any way interfering with constitutional rights."[1] President Lyndon B. Johnson appointed the Commission in January 1968, funds were appropriated six months later, and on September 30, 1970, President Richard M. Nixon received the Commission's *Report*.

It was a daunting bundle, packed with charts and tables; even excluding the series of "Technical Reports" that accompanied it, it ran to seven hundred closely printed pages. Before a month was out, however, a mass-market paperback edition had been published, indicating a more widespread interest in the *Report* than usually greets such governmental utterances. Part of its popularity was due to the nature of its findings and recommendations, which surprised many observers and unsettled others so profoundly they refused to accept them. Part also came from the acrimony that had infested the Commission throughout its existence and was fully reflected in the *Report*. It is a curious document, the last third of which endeavors to discredit everything that precedes it. Taken as a whole, the *Report* proves only that huge amounts of labor and expertise— not to mention money—had been spent on producing a definitive statement of utter confusion. Read in detail, however, it provides an exhaustive survey of what is, to us, familiar terrain. The features of this landscape, this interminable battleground, had not significantly changed since Lord Campbell and Justice Cockburn ventured on it a century earlier; but, as the *Report* demonstrates, by 1970 the lines had become so deeply entrenched that nothing short of an ultimate weapon could break the impasse.

The majority report—to which twelve of the Commission's eighteen members subscribed, while five dissented and one abstained— set out to refute all the fantasies about pornography that had led to the passage of Public Law 90-100. The size of the "industry" had been variously estimated at between $500 million and $2.5 billion per year—"always without," according to the Commission, "supporting data or definitions which would make such estimates meaningful." The Commission's findings, admittedly fragmentary and inconclusive, placed the total considerably below the lower of these, at less than $200 million in 1969. There was also no evidence that the smut business was "monolithic"; instead, it seemed to consist of "several distinct markets and submarkets," some well organized but others "extremely chaotic." The myth that vast fortunes were to be made peddling obscenity was unfounded: the largest dealer in "mail-order erotica," for example, probably turned a profit of only $200,000 per year, before taxes. As to the popular belief that "organized crime" controlled the industry, the Commission had "insufficient data" to support any conclusion. The *Report* rather wryly comments, however, that the "adult bookstore" trade "tends to involve individuals who have had considerable experience with being arrested."[2] There was no need to point out that since the days of Anthony Comstock, existing laws had guaranteed this connection.

Obeying its mandate to investigate the effects of pornography, the Commission waded into the morass of psychological and sociological studies that had accumulated in the last twenty years. Earlier treatments of the subject had been hampered (their authors complained) by a shortage of empirical data; by 1970, that complaint could no longer be made. The field had flourished alarmingly and would continue to do so at a rate that mimicked the burgeoning of "pornography" itself.[3] Information was still sketchy in certain areas, but the *Report* was nevertheless able to conclude unequivocally that "empirical research designed to clarify the question has found no evidence to date that exposure to explicit sexual materials plays a significant role in the causation of delinquent or criminal behavior among youth or adults."[4] Research would go on, however, mainly because any such conclusion is bound to be unsatisfactory, even to those who arrive at it. No matter how forcefully a statement of "no evidence" is made, it has an air of tentativeness, as if evidence were available but had simply not been discovered yet. One might also mention the researcher's enduring need for funding—in order, if nothing else, to remain a researcher. Funding is motivated first of all by a desire that positive results be obtained, and that desire can never be stilled by conclusions of "no evidence."

The most radical section of the *Report* came under the heading of its fourth task, to recommend legislative or administrative action in regard to "pornography." This was inseparable from the first task—to define what the word meant—since the justice and effectiveness of any law depend on the precision with which its object is identified. Surveying the present federal and state antiobscenity laws—and remarking on the formidable cost of their enforcement—the *Report* observed that "obscene" was generally not defined at all in them, and when it was, the definition merely adapted the language of the Supreme Court's *Roth* decision. Despite the apparent objectivity of its three criteria—prurient interest, patent offensiveness, and lack of social value—*Roth* was inadequate in the Commission's view:

> It is impossible for a publisher, distributor, retailer or exhibitor to know in advance whether he will be charged with a criminal offense for distributing a particular work, since his understanding of the three tests and their application to his work may differ from that of the police, prosecutor, court or jury.[5]

In the end, the *Report* provided no definition of obscenity and recommended that none be attempted by any legislative or administrative body. This was not, however, a throwing up of hands or acquiescence in the status quo. It represented a logical and consistent stance, because it came in tandem with another recommendation: "The Commission recommends that federal, state, and local legislation prohibiting the sale, exhibition, or distribution of sexual materials to consenting adults be repealed."[6]

It is remarkable, given the history of the subject and of governmental commissions in general, that such an organization arrived at a conclusion that not only conformed to logic but also demolished the basis on which the Commission itself had been established. The conclusion was not, of course, new: it had been reached by Ernst and Seagle in 1928 and by virtually every literary artist (except D. H. Lawrence) whose works had been tried as obscene; it was also the long-standing position of the American Civil Liberties Union and of the two Supreme Court justices, Hugo Black and William O. Douglas, who had dissented from *Roth* on the grounds that the First Amendment guaranteed freedom of all speech, without reservation. Quixotism, however, is built into this stance, and not merely because there has always been a multitude of people eager to speak out against logic. Those who agree with the *Report* that antiobscenity laws should be repealed, that there is no predictable correlation between lewd representations and lewd acts, must also agree that there is no predictable correlation between any image and any act—that the problem we have been haggling over all these years is no problem, only an illusion. To take this position means, in effect, to advocate silence or exact repetition: *No censorship of any kind, any time, anywhere* is all that can be said, over and over again, until it takes on, even in the speaker's ears, the weirdness that invests any statement if you make it often enough. The supposed liber-tarians who would deregulate pornography are, in this sense, more modest than those who would prosecute it. The libertarians would simply have us shut up and get on with our lives, while the others would demand endless talk about sex, in the courtroom and out of it.

What I have been calling the *Report* is only about two thirds of the document, the majority report. It was accompanied by 150 pages of dissents, some (apparently justified) complaining of how the Commission had been conceived and run, others directed at its conclusions, which several members found to be as shocking and dangerous as pornography itself. Commissioners Morton A. Hill, S.J., and Winfrey C. Link made the plausible objection that the absence of a demonstrable bond between pornography and crime did not support the inference that pornography was harmless. But they trod on treacherous ground when they declared that the "basic question" was "whether and to what extent society may establish and maintain certain moral standards." Hill and Link claimed that the majority report had "deliberately and carefully avoided coming to grips with this issue,"[7] when in fact the report spoke on the subject rather eloquently:

> The Commission recognizes and believes that the existence of sound moral standards is of vital importance to individuals and to society. To be effective and meaningful, however, these stan-dards must be based upon deep personal commitment flowing from values instilled in the home, in educational and religious training, and through individual resolutions of personal confron-tations with human experience. Governmental regulation of moral choice can deprive the individual of the responsibility for personal decision which is essential to the formation of genuine moral

standards. Such regulation would also tend to establish an official moral orthodoxy, contrary to our most fundamental constitutional traditions.[8]

By identifying "society" with "government," as they too easily did, Hill and Link became advocates of just the tyranny the majority had sought to forestall.

It is unnecessary to discuss in detail the diagnoses and remedies furnished by Hill and Link—or those of Charles H. Keating, Jr., a third dissenting commissioner, who concurred in Hill and Link's report and attached one of his own, almost as long. "Children cannot grow in love if they are trained with pornography," said Hill and Link, commenting on sex education in schools (which they also opposed). "Pornography is loveless; it degrades the human being, reduces him to the level of animal."[9] According to Keating, "our nation is imperiled by a poison which is all-pervasive"[10]—exactly Comstock's belief, and a metaphor that Aldous Huxley thought he had laid to rest in 1928. The most lifeless feature of these latter-day denunciations of pornography is their rhetoric, the extremely limited stock of metaphors they are able to draw on. Metaphors are essential in this realm of discourse, because there seems, and always has seemed, to be no possibility of a literal statement. Comstock, when he turned literal and asked his readers to look around at America's youth dropping in its tracks, obtained no response: if his readers looked, they saw no such thing. But when he spoke of poisoned swords piercing tender flesh, or of diabolical parents giving their children scorpions to play with, he could count on arousing powerful emotions. The history of "pornography" is a political one, and the connection shows itself nowhere more clearly than here—in the similarity of two rhetorical systems, both of which sidestep the literal at every opportunity.

Exhausted metaphors have never been a liability to politicians, and the moment the *Report* appeared, at the end of September 1970, its doom was sealed. The majority who signed it must have known that this would happen; they are to be commended—truth or error notwithstanding—for their courage in sticking with conclusions that were bound to win them nearly universal denunciation. The United States Senate reacted with more than customary pusillanimity, no doubt thanks to the impending elections, scheduled for November 8. On October 13, by a roll-call vote of sixty to five, it rejected the *Report* out of hand; a few days later, the President did the same. Campaigning in Baltimore, Maryland, on behalf of local Republican candidates, Nixon delivered a brief address which offers a catalogue of the censors' major clichés in the post-pornographic era. The Commission's conclusions and recommendations were, he said, "morally bankrupt"—a quality which may or may not have been related to the Commission's appointment "in a previous Adminstration." "So long as I am in the White House," he vowed, "there will be no relaxation of the national effort to control and eliminate smut from our national life." Nixon went on to make a provocative analogy that had seldom been put in such forthright terms. He was well aware, he said, of the importance of protecting free expression, but "pornography is to freedom of expression what anarchy is to liberty; as free men willingly restrain a measure of their freedom to prevent anarchy, so must we draw the line against pornography to protect freedom of expression." He concluded with a grand extension of the analogy that reflected the nervous political climate of 1970: "Moreover, if an attitude of permissiveness were to be adopted regarding pornography, this would contribute to an atmosphere condoning anarchy in every other field—and would increase the threat to our social order as well as to our moral principles."

One is not accustomed to look to political speeches for insight into any viewpoint or problem, but this terse declaration of Nixon's provides that for the question of pornography in the late twentieth century. The infection of the President's writers by his personal paranoia may have contributed to the eloquence with which they expressed the true reasons why pornography has always inspired anxiety in the wielders of power. It is indeed a symbol for anarchy, as it has been ever since women, children, and the poor were barred from the Secret Museum. On the surface, pornography threatens nothing but the unleashing of sexuality; but that unleashing, as

Nixon said, turns immediately into wantonness of every other kind, including the promiscuous redistribution of property. The fear that this will follow, that sex will become self-conscious and recognize its own political nature, constituted "pornography" at its origin and fuels it now.

Nixon's speech specified another, even more fundamental component of "pornography," one that also had rarely been stated with such concision. "The commission," he said, "contends that the proliferation of filthy books and plays has no lasting harmful effect on a man's character. If that were true, it must also be true that great books, great paintings and great plays have no ennobling effect on a man's conduct. Centuries of civilization and ten minutes of common sense tell us otherwise."[11] Whatever common sense may say, history provides no proof that "great" representations have had any such effect on anyone's actual behavior. The supposedly ennobling effect of good words and pictures is, however, inseparable from the supposedly harmful effects of bad ones; Nixon was correct to suggest that, if we accepted the innocuousness of pornography, we would have to ascribe equal impotence to our most treasured cultural inheritances—including religious texts and pictures. The result is unthinkable: we would find ourselves bereft of our myths of instruction, compelled to reexamine the very bases of our entire religious, educational, and political systems. It is supremely ironic that "worthless trash" like pornography should drive even a President to the brink of that abyss. Only to the brink, however: the unthinkable step was never taken.

Some, at least, had gone so far as to think it. The most famous of them was Marshall McLuhan, who in a series of books including *The Gutenberg Galaxy* (1962) and *Understanding Media* (1964), examined past and contemporary Western culture in terms of medium rather than content, the form of communication rather than the thing communicated. McLuhan's catchy and much-misinterpreted slogan, "The medium is the message," ought to have been applied—though it was not—to the pornography debate; it went instead to trendy chitchat about the brave new world of the electronic future, a watering-down instigated by McLuhan himself. McLuhan's earlier, more valuable, work intends to demonstrate that the medium of which a representation is made—print, paint, film, and so on—produces its deepest effects irrespective of what is being represented: " 'the medium is the message' because it is the medium that shapes and controls the scale and form of human association and action. The content or uses of such media are as diverse as they are ineffectual in shaping the form of human association. Indeed, it is only too typical that the 'content' of any medium blinds us to the character of the medium."[12] In this view, *The Mysteries of Verbena House* and *The Little Flowers of St. Francis* are more alike than they are different. Both are printed books and hence influence their readers' perceptual organization in precisely the same way; that one praises flagellation, the other sanctity, is irrelevant.

No one, perhaps, would be willing to adopt this proposition in its baldest form. It is apparent, however, that during the course of the pornographic era—from approximately the 1840s to the 1960s—representations of all kinds proliferated at a wildly accelerating pace in both quantity and medium. Printed books followed that path, along with every new medium invented during the period, from photography at its beginning to television near its end. The trend in all cases was toward ever wider dissemination of ever more representations, saturating the culture with words and pictures. Simultaneously, the range of content steadily broadened, in an apparently unstoppable drive toward the total availability of total detail. If the smut of fifty or even twenty years ago looks tame by comparison with today's, the reason may have nothing to do with pornography itself. Every mode of representation has become explicit in the same years, in every nonsexual realm; it has become possible to photograph the earth from outer space, a fetus in the womb, and Vietnamese children in the process of dying. The only difference in the case of pornography is that it faces steady resistance, while these other advances in explicitness win praise for contributing to the enrichment of knowledge. Yet resistance has always been futile; the march of knowledge is evidently stronger.

It is a familiar fact that our culture's ability to grasp technological innovations, to accommodate them morally and ethically, lags far behind the progress of technology itself. This discrepancy is especially apparent in the area of pornography, which has kept in step with the development of new media though the terms used to argue about it have hardly changed. The fear of images is so deep-rooted that its dislodgement must be very slow; at a time when men had walked on the moon (and been taped in the act), intelligent people were still using their grandparents' vocabulary to talk about pornography. Another reason for the retardation of pornographic discourse is that the best thinkers of any time have seldom paid much attention to it, except to reject the label when it was attached to works of art. The issue was customarily treated as a legal one, requiring only procedural analysis. The overweighted shelf of books on pornography holds few contributions by distinguished cultural analysts; most such books are either drearily statistical or blatantly polemical, sometimes both. The lack has to do in part with disdain for this lowly subject—disdain grounded, as I have attempted to show, in social as well as intellectual presuppositions. But it may also be that the solution of the problem, in which ordinary minds have been ensnaring themselves for more than a century, is too obvious for even a moment's cogitation.

At the end of the pornographic era, in the United States, two significant literary figures did comment on pornography, gaining heightened public attention. Steven Marcus's *The Other Victorians* (1964) was a cross-over book, academic in method but popular in style and subject. It contained the first serious, detailed analysis of *My Secret Life*, and it was informed throughout by erudite sympathy with the Victorians and their foibles. It was also pervaded, however, by the desire to show that pornography was and had always been both regressive and debilitating—on the one hand because it aimed at the gratification of infantile wishes, on the other because it inhabited "pornotopia," a place utterly unrelated to the real world. Marcus's unquestioning reliance on the Freudian norms of "maturity" and "reality"—their absolute superiority to anything childish or fantastic—allowed him to shore up popular prejudices with pseudo-psychoanalytic underpinnings. His Freudianism, too, was of the garden variety, persuasive to nonspecialized readers because it called for no special knowledge of what Freud wrote. The importance of *The Other Victorians* is unquestionable, but it is lessened by the very modern nature of the wish it fulfills, and also by its anachronistic use of the word "pornography." In 1964, "pornography" meant worthless portrayals of sex; for the Victorians, the question of value was only starting to arise, and a century would have to pass before an answer came. Marcus possessed what he thought was the answer before he began.

Susan Sontag's essay "The Pornographic Imagination," first published in 1967, had greater immediate impact than Marcus's book and seemed to be more radical. But it was something of an anachronism, too, because it treated "pornography" as a designation for certain kinds of "art." The courts, belatedly codifying public opinion, had already ruled that these terms were mutually exclusive; nevertheless, Sontag began by distinguishing among three species of pornography—"an item in social history," "a psychological phenomenon," and "a minor but interesting modality or convention within the arts."[13] She did, it is true, argue cogently against the reasons usually given why "art" and "pornography" could not coincide: most often, pornography had been denied artistic stature on the basis of definitions of "art," not "pornography," and these conceptions of art were limiting, even stultifying. "A definition of literature," Sontag pointed out (probably with Marcus in mind), "that faults a work for being rooted in 'fantasy' rather than in the realistic rendering of how lifelike persons in familiar situations live with each other couldn't even handle such venerable conventions as the pastoral, which depicts relations between people that are certainly reductive, vapid, and unconvincing."

It is unfortunate that Sontag's intellectual elitism led her to confine her attention to the narrow enclosure of "art," specifically its literary precincts. Her discussions of such French modernist works as *Story of O* and Georges Bataille's *Histoire de l'Oeil* are provocative, but these books had already been granted artistic stature without fighting for it. Art was no longer under attack and might portray whatever it liked; it could not, therefore, be pornographic by any stretch of the imagination, because "pornography" is a fighting word, and popular culture had decided not to fight about "art" anymore. Some of Sontag's best observations would have been better applied to under-the-counter porno loops and would have been equally valid for them:

> What's really at stake? A concern about the uses of knowledge itself. There's a sense in which *all* knowledge is dangerous, the reason being that not everyone is in the same condition as knowers or potential knowers. . . . It may be that, without subtle and extensive psychic preparation, any widening of experience and consciousness is destructive for most people. Then we must ask what justifies the reckless unlimited confidence we have in the present mass availability of other kinds of knowledge, in our optimistic acquiescence in the transformation of and extension of human capacities by machines. Pornography is only one item among the many dangerous commodities being circulated in this society and, unattractive as it may be, one of the less lethal, the less costly to the community in terms of human suffering.[14]

This, I would say, is exactly true; but the force of Sontag's argument had been vitiated in advance by her insistence that it had relevance only to art.

"The Pornographic Imagination" was also weakened by Sontag's definition of what separated the artistic from other forms of expression. The definition remained implicit in that essay and her earlier work in general, but it became overt in later books like *On Photography* (1977). One of her principal strategies for defending "pornography" was to remark that modern pornographic art makes frequent reference to earlier books in the same genre; by employing this tactic, *Story of O*—for example—declared that it belonged to a literary tradition, that its principal affinity was with other books, not with anything so visceral and fleeting as "real life." The postmodern name for this affinity (Sontag does not use it) is "intertextuality," the relation of texts among themselves rather than to extra-textual reality.

If intertextuality is taken as the identifying characteristic of "art," then any question of "pornography" becomes pointless, since pornography is defined as working on minds and bodies, not other texts. The sealing up of art in a museum where only art was to be found would easily eliminate the need for court trials and book burnings. It would also, however, remove the last vestiges of art's legendary power to move and alter a nonartistic audience. It may well be that art in fact never possessed such power. For centuries, nevertheless, it had been thought to possess it: not until the dawn of the post-pornographic era did public and elite reach a final consensus that art was only art when it had nothing whatever to do with the nonartistic world. If a representation did otherwise, if it reached rudely out of its proper sphere, it certainly was not art. It might, indeed, be dangerous.

Sontag confronted the perils of nonart in *On Photography*, a curious diatribe against a medium of representation whose artistic status had been equivocal ever since the process was invented, in the 1830s. In Sontag's view, the modern cult of the photograph was deeply pernicious, because it involved a reversal of values in which real experience lost priority over its image: "photographic images," she complained, "tend to subtract feeling from something we experience at first hand and the feelings they do arouse are, largely, not those we have in real life."

> Photography does not simply reproduce the real, it recycles it—a key process of a modern society. In the form of photographic images, things and events are put to new uses, assigned new meanings, which go beyond the distinctions between the beautiful and the ugly, the true and the false, the useful and the useless, good taste and bad. Photography is one of the chief means for producing that quality ascribed to things and situations which erases these distinctions: "the interesting."[15]

The chief source of Sontag's anxiety seems to be that excessive exposure to photographs blunts and spoils one's responses to the nonphotographic world. One becomes morally listless, uninterested in beauty and goodness; one becomes just as depraved as Comstockian masturbators did, though in a more sophisticated style. Following McLuhan, Sontag does not ascribe the corrupting effects of photography to anything in the content of its images. Rather, photography does its worst damage when it dulls one's sensitivity to the real existence of that content, the moral and ethical qualities it possesses as a thing, not as an image. But the upshot is a reversion to a fear older than Plato—that images will invade reality and warp it.

The Commission on Pornography and Obscenity had been remarkably free of that fear, in regard to both medium and content. According to its *Report*, the American people was unable to make up its mind on the issue; there was "no consensus among Americans" on either the effects of pornography or the value of those effects:

> Between 40% and 60% believe that sexual materials provide information about sex, provide entertainment, lead to moral breakdown, improve sexual relationships of married couples, lead people to commit rape, produce boredom with sexual materials, encourage innovation in marital sexual technique and lead people to lose respect for women. Some of these presumed effects are obviously socially undesirable while others may be regarded as socially neutral or desirable.[16]

Again, however, those who feel that no harm is being done are unlikely to form pressure groups in order to advance that view. Contentment and indifference are silent, while fear and outrage bellow; and in the pornography debate, hysteria on the part of a few has traditionally been given free rein by the obliviousness of the many.

Whether or not the Commission's recommendations accurately reflected majority opinion in the United States, its definition of "pornography and obscenity" certainly did so. To provide such a definition had been its first Congressional mandate, but the *Report* gave none in explicit terms. Implicitly, however, by means of the materials it analyzed and the milieux in which it located them, the

Report defined pornography as "worthless trash," the same definition the courts had come to after a century of labor. After 1966, "pornography" and "art" no longer overlapped; despite Sontag's ingenuities, the issue of value had been permanently settled. This was the only question a century of argument had managed to dispose of, yet its effects were decisive. They have led me to mark the period 1966–70 as the end of the pornographic era and the start of a new one, which in the absence of an identifying characteristic of its own I have labeled "post-pornographic." Like the coeval label "postmodern," "post-pornographic" is meant to suggest how darkly a later age has been overshadowed by its precursor. It means to imply, too, that this monster, when it died, rose again at once. In 1970, the Commission wished to throw the last shovelful of earth upon the unquiet grave of "pornography." The apparently immortal Young Person, however, was having none of that.

She rose slowly, and in a weird, degenerate form. Her sex had been ambiguous all along; she had been female and male by turns and simultaneously, depending on the bias of her self-appointed defender. At first, she had been young; later, youth expanded to include retarded adulthood. She had always been poor, in either money or wisdom; this attribute stays with her. As befits her stunted intelligence, she reads little, preferring the more immediate stimulation of pictures, videotapes, and live performances. The danger she poses is as great as ever, perhaps greater, because now she threatens actual physical harm to others. She no longer wastes away in solitude, the victim of a private vice that will eventually doom the race but at present wrecks only one person. Her internal decrepitude is no longer of special concern; she can masturbate till her brain rots, and no one will lift a finger to stop her. What makes the reborn Young Person frightening is that, like the media she favors, the crimes she commits are direct and violent. She oppresses, degrades, batters, and rapes women—not in imagination, but in grim reality. She does this because, after a century of ambivalence, she has emerged unequivocally and exclusively male.

This new Young Person shares with her deceased sisters the fact of being a primarily political animal. Unlike them, however, she does not repress her politics; her sins are civil, not moral, and religion has no bearing on them. Her most extreme opponents appear to be motivated by categorical hatred of all human beings who possess, as she does, a penis; this motive is the exact mirroring of the ancient male attitude toward those who lack this crucial organ. But the new Young Person dwells explicitly in the realm of power relations, where words like "vice" and "virtue"—not to mention "art"—are meaningless. She is different, too, in that she was conceived principally by women, while her predecessors were male inventions. She is still, however, nourished by fear, a fear that has not changed much since Socrates proposed the expulsion of poets from his ideal Republic. That fear bellows more loudly than ever, and no longer in unconvincing tones of moral or aesthetic outrage. Now it screams in bitter pain.

The post-pornographic Young Person came of age in the years just after the rejection of the Pornography Commission's *Report*, in a social atmosphere of disgruntlement and stagnation. She was the offspring of several feminist organizations, most notably the Women Against Pornography (WAP), founded in 1976. The events leading up to Nixon's resignation in August 1974, together with the whimpering end of the Vietnam War almost a year later, had lent fresh conviction to the traditional American belief that public authorities, left to themselves, will either do nothing or make matters worse. But the equally endemic faith survived that private activism, operating by strictly legal means, could awaken the sleepy guardians of justice. It was in this spirit that WAP and other organizations set about righting what they saw as the most grievous of social inequities—a sexual tyranny that fostered violence against the minds and bodies of women.

An early statement of their position was provided by Susan Brownmiller's *Against Our Will: Men, Women and Rape*, published in 1975. Brownmiller sought to investigate the entire phenomenon of rape, in all its aspects and throughout Western history; she defined rape broadly and in different terms from those of the law:

A sexual invasion of the body by force, an incursion into the private, personal inner space without consent—in short, an in-

ternal assault from one of several avenues and by one of several
methods—constitutes a deliberate violation of emotional, physical
and rational integrity and is a hostile, degrading act of violence
that deserves the name of rape.[17]

She demonstrated with clarity and precision how traditional definitions of rape, embodied in laws written by men, derived from a
conception of women as male property: for all the severity of the
punishments they prescribed, such laws were part and parcel of
the same system that produced rape itself. She proposed a radical
transformation of attitudes and values as the only sure means of
rectifying this ancient, pervasive injustice. And she had rather little
to say about pornography, treating it as only the most blatant
reflection of myths visible everywhere in contemporary culture:

> Pornography, like rape, is a male invention, designed to dehu-
> manize women, to reduce the female to an object of sexual ac-
> cess. . . . The staple of porn will always be the naked female
> body, breasts and genitals exposed, because as man devised it,
> her naked body is the female's 'shame,' her private parts the
> private property of man, while his are the ancient, holy, universal,
> patriarchal instrument of his power, his rule by force over *her*.[18]

This is a distinctly post-pornographic definition of "pornography," though one would never know this from Brownmiller herself.
Like most writers on the subject, she treated pornography as an
ahistorical phenomenon, which had always looked much as it did
at the time of writing—in this case, 1975. In fact, however, she
relied wholly on the rather recent equation of "pornography" with
"worthless trash"; her archetypal pornographic image was that of
the stag film, a modern genre in both medium and content, and
one that no one had ever tried to defend on aesthetic grounds.
Brownmiller's casual employment of the abbreviation "porn"—which,
along with "porno," had become almost universal in the post-
pornographic era—suggests her assumption that any well-informed
reader, male or female, would be familiar with such materials, at
least by repute. Twenty years earlier, that familiarity did not exist,

but the 1970 *Report* had indicated that 85 percent of adult men and 70 percent of adult women in the United States "have been exposed at sometime during their lives to depictions of explicit sexual material in either visual or textual form."[19] A polysyllabic, technical-sounding word like "pornography" no longer seemed appropriate to such a commonplace article—a curious fate for a concept that had begun its career in the locked cases of museums and libraries. Familiarity, of course, had bred contempt; but it had also produced a contrary tendency that clashed oddly with the insistence that pornography was worthless by definition. Trashy though stag films were, Brownmiller read them in a manner best described as mythic: the raw exposure of a woman's genitals became a statement about her social and political status; a penis became an "ancient, holy, universal, patriarchal instrument." The tacit presupposition that the makers and viewers of these displays were unconscious of their mythic meaning only lent greater impact to Brownmiller's interpretation. Like Freud reading dreams, she was able to find in apparently trivial images a profound significance of which the pornographer, like the dreamer, was unaware.

The mythic reading of pornography also shares with psychoanalysis the advantage (for the interpreter) that its conclusions are irrefutable and always the same. But it is split down the middle by a contradiction that does not trouble psychoanalysis. Freud maintained that dreams were only *apparently* trivial; in fact, they were neither "meaningless" nor "absurd," but rather "psychical phenomena of complete validity."[20] Brownmiller and her followers, in contrast, wished to interpret pornography in the most portentous possible manner, while at the same time maintaining that it was poisonous garbage, worthy only of destruction. The contradiction reached a sort of apotheosis in Andrea Dworkin's *Pornography: Men Possessing Women* (1980), the most vitriolic entry in a genre not noted for self-restraint. There had been anger enough in Brownmiller; in Dworkin there was nothing *but* anger, a scalding flood of it for more than two hundred pages. Dworkin's arguments were much the same as Brownmiller's, padded to bursting with polemic. Her interpretive techniques were similar, too, though she wielded them with a hamhanded brutality that made Brownmiller look namby-pamby by comparison. A virtuoso instance comes early in *Pornography:* a five-page analysis of a photograph from *Hustler* magazine representing two men dressed as hunters, with a naked woman tied spread-eagle to the hood of their Jeep like an animal trophy. From this photograph, its title ("Beaver Hunters"), and a brief accompanying text, Dworkin reads out every feature of the violent male hegemony that, in her view, has characterized Western culture since its dimmest origins. The reading is ingenious:

> Sex as power is the most explicit meaning of the photograph. The power of sex unambiguously resides in the male, though the characterization of the female as a wild animal suggests that the sexuality of the untamed female is dangerous to men. But the triumph of the hunters is the nearly universal triumph of men over women. . . . The hunters are figures of virility. Their penises are hidden but their guns are emphasized. The car, beloved ally of men in the larger culture, also indicates virility, especially when a woman is tied to it naked instead of draped over it wearing an evening gown. The pornographic image explicates the advertising image, and the advertising image echoes the pornographic image.[21]

Staccato, repetitive, incantatory, Dworkin's style is that of an enraptured demagogue; her aim is not, as Brownmiller's was, to enlighten and persuade, but rather to excite preexisting feelings. Already by 1980, the feminist antipornography campaign had acquired an extremist faction.

Dworkin also went far beyond Brownmiller in insisting upon pornography as not only the clearest depiction but also the cause of violence against women. Her rhetorical repertoire does not include techniques of logical explanation; she never outlines how this causation is supposed to operate. But there is no question of her belief in it: "The woman's sex is appropriated, her body is possessed, she is used and she is despised: the pornography does it and the pornography proves it."[22] The conclusion—unexplicated but very plain throughout the book—is that an entire system of inherited and inculcated values would somehow vanish, or at least become innocuous, if its rudest embodiment were made unavailable. It is not difficult to imagine that pictures like "Beaver Hunters" might reinforce and justify the prejudices of men who look at them; they might also—though this deduction is shakier—encourage those men to act out their prejudices in ways they would not have thought of on their own. Even according to Dworkin's argument, however, it is impossible to conclude that pornography creates attitudes in men who did not have them already. There is a strange incongruity in tracing a violence said to be endemic in Western culture back to some pictures and films that could not have existed a century ago and that have been promiscuously on sale for only about twenty years. The removal of pornography from view would amount only to a kind of window dressing; the supposed attitudes it reflects would then merely go underground, where they might fester.

Nevertheless, it was to this goal that WAP and related organizations turned their attention. Their methods were principally the traditional ones of picketing, protest marches, and the distribution of leaflets, along with the latter-day addition of T-shirts. By 1983, however, they had advanced to a new tactic, the proposal of legislation. A century and more of futility might have taught them that any such law is bound to be ineffectual, even to foster the very thing it would suppress. They might also have seen that their new Young Person—a brutal, low-minded male, or indeed any male at all—was only a weirdly transmogrified version of a fantasy that, in the past, had abetted the oppression of the very people (women) who now wished to appropriate it. But if the antipornography feminists glanced at history, the only lesson they learned was that past procedures had been incorrect, not that the effort itself was both tyrannical and hopeless. With law professor Catharine A. MacKinnon, Dworkin collaborated on the drafting of an ordinance that made its first official appearance before the City Council of Minneapolis, Minnesota, in December 1983. After two days of public hearings, the Council approved it by a one-vote margin; Mayor Donald Fraser vetoed it immediately and did so again a few months later, when a revised version was approved by the Council. Revised again, it was signed into law by Mayor William H. Hudnut

III of Indianapolis, Indiana; this time, it was declared unconstitutional by District Judge Sarah Evans Parker. In yet another form, it was voted down by the County Council of Suffolk County, New York.[23] None of these defeats served to convince MacKinnon, Dworkin, and their supporters that the very concept of the ordinance was indefensible, let alone illegal. They persisted in believing that the trouble lay in details, which a little more tinkering would set straight.

In all its incarnations, the MacKinnon-Dworkin ordinance bears little overt resemblance to earlier legislation against pornography. The most striking innovation is that the vicious old circle of synonyms—"lewd," "lascivious," "obscene," and so on—is completely absent from it. The manufacture and distribution of pornography are also no longer criminal offenses; pornography has become a civil matter, specifically a matter of civil rights. As it stood in April 1985, the ordinance (then in "model" rather than practical form) defined pornography as

> the graphic sexually explicit subordination of women through pictures and/or words that also includes one or more of the following: (i) women are presented dehumanized as sexual objects, things, or commodities; or (ii) women are presented as sexual objects who enjoy pain or humiliation; or (iii) women are presented as sexual objects who experience sexual pleasure in being raped; or (iv) women are presented as sexual objects tied up or cut up or mutilated or bruised or physically hurt; or (v) women are presented in postures or positions of sexual submission, servility, or display; or (vi) women's body parts—including but not limited to vaginas, breasts, or buttocks—are exhibited such that women are reduced to those parts; or (vii) women are presented as whores by nature; or (viii) women are presented being penetrated by animals; or (ix) women are presented in scenarios of degradation, injury, torture, shown as filthy or inferior, bleeding, bruised, or hurt in a context that makes these conditions sexual.[24]

This is, no doubt, the longest, most detailed definition of "pornography" ever composed. By any prior standard, it is pornographic in its own right; an enterprising filmmaker might well take it as a blueprint for outraging everybody, even in the jaded late twentieth century. Yet for all its gruesome explicitness, its utter lack of attention to "art" or "value," it is pornography's most aesthetic definition, too. Every clause demands some judgment upon the manufacturer's intentions or the viewer's response, the same dreary problems that used to call "experts" into court. Who but an expert could determine, for example, whether some portrayal of a "bleeding, bruised, or hurt" woman had been placed in "a context that makes these conditions sexual"? Women (and men) bleed and get hurt in an immense variety of contexts, and sexuality is immensely variable. We return once more to our starting point, as we seemed doomed to do.

In mid-1985, yet another official investigation of pornography was launched, this time under the jurisdiction of the Attorney General. Its *Final Report*, issued a year later, seemed designed to obliterate the 1970 *Report*—indeed, the entire twentieth century—and return the United States to the days of Comstockery, though with a few up-to-date flourishes that camouflaged the atavism. Predictably unable to define "pornography," the 1986 Commission nevertheless used the word on virtually every one of its 2,000 pages; unable to establish any definite connection between pornography and antisocial behavior, it nevertheless asserted that the connection was automatic and inescapable. According to the new *Report*, the nature of pornography had changed radically since 1970, exhibiting an intensified focus on violence toward women and the violation of children. Immediate action was therefore necessary, on all levels of government, to halt the advance of this brand-new plague.

Unlike its predecessor, the 1986 *Report* is an unbelievably fatuous document, riddled with false reasoning and bad prose. It is also blatantly pornographic. Evidently intending to inform the reader exactly how grotesque trash can be, the Commission provided three hundred pages of summaries and descriptions, some with dialogue: "I want to taste your cum. I want you to come in my mouth. I want to feel your hot cum squirt in my mouth," and much, much more in the same vein.[25] No doubt this established a landmark in the history of government publications. Perhaps, however, according to the Commission's reasoning, such vile drivel could have no deleterious effect because it appeared in words, not pictures. The *Report* exempts the written or printed word from all prosecution, on the grounds that "the absence of photographs necessarily produces a message that seems to necessitate for its assimilation more real thought and less almost reflexive reaction than does the more typical pornographic item. There remains a difference between reading a book and looking at pictures. . . ."[26] The real difference, of course, had to do with the nature of the Young Person, late-twentieth-century style. He was a functional, if not a total, illiterate; the danger he posed was heightened rather than reduced by this disability.

The *Report*, despite its overall backwardness, reflected the temper of its time when it recognized the impotence of words. It was also timely in maintaining an absolute silence on questions of morality. It speaks instead—following the antipornography feminists—of "harms," by which it means physical or psychological damage wrought upon women and children by the manufacturers and "consumers" of smut. This apparent objectivity merely masked the old desire whose course I have attempted to chronicle: the urge to regulate the behavior of those who seem to threaten the social order. By 1986, though women and children stood in need of as much surveillance as ever, the category of "the poor" had definitively altered from those who lacked money to those who lacked enlightenment; the threat, however, was the same. Women do get raped and battered; pictures of rape and battery often abet these crimes. It remains absurd, however, to suppose that the suppression of the image can prevent the perpetration of the deed. Sexual violence and representations of sexual violence emanate from the identical source, a tangled web of attitudes that cannot possibly be unraveled by setting a few bonfires. Yet the myth persists. Even the most sanguine observer feels the approach of despair at the spectacle of such stubborn ignorance, such stiff-necked denial of history.

The most remarkable fact about "pornography" in the post-pornographic era is not that the argument refuses to die—earthquakes generate aftershocks—but that it has made some progress and produced some results. We are no longer concerned with "art" and "value"; I have emphasized the dismal side of this development, but it does grant the arts a freedom unprecedented in human history, and the freedom is still too new for any evaluation of its effects. We are no longer so frightened of "sex" as we used to be; in the MacKinnon-Dworkin ordinance, for example, sex plays a surprisingly ancillary role, because the real target is violence, with sex as an enabling attribute though possibly not an essential one. The latest phase of the pornography debate seems to entail its elevation from morals to politics, the long-overdue recognition that what we have been arguing about the entire time is a matter of power, of access to the world around us, of control over our own bodies and our own minds. For two hundred and fifty years—ever since the first obscene artifacts were unearthed at Pompeii—a certain problematic of power has been unfolding; and now, at last, the naked truth of it seems to stand exposed.

Unfortunately, this is only one level of the story, and not its deepest one. Below the interminable jockeyings for power, fueling them, lurks the old fear that representations direct our lives in ways we cannot govern or even understand. Unlike the level above it, on which some light appears to have dawned, where this fear dwells nothing much has changed between Plato in the fourth century B.C. and the Women Against Pornography more than two thousand years later. It might be supposed that the very durability of the idea is proof of its truth, that nothing can endure so long if it is simply a mistake. Yet other equally venerable notions—the natural inferiority of certain classes or races, the right of their natural superiors to own them as slaves, the intrinsic subordination of women—are being discredited despite their ancientness. The simplicity of the mechanism should make it suspect: one reads an episode or views a scene, whereupon one is uncontrollably moved to imitate it in three dimensions instead of two, flesh instead of ink or film. Nothing in human behavior is so simple as that; we do not recognize reality, we fulfill wishes, when we dream that even the most trivial human action can be accounted for in such a simpleminded fashion.

The grimly comic history of "pornography" shows that all aspects of the problem have altered utterly except these two: power and fear. The Pompeiian artifacts that shocked and puzzled our ancestors may still look a bit outrageous to us, but we put them on display before the three groups—women, children, and the poor—to whom they were at first forbidden. We now admit that the sight of a yard-long penis painted on a wall, or of a marble satyr locked in eternal coition with a marble goat, is unlikely to drive even susceptible souls to acts of lewdness. We do so, in part, because we see such objects as "art," insulated from impact by the awe with which they ought to be greeted. We also, I think, feel a certain nostalgia (felt by our Victorian forebears, too) for a time when a pictured erect penis at an intersection signified not the morbid hostility of some stranger we hope we never meet, but the sanctified assurance of fruitfulness. Today's pornography, with its ghastly detail and devotion to cruelty, is as different as it could be from those benign images; yet the indignation of those who would burn today's worthless trash resembles exactly what Victorian curators felt, when Pan or Priapus came before them in undaunted lubricity.

The first question they asked was *What on earth were the Romans thinking of?* The second followed immediately: *What will happen if vulnerable people see these things?* The answer to the first question is still being worked on by classicists; the answer to the second came as quickly as the question: depravity will settle on women, children, and the poor (they are predisposed to it); lust will flower in them (they bear its seeds already); they will rise up in wantonness, wrecking the achievements of three millennia—including us, their appointed guardians. Measures were taken. Gates were set up and guards were set at them, under orders to admit only grown-up, well-to-do males into the Secret Museum. Gentlemen could be trusted not to tear the edifice down, because gentlemen owned and had built it. If lust should enflame them, too, there was still no risk; sluices like prostitution were waiting to receive it. "Pornography" was the name they gave to the strange zone where chaos subsisted safely within order.

All worked well for a while; then the worst happened. "Pornography" slithered out between the bars, polluting streetcorners once again, as if they were its proper dwelling place. Suddenly it was everywhere, in magazines, newspapers, and novels, invading even the sacred confines of the home; the patina of age had been stripped away and replaced by flashy up-to-dateness. There was no shielding the vulnerable from this monstrous modern brand of filth, so new strategies were called for. "Pornography" had to be hunted down, confiscated, burned. But the dismaying consequence was that "pornography" had to be named and characterized, its nature made so public that the effort to stifle it became a corrupting influence. The real problem—though no one recognized this—was publicity itself, the permeation of the culture by images. Once the process was fully underway, as it was by the middle of the nineteenth century, any attempt to mark out a certain category of representations, to forbid them while permitting the rest, could only be futile. So it proved: "pornography" spread irresistibly, flourishing in direct proportion to the energy of its combatants. It seemed, vampirelike, to batten on their strength, to rise up refreshed from each new campaign to put it down.

Meanwhile, the gentlemanly enclosure, the first target of pornography's disruption, fell into ruins. Pornography itself was not the destroyer, though pornography had always ranged itself on the side of leveling, the breaking down of barriers and hierarchies, the dissolution of differences, and these forces were the victors. Gentlemanly censorship had been vitiated at its origin by a crippling ambivalence about value: Pompeiian artifacts, risqué novels, and graphic paintings had to be quarantined, not destroyed, and this double-mindedness invited eventual anarchy. History would no doubt have followed the same course, but it is interesting to speculate on what might have happened if the excavators of Pompeii, instead of putting Priapus on private show, had simply burned him. We might then have been spared all the rest, the tons of paper and occasional gouts of blood, that constitute the "pornographic" story I have told. We would be living, then, in a safer though unutterably more arid world.

Ambivalence ended when "pornography" did, though the gentleman rose again like the Young Person, his natural foe. This new gentleman—female, as his new protégée is male—still desires to prevent the ignorant and vicious from obtaining access to dangerous representations, and this desire still masks a lust for power. The female gentleman, however, feels himself disenfranchised; power already belongs to the ignorant and vicious, and it must be wrested from them, though without changing the nature or structure of power in the slightest degree. The most dismaying aspect of the feminist antipornography campaign is its exact resemblance to every such effort that preceded it, from Lord Campbell's and Justice Cockburn's, through that of Comstock and all the Societies for the Suppression of Vice, to the modern vigilantism of Leagues and Legions of Decency. Whatever its guise, the pornographic urge remains unchanged—immune to argument, invincibly self-righteous, engorged with indignant passion. If the twisted history of "pornography" shows nothing else, it shows that forgetfulness of history is the chief weapon in the armory of those who would forbid us to see and know. "Pornography" is not eternal, nor are its dangers self-evident; to remember that is to win strength against fear. I have written this book in the hope of reminding us that we have fought ignorant battles, and that we ought not to be so stupid as to believe that we must fight them again.

AFTERWORD

I FINISHED WRITING *The Secret Museum* in the summer of 1986, just in time to plod through the *Final Report* of the U. S. Attorney General's Commission on Pornography, better known as the "Meese Commission Report" after Attorney General Edwin Meese. As I noted then, the Meese Commission was only the latest in a long series of paroxysms into which the American public (or at least the American government) had been throwing itself since the days of Anthony Comstock a century earlier. For me, the most depressing aspect of this sadly repetitive history was that no one seemed to learn anything from past mistakes. Like vampires, the same bugaboos kept rising again, to be wrestled with again on the same bloody ground; the same fears kept returning, the same circular arguments spinning and spinning. Greeted by a predictable chorus of jeers, the *Final Report* sank into deserved oblivion, having affected practically nothing. But there have been enough flare-ups since 1986 to show that the pornographic vampire is still not finally dead, and it has lately (as of the summer of 1996) been showing a disposition to pick some bigger fights.

It strikes me now that the most remarkable aspect of this cultural neurosis is its Americanness. The later chapters of *The Secret Museum* grow steadily more American in focus—partly because of my own bias as an American, but mostly because the story of arguments about pornography has been, for the last fifty years at least, largely an American one. It is by no means obvious why this should be so. The U. S. prides itself, after all, on being the land of the free, a message it loves to send itself and to broadcast outside its borders. American freedom, however, is a much thornier matter than such propaganda suggests, particularly where sex is concerned. American sexual freedom is hemmed in by all sorts of confusions, uncertainties, and fears that seem not to plague other nations, at least to such a ludicrous degree. It no doubt appears to other nations that Americans are obsessed with sex, because they talk about it all the time and are constantly flashing pictures of it. Certainly, though, Americans do not *have* more sex than other people; nor, by all accounts, are they notably inventive in the sex they do have. The fact is, Americans concern themselves much less with sex itself than with representations of sex, any words or pictures that convey or may arouse sexual feelings. The American obsession with sex reflects a deep ambivalence about the power of representations; it is the by-product of a passion for image making, uneasily yoked to a passionate fear of images.

Other nations tend to manage pornography in one of two more or less rational ways. Either there is a smoothly running, relatively silent state mechanism of control, or else there is no control whatever. Canada and the United Kingdom exemplify the former approach, while the Scandinavian countries have gone about as far as it is possible to go in the latter direction. In neither case do arguments about pornography play a significant role in public discourse. The United States, however, is stuck in between. There are numerous, no doubt too many, national and local control mechanisms, but they operate with what often seems like deliberate inefficiency. Legislators eagerly pass laws banning or regulating sexual representations, but the laws are enforced sporadically if at all. Special-interest groups campaign enthusiastically for the closing of outlets for pornography, but the usual result is that the outlets move a few miles, or only a few blocks, away. Legal prosecutions may succeed at the local level, but they are routinely contested in higher courts, which routinely overturn convictions. America vacillates hysterically between controlling sexual images and letting them run free; the country is unable to settle down on one side or the other, which means that arguments about pornography keep flaring up anew.

The past ten years have seen no fundamental change in the pattern of American vacillation. A couple of instances, however, have shown that though the argument remains the same, the terms in which the battles are fought continue to shift. The Meese Commission's report turns out to have contained one truth: printed words are no longer "pornographic," or at least they are no longer worth fighting about. "Pornography" now means pictures, preferably moving pictures; sexually, the printed word is dead. None of the recent major battles over pornography has involved the naked word, and it seems unlikely that any future *Ulysses* or *Lady Chatterley's Lover* will be able to arouse the fury those books caused when they were new. This remains an ambiguous step forward. One is grateful to see the end of literary prosecution, but one cannot help regretting that the printed word no longer has the power to generate passions, either pro or con.

It is heartening to note, however, that the past ten years have seen a boom in the publication of what is called "erotica," much of it written by women to be read by women or by gay men and lesbians for their own constituencies. These numerous books (few of which contain pictures) are on sale in respectable bookstores; they are tastefully designed and printed by respectable publishers who would never deign to issue "pornography." In fact, the contents of books like *Herotica*, *High Risk*, and *Flesh and the Word* (to mention three of the more notable short-story anthologies, all of which spawned sequels) would have been judged indubitably pornographic twenty years ago. The death of the printed word has saved them from prosecution, and they have taken refuge under the high-toned label "erotica," which no one would dream of putting on trial. Few purveyors of the new erotica exhibit the honesty of John Preston, veteran pornographer and editor of *Flesh and the Word* (1992), a collection of stories by and about gay men. "Pornography and erotica are the same thing," Preston wrote in his introduction. "The only difference is that erotica is the stuff bought by rich people; pornography is what the rest of us buy."[1] As *The Secret Museum* chronicles, this was certainly true throughout the nineteenth century and even as recently as the 1960s. But it is not true of the new erotica, which comes moderately priced, often in paperback. Nevertheless, that word lends such books an air of respectability that aligns them, however falsely, with art. And art, as a century and a half of trials has painfully shown, is the very antithesis of pornography.

Like "pornography," "erotica" is a modern coinage with a specious aura of antiquity. The OED dates its first English usage 1853 (just three years, that is, after the first published use of "pornographers"), as a category heading in a bookseller's catalogue. Along with "curiosa" and "facetiæ," it continued to perform that esoteric function for at least a century, signaling to the initiated (bibliophiles in the tradition of Henry Spencer Ashbee) books that might please their specialized tastes. "Erotica" seems to have entered the general vocabulary only in the 1950s and 60s, as "pornography" became increasingly tainted with low-class associations. A word was needed to designate the increasing number of books that, though they dealt with sex, somehow did so in a safe and classy way.[2] "Erotica" filled the bill, and in the 1990s it can be found on signs in many American bookstores, not far from HORROR and LITERATURE.

One latter-day "erotic" book, a hybrid of words and pictures, is noteworthy for the furor it did not arouse. Madonna's succinctly-titled *Sex*, published late in 1992, garnered all the media attention it was designed to elicit, but except for a few public libraries that declined to order it, the book met with no resistance. Like the new erotica, *Sex* would have been instantly quarantined as pornographic if it had been published twenty years before. Yet, of course, *Sex* could not have been conceived of, let alone produced, in 1972. Its heavy, dangerously sharp-cornered aluminum covers, its thick paper and extremely stylish layout, along with its steep price ($49.95), marked it as "erotica" in Preston's old-fashioned sense of the term, though its first printing amounted to 500,000 copies for American distribution alone, of which 150,000 were sold on the first day of publication.[3] *Sex* also offered full-frontal nude pictures of an international celebrity who had made a career out of exposing almost everything else. The prerequisite for *Sex* was Madonna; her prerequisite was the hype network that had grown up in the previous decade and that she had consistently, brilliantly exploited.

Sex was titillating, not shocking, to the affluent, upper-middle-class public that bought it. It therefore furnishes a handy index to the location of the line between the acceptable and the forbidden in the United States, late in 1992. Needless to say, *Sex* is tawdry, vulgar, and cheap in all senses, despite its high price. Those qualities were probably deliberate; Madonna owed her fame to carefully managed cheapness, staying always just on the safe side of what the American middle class found repellent and would not pay for. Above all else, Madonna aspired to be paid. Given this caution, the most remarkable thing about *Sex* wasn't the star's nudity; it was the book's persistent flirtation with homosexuality and sadomasochism both gay and straight. Naked male dancers at The Gaiety (a venerable gay night spot in Manhattan) were shown fully frontal, too, though flaccid and apparently distracted. Madonna herself appeared in bondage gear, in the company of both men and women similarly decked-out. Men fondled men, and women nuzzled women, in a manner that by 1992 had evidently come to seem acceptable, if a little naughty.

The reception of *Sex* reflected another peculiarly American disjunction that keeps the United States in an intermittent tizzy about pornography. In their wisdom, Madonna's managers saw—as the official arbiters of morality consistently fail to see—that the general public's tolerance of sexual imagery is far broader in practice than in theory. Many of the acts hinted at in *Sex* are illegal in most parts of the country, and most Americans would probably balk at the lifting of official bans on homosexuality, torture, fetishism, and other supposedly marginal activities. Yet such laws are seldom enforced, such activities are engaged in with relative impunity, and it has lately become apparent that conventional Americans are willing to look at pictures of marginal acts, if not to perform them. In practice, that is, Americans are far less timid and censorious than their laws suggest or their clergy and civil legislators care to admit.

There are still limits, however. An intriguing one was breached in the summer of 1989, when an exhibit of Robert Mapplethorpe's photographs was to have opened at the Corcoran Gallery of Art in Washington, D.C. Most of Mapplethorpe's work—stylish photos of lilies and celebrities—was inoffensive, even tedious in its good taste. But a few of his pictures, the provocatively-named "Portfolio

X," aroused official ire because they showed men, some with erect penises, engaged in sadomasochistic homosexual acts. Perhaps the most shocking aspect of these pictures was that in composition, lighting, and style, they preserved the slick decorum that marked Mapplethorpe's innocuous work. Only the subject matter offended; it was immediately construed as a posthumous effort by Mapplethorpe (who had died of AIDS earlier that year) to foist his own dangerous sexual habits on an innocent world. The would-be exhibit had been funded in part by the National Endowment for the Arts, which brought the federal government into the fray and allowed Jesse Helms of North Carolina to announce in the U. S. Senate, "It is an issue of soaking the taxpayer to fund the homosexual pornography of Robert Mapplethorpe, who died of AIDS while spending the last years of his life promoting homosexuality."[4]

The exhibit did not open in Washington, but the following spring it moved to the Contemporary Arts Center in Cincinnati, Ohio, where the public prosecutor promptly slapped it with obscenity charges. The outcome of the ensuing trial was predictable: art won out over subject matter, as it had been doing with some regularity since the prosecution of *Madame Bovary* 133 years before. The show went on in Cincinnati, and (another predictable result) Mapplethorpe gained far more publicity from the brouhaha than his work would have won on its own. In its general outlines, the Mapplethorpe furor followed a thoroughly traditional pattern. But there was one provocative difference: for the first time in history, the offensive images represented men and only men—presumably homosexual men, too, sporting erections. It is difficult to imagine that the rather bleak scenes portrayed in "Portfolio X" could persuade weak-minded museum patrons to rush out and imitate them, as Helms and his cronies seemed to fear. That, I think, was not the true scandal. Rather, it was the public, sanctioned display of the erect penis. The Mapplethorpe uproar established that, in the words of historian Peter Brooks, "the erect penis is virtually the only object still rated obscene in contemporary American society—the very definition of 'hard core'—and subject to restrictions."[5]

Yet the Cincinnati jurors swallowed whatever revulsion (or titillation) they might have felt, because Mapplethorpe's photographs, even the most outrageous, were unquestionably art. One hardly needed expert courtroom testimony to establish that fact: the pictures were displayed not on streetcorners or TV but in the sanctified hush of a museum. They had therefore already passed expert muster. They were also shut away from promiscuous view: nobody stumbles into a museum by mistake (the jurors may have reasoned), and besides, "Portfolio X" had been confined to its own area, not behind a locked gate as at the old Museo Borbonico but nevertheless quarantined. Susceptible persons had sufficient warning; if they chose to defy it, their disgust or inflammation was their own affair, not the museum's or Mapplethorpe's. All parents, of course, would bar their children from the danger zone. That was so obvious it went without saying.

The Mapplethorpe case was extraordinary only in content; otherwise, prosecution, defense, and verdict all followed a time-worn course. The case may prove a harbinger in one respect: the last decade has seen burgeoning exploitation of the male body in the public media, from Calvin Klein underwear billboards to unclothed hunks on daytime TV, and as this development continues, the exploiters are likely to take ever greater risks.[6] (In 1995, for instance, the English film *Angels and Insects* was released in the U.S. unrated, presumably because the glimpse it offered of a semi-erect penis would have earned it the commercially disastrous "NC-17" rating.) But in all other ways, even at a remove of only six years, the Mapplethorpe case now looks antique. It occurred just before the porn wars underwent another shift, the biggest they had made since the advent of the VCR in the late 1970s. Then, the primary battle site had moved from the "adult" movie theater and bookstore into the home, where videocassettes made explicit sexual pictures easily and privately available. Twenty years later, this threat had largely been tamed: Video stores set up their own secret museums, and parents who rented or bought explicit tapes learned how to lock them away from children's concupiscent little fingers. The video menace had hardly subsided, however, when an even more dangerous, and insidious, conduit for filth opened up. The home remained the battleground, and children were still the hostages, but now the enemy was also the family's ravishing new friend, the computer.

Purveyors of sexual images have traditionally shown great enterprise in exploiting the invention of visual media. Photography seems to have spawned its subspecies of pornography almost at once: Louis Daguerre patented the daguerreotype in 1840, and only ten years later, the French government enacted a law prohibiting the sale of obscene photographs.[7] Since laws, even in France, usually tag after what they are meant to control, one can be fairly sure that explicit sexual daguerreotypes had been in circulation long before 1850, despite the strain of holding poses for them. Motion-picture pornography was another fast arrival; specimens are known from the first decade of the twentieth century. Pornographers were quick to exploit videocassettes, too, and are often given credit for having spurred the adoption of the VCR as a necessary adjunct to any television. By the early 1990s, they had made their way into the fledgling technology of interactive CD-ROMs.[8] No visual medium has ever been devised in order to portray sex, but under-the-counter traffickers in portrayals of sex have followed hard on the heels of every new invention.

In this area, technological progress has had two aims. The first is to bring the experience of represented events ever closer to their real experience. Photography marked an advance beyond lithographs, engravings, and paintings; moving pictures went further yet; both media have seen refinement after refinement—in the case of film, repeatedly enhanced Dolby sound, for example, and the astonishing visual effects of movies like *Jurassic Park* (1993) and *Twister* (1996). The multimedia technology called virtual reality, still in its infancy, promises a giant step in the same direction. The primary rationale of all these advances is to provide the most vivid possible equivalent of sensory stimuli their users would probably never undergo in the course of their actual lives. It remains mysterious (to me, at least) why anyone would wish to approximate the experience of being chased by a tornado or a hungry tyrannosaurus. But the desire is next to universal, and the realm of sex certainly partakes of it. Indeed, insofar as pornography serves to replace or to supplement real experience, it demands verisimilitude with special urgency. Small wonder, then, that the manufacturers of sexual images seek out whatever heightening of illusion new technologies may provide.

In their early stages, new visual technologies are cumbersome, expensive, and therefore public; in order to yield a profit on the high initial investments they require, they must be used by large numbers of people at a time, which makes them unsuitable for the display of explicit sexual images. But the second main thrust of technological progress works toward removing this disadvantage. At an accelerating pace, media advances of all sorts have moved from public to private, as the cost of equipment falls and its operation becomes comprehensible to those who did not take part in devising it. The paradigm for this development is television, which transmitted its first talking pictures in 1927, the same year *The Jazz Singer* revolutionized the movies. Not until the late 1940s, however, when the clarity of broadcasts and the size of screens had also greatly increased, could most American families afford TV sets. By 1960—when television, lagging behind the movies, was transforming itself from a black-and-white into a color medium—eighty percent of American homes contained at least one set, turned on for an average of five hours and five minutes a day.[9]

By then, too, most American households were able to stage their own movie shows. The bills of fare had been written by local stations or national networks, and the films had been, as the phrase still runs, "edited for television," which means butchered for the insertion of commercials and trimmed of words or pictures that some viewer might find objectionable. Nevertheless, movies had been wrenched away from the public places where they had typically been shown. After the mid-1950s, movies could also no longer rely on the universal audience that had been theirs since the turn of the century. Competition with television led to the splintering of the moviegoing public into three main groups—children, teenagers, and adults—for each of which a distinct kind of film was produced and appropriately advertised. In 1968, this balkanization became official in the form of a rating code that labeled films G (for "general" audiences), PG (which children might attend unescorted if they had submitted to a process called "parental guidance"), or X (to which, supposedly, people under seventeen were admitted only if accompanied by their legal guardians). In theory, several factors, including overall maturity of theme, determined a film's rating. In practice, however, sexual explicitness was the only criterion, and Hollywood matched it with the moviegoer's age: Children, the assumption went, were born ignorant of sex and must remain so until their seventeenth birthday, when all would be revealed.

This largely futile rating system (which has been tinkered with and expanded since then) was imposed in response to complaints about the heightened sexual explicitness of mainstream films. But the system had the unexpected effect of boosting the trend, not taming it. The X label served as potent advertising for a few films—notably *Vixen* (1969), *Deep Throat* (1972), and *The Devil in Miss Jones* (1972)—that now, thanks to the certified exclusion of children, could be shown in aboveboard theatres rather than in the "adult" houses to which they otherwise would have been banished. Among certified adult (but predominantly younger) couples, a fad arose for seeing such films—in order, apparently, to demonstrate how liberated and grown-up the couples were. The fad did not last long: the incursion of hard-core images into respectable gathering places represented a violation of the center by the margins, the public by the private, that Americans were not yet ready to tolerate, despite the sexual revolution said to be raging at the time. The VCR, which became affordable a few years later, offered an ideal compromise; it preserved those boundaries of decorum, meanwhile granting pornography wider distribution than ever before.

Until the mid-1990s, battles over pornography followed a pattern that had been familiar for well over a century. During the same years, public tolerance of sexual representations grew slowly but steadily broader—another old trend that shows no sign of waning. By 1995, however, two recent technological developments had conspired to transfuse fresh blood into the slumbering vampire, "pornography," which rose from its shallow grave with sudden vigor and, apparently, a new face. The last paragraph of this book's Chapter Eight looks foolishly optimistic to me now: I never believed that *The Secret Museum* would call a halt to our ignorant battles over "pornography," but ten years ago I did imagine that the Meese Commission *Report* marked the last gasp of that old rhetoric. I thought I saw another dead end in the demagoguery of Andrea Dworkin and Catharine MacKinnon. Their lunatic equation of pictures with deeds made, I thought, a reductio ad absurdum beyond which it was impossible for even them to go.

I may have been right about Dworkin, MacKinnon, and their sympathizers; having arrived at what they take for absolute truth, they have been able, during the last decade, only to restate it in ever more grandiose terms—with some local effect, but also with the loss of whatever slight credibility their rant once possessed. I was wrong, however, about the rhetoric of fear that, for nearly two and a half centuries now, has been building secret museums. The Meese Commission *Report* dealt it a heavy blow, but it was resuscitated by the burgeoning of home computers and the Internet, two technological developments that neither I nor the Commissioners foresaw in 1986. In 1996, the much-touted computer revolution rages on, and I won't try to predict its outcome, if it ever yields anything so clear-cut. The furor over pornography on the Internet is also in full swing as I write this, but here at least a prognosis is possible.

Nothing new has been said by either those who would police the Internet or those who would leave it alone. Nothing new ever will be said, because both sides ground themselves in premises that brook no refutation or compromise. Fear cannot debate with freedom; all that can happen is the continuing repetition of assertions that have been made, without significant difference, for 150 years and more. In the end, freedom will probably win out, as it has repeatedly done, until the next unforeseeable battle flares up. So far, the pattern is monotonous and just as depressing for the historian as it has always been. But the current argument about the Internet does ring a couple of fresh changes on its old themes. The new medium has introduced provocative confusion of the public and the private; it even confuses the material and the immaterial, thereby shaking up the most basic presuppositions of traditional thinking about images of all sorts. And the new argument has made a remarkable lurch backward, all the way to Anthony Comstock, in its conception of the Young Person, that frightening creature who calls for constant vigilance. The information-age Young Person is not an adolescent girl, as she was for the prosecutors of *Madame Bovary* and *Ulysses;* he is not a testosterone-addled adult male, as he remains for anti-pornography feminists. Today's Young Person is, as it was for Comstock, an actual, imaginary child.

It should have surprised no one that sexual words and pictures would find their way into computers and the systems connecting them; that was apparent already in 1986. What surprised most observers was the wildfire spread of home-computer use, along with the explosive growth of the Internet. According to a 1995 estimate, "35 percent of American families and 50 percent of American teenagers" then had access to a home computer; at the same time, the "population" of the Internet was growing at a rate of ten percent a month.[10] Dizzying numbers came accompanied by extravagant hype from politicians and pundits of all stripes, many of whom had but the dimmest notion what they were raving about. The Internet seemed to offer the universal availability of limitless "information" (as its contents were commonly called), which made it a special boon to children. A new, computer-literate generation would somehow—the means were never clear—transform the world, thanks to all that information. Some Internet boosters waxed positively hysterical in its praise. This breathless effusion, taken from the introduction to a 1994 guidebook, is typical:

> The Internet is, by far, the greatest and most significant achievement in the history of mankind. What? Am I saying that the Internet is more impressive than the pyramids? More beautiful than Michelangelo's David? More important to mankind than the wondrous inventions of the industrial revolution? Yes, yes and yes.[11]

The Internet, however, soon revealed its dark side, which at first seemed to be merely the transmission of sexually explicit words and pictures along its innumerable metaphorical highways.

But if that had been its only threat, the Internet could be furnished with a secret museum analogous to those that sometimes still worked for statues, paintings, books, photographs, films, and videos. The trouble was that this vast network, though usually spoken of in spatial terms (cyberspace, sites, Web pages, and so on), occupied no dimension; its contents could not be stashed away in a guarded room or a locked case. Its contents, indeed, were not things, at least not until some user downloaded them and printed them out. They weren't even transmissions in the usual sense, because no locatable source broadcast them for reception in the manner of radio and television. The traditional language of censorship and control broke down in the face of the Internet, which also saw no difference between an image of the Mona Lisa and one of a satyr *in coitu* with a goat. Both pictures constituted "information"; both were equally available to all comers, including those computer-wise children, whose prospects suddenly looked less rosy. With an ironic lurch, America's latter-day pastors and masters found themselves thrust back 250 years, into the shocked company of Pompeii's first curators. Those long-dead worthies had quailed before the vision of a city where frescoes portrayed erect penises and bouquets of flowers side by side and let everybody see everything. Their descendants gazed horrified into the abyss of a dimensionless electronic world where improvement and damnation came beaming indiscriminately into the home at the call of anybody's keystrokes. The horror spanned centuries and was the same: absolute promiscuity of knowledge.

The Internet was never so democratic as its early attackers and defenders made out. Some sites could not be entered without passwords; some attached stiff access or subscription fees; it was in such home-made secret museums that most of the dirty stuff lurked. But both cyberlibertarians and would-be cybercensors found it convenient to pretend that the virtual world flourished in perfect anarchy. Supporters exploited the mythic power of Daniel Boone and Davy Crockett, portraying the Internet as a final frontier, where every user was free to set up his or her own Web page, like a settler's cabin in the long-vanished American West. Opponents drew on more equally hoary notions of mean city streets, where depraved men held out candy toward babies. Very early, the lore of cyberspace spawned tales of brave hackers who, thanks to ingenuity or accident, tapped into classified files; the first mass-market example was the film *War Games* (1983), in which a lone teenager at his keyboard terrifies the Pentagon. Ten years later, though such myths persisted, their appeal had tarnished. By then, the hottest myth had become that of a child who, while cruising the Internet in search of wholesome enlightenment, stumbles across satyrs and goats and gets debauched on the spot.

Alarm was fueled by the heavy promotion the Internet continued to receive as a learning tool for children, and by the sense shared by many adults that their computer-wise offspring were already sophisticated enough to evade any attempt to protect them. Besides, the sheer size and multifariousness of the Internet frustrated all efforts to measure it or to evaluate its contents. The most ambitious such undertaking, a year-long study conducted at Carnegie Mellon University in 1994–95, plainly proclaimed its own futility; public response to the study demonstrated the intensity of fear that the Internet, a purportedly unalloyed boon to mankind, could arouse. The Carnegie Mellon researchers focused on the Usenet (an international interlinkage of some 14,000 "newsgroups") and on thirty-five commercially operated BBS's ("bulletin-board systems").[12] They meticulously analyzed the contents of such newsgroups as "alt.binaries.pictures.erotica" and "alt.binaries.pictures.tasteless" and of BBSs with less frank names like Amateur Action and Windy City Freedom Fortress.[13] The study, published by "Principal Investigator" Marty Rimm in the June 1995 issue of *The Georgetown Law Journal*, was a daunting document, bottom-heavy with footnotes and bloated with tables, bar graphs, and pie charts. On its own, it might have made little public impact. But a national news magazine got hold of it, and a silly little tempest broke out.

The July 3, 1995 issue of *Time* bore a striking cover picture that is more eloquent than anything inside the magazine. An androgynous, evidently hydrocephalic child stares out at you—you, the equally innocent soul who has just picked up *Time*. The bottom of the picture is formed by a slightly out-of-focus field of white trapezoids and lavender rectangles that any informed observer would recognize as a computer keyboard of the IBM-clone variety. The child's pudgy fingers rest, uplifted, against its edge, as if just pulled back in shock at what the keys have conjured up. The child's face, which fills most of the picture, registers horror: wide, unnaturally large blue eyes and a gaping, pink-lipped mouth, all bathed in the weird white glare of an unseen computer monitor. In case you missed the point, between the child's chin and the keyboard, in big blue capitals, stands the coy neologism CYBERPORN. Even without text, the message is plain: This hapless cherub (who is all the more poignant for being very white indeed) has encountered the ultimate horror, sex, on the Internet.[14]

Maybe the child has stumbled upon "SHE CHOKES ON THICK DOG COCK! DOG SPERM ON HER SEXY LIPS!" (the Carnegie-Mellon researchers downloaded an image with that label, but they found the description inaccurate[15]). *Time*'s writer, Philip Elmer-DeWitt, furnished no details, remarking rather primly that none of the descriptions listed in the Carnegie-Mellon study were fit to print in his magazine.[16] On the whole, Elmer-DeWitt's article was considerably less sensational than the graphics that accompanied it, but together they made the same two points that Rimm had stressed: explicit sex was "ubiquitous" in cyberspace,[17] and, as Rimm put it, "The 'adult' BBS market is driven largely by the demand for paraphilic and pedo/hebephilic imagery"[18]—or, in the words of *Time*'s cover, cyberporn is "pervasive" and "wild." Rimm reveled in huge numbers—917,410 sex items, 8.5 million downloads, and so on—and Elmer-DeWitt borrowed many of them. But while Rimm and his colleagues spent days and nights attempting, rather comically, to distinguish various forms of "paraphilia," Elmer-DeWitt cut to the chase:

the adult BBS market seems to be driven largely by a demand for images that can't be found in the average magazine rack: pedophilia (nude photos of children), hebephilia (youths) and what the researchers call paraphilia—a grab bag of "deviant" material that includes images of bondage, sadomasochism, urination, defecation, and sex acts with a barnyard full of animals.[19]

In both its technical and popular formulations, the upshot looked scary: The Internet swarmed not only with sex but also with styles of sex that even Madonna would shy away from. And America's children stood in dire peril.

Though *Time*'s cover emphasized that last point, Elmer-De-Witt's article debunked it, citing no less formidable authority than a sixteen-year-old "veteran Internet surfer." "If you don't want them [sex pictures] you won't get them," said David Slifka. "The chances of randomly coming across them are unbelievably slim." Rimm's big numbers could be misleading, too. Busy as the pornographic image files were, they constituted only three percent of the Usenet, which itself amounted to 11.5 percent of the Internet.[20] If the Carnegie-Mellon findings were taken to be absolutely accurate (unlikely), cyberporn was a minuscule district, about one third of one percent of the Internet, and rather difficult to get into: a perfectly traditional secret museum. As usual when pornography is at issue, however, facts made little difference. *Time*'s lurid cover picture made a far stronger impression than the words inside, and it seemed for a while that the Carnegie-Mellon study would help push through the amended Communications Decency Act, which had recently been passed by the U.S. Senate. Then an odd thing happened.

Read attentively, Rimm's and Elmer-DeWitt's articles debunked themselves, but their unexpected sequel was the personal debunking of Marty Rimm. An Atlantic City, New Jersey, newspaper revealed that in 1981, when he was sixteen, he had dressed up as an Arab sheikh and gambled illegally at the Playboy Hotel there. In 1990, he had written a "licentious" novel and posted selections from it on the World Wide Web. Most damningly, he had planned to use the Carnegie-Mellon data in a book of his own, to be called *The Pornographer's Handbook: How to Exploit Women, Dupe Men and Make Lots of Money*. Rimm, it appeared, "had gained access to pornographic bulletin boards by promising to advise operators on how to improve their marketing techniques, and had then used the data as the basis for his study denouncing the marketing techniques of cyberspace pornographers."[21] Rimm's study denounced nothing in particular, and data need not be false because they are obtained by shady means. But the Senate Judiciary Committee, before which Rimm had been scheduled to appear as an expert on cyberporn, dropped him; with evident relief, the public media did the same to his briefly shocking study. The sideshow ran its course in about six weeks.

For once, civil libertarians and advocates of censorship had been able to join forces against a common enemy, the luckless Rimm. His data, especially when sensationalized in the manner of *Time*'s cover, made libertarians uncomfortable; would-be censors felt reluctant to accept even potent ammunition from such a questionable source. Neither side had been influenced in the slightest by Rimm's rise and fall, because the porn wars had long since passed the point (if there had ever been one) where even unimpeachable facts possessed the power to alter anyone's convictions. Meanwhile, the Communications Decency Act, a provision of the Telecommunications Reform Bill, went its slow way through Congress; it reached President Bill Clinton's desk on February 8, 1996, and was signed into law as part of the Telecommunications Act of 1996. A lawsuit followed quickly, filed by a coalition of forty-seven groups, including the ACLU and the American Library Association. Less than two weeks later, Judge Ronald L. Buckwalter of Federal District Court in Philadelphia temporarily blocked enforcement of the Act on account of vague language. Four months later, a panel composed of Buckwalter and two other judges found the Act emphatically unconstitutional. Further litigation seems inevitable, but that doesn't matter; it is business as usual.

The Communications Decency Act was a radically ignorant and atavistic piece of work. Avoiding such long-contested terms as "obscene" and "pornographic," it dredged up instead the quaint "indecent," which it applied to "any comment, request, suggestion, proposal, image or other communication that, in context, depicts or describes, in terms patently offensive as measured by contemporary community standards, sexual or excretory activities or organs."[22] Senators James J. Exon of Nebraska and Dan Coats of Indiana, co-sponsors of the bill, had evidently consulted Supreme

Court obscenity decisions, notably *Miller* v. *California* (1973), which introduced the troublesome concept "community standards" into arguments about pornography. The idea had already been old-fashioned in 1973, since it presupposed an America made up of homogeneous, discreet settlements (separated by cornfields, presumably), each of which could reach a consensus on what the locals found objectionable. The idea was absurd in 1996, especially when applied to the Internet, which allowed instantaneous communication all over the world. As if to fossilize the Act completely, at a late stage Representative Henry J. Hyde of Illinois added a provision prohibiting the electronic distribution of information about abortion. This, of course, harked directly back to the Comstock Act of 1873.

The Act was also retrograde, though not quite so severely, in its conception of the Internet as a broadcast medium analogous to television or radio. Exon and Coats seemed to imagine that cyberspace consisted of a definable number of broadcasters beaming their stuff into home receivers; they therefore felt justified in imposing stiff penalties (fines of up to $250,000 and prison sentences of up to five years) for the electronic transmission of material that would never be prosecuted if it appeared as ink and paper. For the Act's opponents, however, the Internet looked more like print than like network TV. In the words of Jonah Seiger, a policy analyst at the Center for Democracy and Technology, "On the Internet, everybody is essentially a publisher. There's virtually no difference between someone who operates a Web page and the publisher of a magazine."[23] A good deal is fudged in that "virtually," including the difference between material objects and electronic images. Little as it resembles broadcasting, the Internet is hardly similar to magazine publishing either, since every electronic reader is also a potential "publisher." But print and broadcasting were the only available analogies, and it was in those terms that the case framed itself when, at the end of March 1996, it went before a panel of three federal judges—Buckwalter, Delores K. Sloviter, and Stewart Dalzell—in Philadelphia. The judges, as backward as Congress when it came to cyberspace, had to be led by the hand through "web-surfing sessions" in the courtroom. Rather touchingly, they got no direct look at steamy sites like Bianca's Smut Shack: "Sites that might have been objectionable did not appear on courtroom screens. Judges saw photocopies of them bound in thick black Government exhibit volumes."[24] No doubt the solid heft of the tomes reassured the judges somewhat.

In early June, they handed down their ruling. It was no surprise that Buckwalter's two colleagues joined him in finding the Act unconstitutional, but the tone of their 175-page memorandum was unexpectedly gung-ho for the Internet. The judges' surfing practice seems to have converted them violently. Speech on the Internet, they declared,

> can be unfiltered, unpolished, and unconventional, even emotionally charged, sexually explicit, and vulgar—in a word, 'indecent.' But we should expect such speech to occur in a medium in which citizens from all walks of life have a voice. We should also protect the autonomy that such a medium confers on ordinary people as well as media magnates.

"Just as the strength of the Internet is chaos," the judges added, "so the strength of our liberty depends upon the chaos and cacophony of the unfettered speech the First Amendment protects.[25] No doubt "indecency" deserved the rude slap they gave it, but never before, to my knowledge, had such a paean been bestowed on "chaos." Traditionally, human chaos has always been a frightening state, as at the end of Alexander Pope's *Dunciad* (1743):

> Lo! thy dread Empire, CHAOS! is restor'd;
> Light dies before thy uncreating word:
> Thy hand, great Anarch! lets the curtain fall;
> And Universal Darkness buries All.[26]

Pope, however, never went web-surfing.

Whatever one calls it—smut, obscenity, pornography, or indecency—the representation of sex has not lost its power to make otherwise intelligent people do silly things. Meanwhile, just as pre-

dictably, the trend toward ever greater explicitness continues un-
abated, though so gradually that it seldom attracts attention.
Movies and TV say more and show more than they did ten years
ago; certain words, for instance (such as "ass," "bastard," and
"bitch"), that were never spoken on network television in 1986 are
common in 1996. Subjects that were hardly alluded to then are discussed at length now, especially on TV talk shows. Many factors
have contributed to this development—such as the aids epidemic,
which has compelled new public frankness about sexual organs and
acts. In the long view, however, proximate causes seem not to matter much. For most of the twentieth century, the trend has been
moving at a steady rate, and no legislation or protest has been able
to retard it. We remain, apparently, under the compulsion to show
all that is capable of being shown; we will not rest until every image
is available at every moment to every person on earth. I cannot
imagine that world and don't think I want to live there, but the Internet has brought us a large step closer to realizing it.

Censorship efforts will continue till the end, and in the end they
will lose, as they have always done. Along the way, the only interest
they possess, or have ever possessed, is the insight they yield into
the inchoate, largely unconscious fears of the society that spawns
them. During the two hundred years that I have called the "pornographic era," Western society embodied its sexual fears chiefly in
the Young Person, a label I borrowed from Dickens's 1865 novel,
Our Mutual Friend. Dickens's Young Person dwells exclusively in
the minds of the archbourgeois Mr. Podsnap and middle-aged,
power-wielding men like him; she is the apotheosis of Mr. Podsnap's
eighteen-year-old daughter, Georgiana, but she bears no real resemblance to that exploited and suffering creature. Rather, as Dickens
demonstrates in the tour de force of a single paragraph (quoted in
Chapter Two above), the Young Person is Mr. Podsnap's unacknowledged nightmare of female sexuality. Absolutely innocent,
she nevertheless blushes uncontrollably, all the time: "There appeared to be no line of demarcation between the young person's excessive innocence, and another person's guiltiest knowledge." Such
promiscuous engorgement of the cheeks implies equally wanton

flows of blood to lower regions, a suggestion underlined by Dickens's metaphoric transformation of Mr. Podsnap's blushing damsel into the ultimate emblem of male potency: "Take Mr. Podsnap's word for it, and the soberest tints of drab, white, lilac, and grey, were all flaming red to this troublesome Bull of a young person." Being red in the cheeks becomes seeing red, which becomes being red again, this time in an organ that women do not own but that they can, at least in the male imagination, appropriate. According to Podsnap, the Young Person must be prevented from blushing because women are delicate and easily bruised. What Mr. Podsnap really thinks (though he doesn't know he thinks it) is that women's innocence is just depravity on hold. Give women half a chance and they'll run riot, subjecting men to the worst of all indignities, which is not castration. It is the discovery that women indeed have penises, and that they work better than men's.

In this guise, the Young Person presided over a long tradition of efforts to sequester sexual representations—from the original Secret Museum in Naples through the trials of *Madame Bovary*, *Ulysses*, *Lady Chatterley's Lover*, and many other books. To the annoyance of literary critics and other experts, the censors (bourgeois gentlemen all) cared nothing about artistic value; they worried about an imaginary Georgiana Podsnap, whom exposure to arousing words or pictures would surely galvanize into debauchery, demolishing the walls that the gentlemen had taken so much trouble to erect. In *The Secret Museum*, I found this paradigm useful for understanding all battles over "pornography," up to but not quite including the 1986 Meese Commission *Report*. There, and in the rhetoric of anti-pornography feminists, I thought I saw a shift toward a new Young Person, a truly depraved adult male rather than a falsely innocent adolescent female. In this revised nightmare, the structures of power remained unchanged, only the gentlemen's place was to be shared by certain enlightened women. It would be their task (self-appointed, of course) to protect other women from the "harms" inflicted on them by unenlightened men, for whom pornography was both the cause and the effect of the desire to batter women.

The past ten years have shown that I overestimated that new paradigm; it marked only a swerve, not a permanent shift, in the march of the Young Person. This may be because the clamorings of Andrea Dworkin, Catharine MacKinnon, and their acolytes tumbled into absurdity with remarkable dispatch.[27] More likely, though (since mere absurdity is seldom a deterrent in such matters), the Dworkin-MacKinnonite Young Person failed to fulfill his early promise because too few women wished to see themselves as his pathetic, impotent victims. Besides, the identification of all penetrative intercourse with rape—to which Dworkin and MacKinnon's impeccable logic very soon led—would make heterosexual female desire even more problematical than it was when Victorian gentlemen sought to deny its existence. The rhetoric of anti-porn feminism had some influence on the Meese Commission *Report*, but that document had next to no influence of its own. And so far, in the United States at least, Dworkin and MacKinnon's Model Ordinance has nowhere been enacted into law.[28]

Today's most popular Young Person, who governs the controversy over the Internet and television, is not a battered woman but a child. This creature (classically envisioned in *Time*'s digital cover picture) is of indefinite age and irrelevant sex; she or he is not so liable to be physically harmed by electronic pornography as to be led by it down some equally vague primrose path into unimaginable (at least, unimagined) degradation. All that can be said with certainty about this Young Person's age is that he or she, unlike the traditional version, is prepubescent; any possibility of the child's sexual initiative or responsiveness can therefore be dismissed out of hand. Yet, rather mysteriously, "the child" is even more susceptible to instantaneous debauchery than Georgiana Podsnap was. As an object of pathos, hardly anyone can resist an endangered child, and real children should of course be protected from whatever dangers threaten them. But in the discourse of "pornography," we are not dealing with real children. Like the Young Person in all its other guises, "the child" is a rhetorical figure, which lives in the realm of discourse and nowhere else. Rhetorically, the traditional Young Person was a figure of unconscious irony, meaning the opposite of what it said; in Mr. Podsnap's mind, "excessive innocence" means "guiltiest knowledge," and his need to defend her is really a need to be defended *from* her. "The child" would seem to defy this analysis, because it is defined as presexual and therefore out of the game altogether. Yet in the discourse of "pornography," sex has always been a figure for power, political as well as personal. And when it comes to power, today's Young Person poses a greater threat than Mr. Podsnap ever dreamt of.

America's long-standing ambivalence toward children is a complex subject that might fill several books on its own.[29] In general, it seems to merge two antithetical views with no attempt to synthesize them. On the one hand, children are fallen creatures in the ancient Christian mode, tainted at conception by Original Sin and prone ever after to evil, because they are human. On the other hand, Americans imagine children Romantically, as William Wordsworth did in his "Intimations Ode" (1807):

> Not in entire forgetfulness,
> And not in utter nakedness,
> But trailing clouds of glory do we come
>   From God, who is our home:
> Heaven lies about us in our infancy![30]

The Romantic view leads to the portrayal of children as little vessels of purity, requiring constant protection from an evil adult world. The older view attributes to children an innate potential for evil that requires constant vigilance to prevent its realization. American culture swarms with images of both kinds, from the angelic Shirley Temple of the 1930s to the demon children of William March's *The Bad Seed* (1954), William Peter Blatty's *The Exorcist* (1971), and a host of other novels and films. Like Mr. Podsnap, American culture cannot decide whether it needs to shield its children or to be shielded against them.

In either case, children must be watched over, and the proper site of that surveillance is the home. Since the 1950s at least, children have come not only to inhabit the American home but also to stand for it, with all its connotations of privacy, safety, and sovereignty. Most media images of children in peril feature them, on account of either necessity or parental negligence, away from the home; the best-known such scare tactic is the reproachful question, broadcast every night on many American TV stations: "It's ten o'clock. Do you know where your children are?" Images of domestic violence are doubly horrible because they bring the brutality of the streets into what ought to be a sanctuary. Domestic violence does more than hurt children; it also breaches the barrier between public space, where danger lurks, and private space, which should promise safety. To some degree, radio and television do the same, but they can be controlled fairly readily, if clumsily, by such means as channel blocks and the so-called V-chip.[31] The Internet, with its vast size and potential anonymity of use, goes much further. It brings the whole outside world, pleasures and dangers alike, into the home, and there seems to be no way of policing it. Seen in this light, the Internet's breezy metaphors of cruising and surfing lose their bright promise and turn rather sinister.

To make matters worse, the first generation of American children exposed to home computers attained an expertise that eluded most of their parents. Most often, this imbalance was treated in a jocular spirit, as when *Time* consulted a sixteen-year-old net-surfing expert; it soon became a mildly amusing cliché. But public anxiety about children debauched on the Internet surely arose in part from the unnerving sense that illiterate parents simply could not monitor their literate offspring; it was just as if children saw words on a page where parents saw only squiggles. Innocent or depraved, children handily wielded a power denied to their elders, and no one could dictate what they did with it. When Federal judges need step-by-step instruction in maneuvers that sixteen-year-olds know backwards and forwards, the structure of knowledge, and therefore of power, has certainly gone awry. Like any other Young Person, the imperiled child is also a threat.

This time, I will not be so foolish as to suppose that the history of "pornography" has reached some sort of end point, or even a decisive turn. The current furor over cyberporn will no doubt pass, as

other furors have done; it will no doubt be succeeded by yet another, though no one can predict what that will be.[32] I foresee no final battle in the porn wars, only the continuing repetition, with
small variations, of patterns that were laid down two and a half centuries ago. Meanwhile, however, signs of progress do show up occasionally. In the spring of 1996, for example, the British Museum
saw fit to put on public display, for the first time, some of the wax
phalluses that Sir William Hamilton had collected in southern Italy
late in the eighteenth century. The reviewer of the exhibition for
the London *Times Literary Supplement* was chiefly impressed by
their tiny size.[33]

REFERENCE NOTES

PREFACE TO THE PAPERBACK EDITION

1. Swift, Jonathan, *Gulliver's Travels*, ed. Peter Dixon and J. Chalker (New York, 1967), pp. 221–22.

2. *Ibid.*, p. 230.

CHAPTER ONE
ORIGINS

1. John Ward-Perkins and Amanda Claridge, *Pompeii A.D. 79* (New York, 1978), p. 11.

2. *Critical and Miscellaneous Essays and Poems* (New York, 1860), p. 347.

3. Charles Bonucci, *Pompéi décrite* (Naples, 1830), p. i. John Keats may have had this Pompeiian impression in mind when he wrote, in "Ode on a Grecian Urn" (1820):

> What little town by river or sea shore,
>   Or mountain-built with peaceful citadel,
>   Is emptied of this folk, this pious morn?
> And, little town, thy streets for evermore
>   Will silent be; and not a soul to tell
>   Why thou art desolate, can e'er return.

4. *The Last Days of Pompeii* (1834; rpt. Boston, 1893), p. 12.

5. Egon Caesar, Conte Corte, *The Destruction and Resurrection of Pompeii and Herculaneum* (London, 1951), p. 127.

6. *A Discourse on the Worship of Priapus and Its Connection with the Mystic Theology of the Ancients* (1786), rpt, in *Sexual Symbolism: A History of Phallic Worship* (New York, 1957), p. 65. Because the example from Herculaneum was so familiar, Payne Knight thought it "proper" to include in his book ("for the benefit of the learned") an engraving of a similar Greek statue in Charles Townley's private collection. The interested reader will find two vivid color photographs of the Roman statue in Michael Grant, Antonia Mulas, Antonio De Simone, and Maria Teresa Merella, *Eros in Pompeii: The Secret Rooms of the National Museum of Naples* (New York, 1982), pp. 94–95.

7. Sir William Gell and John P. Gandy, *Pompeiana: The Topography, Edifices, and Ornaments of Pompeii*, 2 vols. (London, 1824), 1:x.

8. *Pompeii*, 2 vols. (4th ed., London, 1836).

9. *Pompeii: Its History, Buildings, and Antiquities* (1875; rev. ed. London, 1883), p. 471. Dyer's authorship of the anonymous *Pompeii* is acknowledged in the preface to this volume.

10. Bonucci, p. 150.

11. *Pompéia décrite et dessinée*, 3rd. ed. (Paris, 1870), p. 360.

12. The most extravagant example of the former breed, a brontosaurian ancestor of the coffee-table book, was *Wandgemälde aus Pompeji und Herculanum nach den Zeichnungen und Nachbildungen in Farben von W. Ternite mit einem erläuternden Text von F. G. Welcker* (Berlin, 1839–58), which was issued to subscribers in ten installments. Welcker later published his text in a separate, octavo volume, since the original, nearly a yard wide and weighing twenty pounds, was impossible to read sitting down. The highest-minded entry in the genre—and a sign of how far the fad had spread—was the Rev. Frederick Wrench's *Recollections of Naples, Being a Selection from the Plates Contained in Il Real Museo Borbonico, of the Statues, Vases, Candelabra, &c. discovered at Herculaneum and Pompeii* (London, 1839); it was published to raise funds for a provincial orphanage. Neither of these, however, aimed at completeness, and so both were exempt from moral complications.

13. *Les Antiquités d'Herculanum, ou les plus belles Peintures antiques, et les Marbres, Bronzes, Meubles, etc. etc. trouvés dans les excavations d'Herculanum, Stabia et Pompeïa, avec leurs explications en françois*, 9 vols. (Paris, 1780), 1:5.

14. *Ibid.*, 4:23–24.

15. *Ibid.*, 7:83.

16. Erasmo Pistolesi, *Antiquities of Herculaneum and Pompeii: Being a Selection of All the Most Interesting Ornaments and Relics Which Have Been Excavated from the Earliest Period to the Present Time; Forming a Complete History of the Eruptions of Vesuvius. To Which Is Added, a Selection of Remarkable Paintings by the Old Masters, Comprising the Principal Objects Preserved in the Museo Borbonico, at Naples*, 2 vols. (Naples, 1842), 1:61. The fractured English is that of the trilingual original, which reprinted for wider circulation Pistolesi's *Real Museo Borbonico descritto ed illustrato*, 3 vols. (Rome, 1838–39).

17. Ward-Perkins and Claridge, p. 188.

18. *Ancient Art and Its Remains; or a Manual of the Archaeology of Art*, trans. John Leitch (London, 1850), p. 619. Leitch translated the second edition of Müller's *Handbuch*, which had been expanded after the author's death by F. G. Welcker. This is the earliest instance of any form in "pornograph-" listed by the OED.

19. *Histoire de la Prostitution chez tous les peuples du monde depuis l'antiquité la plus reculée jusqu'à nos jours*, 6 vols. (Paris, 1851–53), 1:184–85.

20. *Ibid.*, 1:194. The sneering connection between πορνογράφοι ("whore-painters") and ζωγράφοι ("living-body-painters") is made in *Deipnosophistai*, 13:567b. Like Lacroix, C. D. Yonge left both terms in Greek in his "literal" English translation of Athenaeus, 3 vols. (London, 1853), 3:907.

21. Lacroix, 1:168.

22. Giuseppe Fiorelli, *Catalogo del Museo Nazionale di Napoli. Raccolta pornografica* (Naples, 1866).

23. The British Museum had already established a *Museum Secretum* for the housing of obscene artifacts, along with a "Private Case" for books. The damage to scholarship done by such procedures is discussed in Catherine Johns, *Sex or Symbol: Erotic Images of Greece and Rome* (Austin, TX, 1982), chapter 1.

24. *Herculanum et Pompéi, Recueil Général des Peintures, Bronzes, Mosaïques, etc. découverts jusqu'à ce jour et reproduits d'après Le Antichita di Ercolano, Il Museo Borbonico et tous les ouvrages analogues*, 8 vols. (Paris, 1875–77), 8:1.

25. *Ibid.*, 8:6–7.

26. *Ibid.*, 8:11–12.

27. Pistolesi's catalogues, for example, resorted to this expedient.

28. Barré, 8:12.

29. Letter to Walter Theodore Watts-Dunton, July 27, 1896, in Cecil Y. Lang, ed., *The Swinburne Letters*, 6 vols. (New Haven, 1959–62), 6:103–5.

30. Quoted in J. Rives Childs, *Restif de la Bretonne: Témoignages et Jugements. Bibliographie* (Paris, 1949), p. 212.

31. *L'Oeuvre de Restif de la Bretonne*, 9 vols. (Paris, 1930–32), 3:143.

32. *De la Prostitution dans la ville de Paris, considérée sous le rapport de l'hygiène publique, de la morale et de l'administration*, 2 vols. (1836; 3rd ed., Paris, 1857), 1:37.

33. *Ibid.*, 1:6.

34. *Ibid.*, 1:6.

35. *Ibid.*, 1:7.

36. Judith R. Walkowitz, *Prostitution and Victorian Society: Women, Class, and the State* (Cambridge, 1980), p. 36.

37. *The Functions and Disorders of the Reproductive Organs in Youth, in Adult Age, and in Advanced Life: Considered in Their Physiological, Social, and Psychological Relations*, 3rd ed. (1862), p. 101, quoted in Peter Fryer, "Introduction" to *Prostitution* (New York, 1970), p. 12. This passage and similar unenlightened remarks of Acton's have frequently been quoted by twentieth-century writers on Victorian sexuality—notably Steven Marcus, *The Other Victorians: A Study of Sexuality and Pornography in Mid-Nineteenth-Century England* (1966; 2nd ed., New York, 1974), p. 31; and Peter Gay, *The Bourgeois Experience: Victoria to Freud*, vol. 1., *Education of the Senses* (New York, 1984), p. 153.

38. Preface to 2nd ed. (1870), Fryer, p. 24.

39. The story of the public controversies over the Contagious Diseases Acts is told in detail in Walkowitz and in Paul McHugh, *Prostitution and Victorian Social Reform* (New York, 1980).

40. *Prostitution*, p. 144.

41. Quoted in Fryer, "Introduction," p. 15.

42. *History of Prostitution* (1858; "new ed.," New York, 1895), p. 22.

43. *Ibid.*, p. 25.

44. *Ibid.*, pp. 79–80.

45. Anonymous review of *Prostitution*, *Sanitary Review and Journal of Public Health*, 3 (1857–58), 327–35; quoted in Fryer, p. 227.

46. *The History of Sexuality*, vol. 1, *An Introduction*, trans. Robert Hurley (New York, 1978), p. 18.

47. *Ibid.*, p. 25.

48. *Ibid.*, p. 69.

49. *Ibid.*, p. 18.

50. Quoted in Fryer, p. 229.

51. *Ibid.*, pp. 47–48.

CHAPTER TWO

THE PRE-PORNOGRAPHIC ERA

1. Jeffrey Henderson, *The Maculate Muse: Obscene Language in Attic Comedy* (New Haven, 1975), p. 5.

2. "On Translating Homer," in R. H. Super, ed., *The Complete Prose Works of Matthew Arnold*, Vol. 1, *On the Classical Tradition* (Ann Arbor, 1971), p. 138.

3. George Gordon, Lord Byron, *Poetical Works* (London, 1945), p. 683.

4. Henderson, p. 17.

5. Francis MacDonald Conford, ed., *The Republic of Plato* (New York, 1945), pp. 69–70.

6. *Ibid.*, pp. 71–72.

7. *Ibid.*, p. 337.

8. *Ibid.*, pp. 338–39.

9. A sympathetic account of Symonds's struggles with his homosexuality is given in Phyllis Grosskurth, *The Woeful Victorian: A Biography of John Addington Symonds* (New York, 1964).

10. Letter to Henry Graham Dakyns, March 27, 1889, in Herbert M. Schueller and Robert L. Peters, eds., *The Letters of John Addington Symonds*, 3 vols. (Detroit, 1967–69), 3:365.

11. Letter to Benjamin Jowett, February 1, 1889, in *Ibid.*, 3:346–47.

12. S. H. Butcher, *Aristotle's Theory of Poetry and Fine Art with a Critical Text and Translation of the Poetics*, 4th ed. (1911; rpt. New York, 1951), p. 23. In the *Politics*, Aristotle claimed that music, too, can bring about a "release of emotion"; he promised to give a fuller account of what this is supposed to mean, but he never did so. (*The Politics of Aristotle*, trans. Ernest Barker [New York, 1958], p. 349).

13. Butcher, p. 243.

14. W. K. Wimsatt and Cleanth Brooks, *Literary Criticism: A Short History* (New York, 1957), pp. 36–37.

15. *Ars Poetica*, 333–34, 343–44; Smith Palmer Bovie, trans., *The Satires and Epistles of Horace* (Chicago, 1959), p. 285.

16. Preface to *An Evening's Love; or The Mock Astrologer*, in *Of Dramatic Poesy and Other Critical Essays*, ed. George Watson, 2 vols. (New York, 1962), 1:152.

17. Preface to *Lyrical Ballads*, in *Poetical Works*, ed. Ernest de Selincourt (London, 1936), p. 738.

18. Bovie, p. 281.

19. *The Poetry of Catullus* (New York, 1967), p. 8, quoted and corrected in Thomas Nelson Winter, "Catullus Purified: A Brief History of Carmen 16," *Arethusa*, 6 (1973), 258.

20. *Catullus: The Complete Poems for American Readers* (New York, 1970), p. 23.

21. *The Garden of Priapus: Sexuality and Aggression in Roman Humor* (New Haven, 1983), p. 146.

22. John Boswell, *Christianity, Social Tolerance, and Homosexuality: Gay People in Western Europe from the Beginning of the Christian Era to the Fourteenth Century* (Chicago, 1980), p. 73 & 64n.

23. Richlin, p. 146.

24. *My Secret Life* (1966; rpt. Secaucus, NJ, n. d.), p. 2098.

25. "Comic Dramatists of the Restoration," in *Selected Writings*, ed. John Clive and Thomas Pinney (Chicago, 1972), p. 81.

26. Sanger, p. 521.

27. *Ibid.*, p. 522.

28. Macaulay, p. 81.

29. "Science and Culture," in *Science and Education* (London, 1899), p. 149.

30. *Ibid.*, pp. 150–51.

31. "Literature and Science," in R. H. Super, ed., *The Complete Prose Works of Matthew Arnold*, Vol. 10, *Philistinism in England and America* (Ann Arbor, 1974), p. 58.

32. *Ibid.*, p. 71.

33. *Literary Theory: An Introduction* (Minneapolis, 1983), p. 25.

34. *The Classical Tradition: Greek and Roman Influences on Western Literature* (London, 1949), p. 493.

35. *Our Mutual Friend* (Harmondsworth, 1971), chapter 11.

36. Noel Perrin, *Dr. Bowdler's Legacy: A History of Expurgated Books in England and America* (New York, 1969), p. 25.

37. Macaulay, p. 81.

38. *Life of Johnson*, ed. R. W. Chapman (London, 1953), p. 869.

39. Perrin, pp. 52–54.

40. G. Gregory Smith, ed., *The Spectator*, 4 vols. (London, 1907), 1:148.

41. Arthur Sherbo, ed., *Johnson on Shakespeare*, Vol. 7 of *The Yale Edition of the Works of Samuel Johnson* (New Haven, 1968), p. 704.

42. *The Faerie Queene*, ed. J. C. Smith, 2 vols. (Oxford, 1909), 2:27.

43. Perrin, pp. 189–90.

44. M. H. Abrams et al., eds., *The Norton Anthology of English Literature*, 2 vols. (1962; rev. ed. New York, 1968), 1:194.

45. Rpt. in Mark Caldwell and Walter Kendrick, eds., *The Treasury of English Poetry: A Collection of Poems from the Sixth Century to the Present* (New York, 1984), p. 10.

46. Preface to *Fables Ancient and Modern, Translated into Verse from Homer, Ovid, Boccace, and Chaucer, with Original Poems*, in *Of Dramatic Poesy*, 2:284–85.

47. F. N. Robinson, ed., *The Works of Geoffrey Chaucer* (Boston, 1957), p. 265.

48. Gilbert Burnet, *Some Passages of the Life and Death of Rochester* (1680), in David Farley-Hills, ed., *Rochester: The Critical Heritage* (New York, 1972), p. 84.

49. David M. Vieth, ed., *The Complete Poems of John Wilmot, Earl of Rochester* (New Haven and London, 1968).

50. Farley-Hills, p. 19.

51. *Ibid.*, p. 21.

52. See Graham Greene, *Lord Rochester's Monkey, Being the Life of John Wilmot, Second Earl of Rochester* (New York, 1974), pp. 108–13, for a full account of this zany episode.

53. John Hayward, ed., *Collected Works of John Wilmot, Earl of Rochester* (London, 1926).

54. Greene, p. 9.

55. Vieth, p. 45.

56. David Foxon, *Libertine Literature in England 1660–1745* (New Hyde Park, NY, 1965), p. 5.

57. *Lives of the Most Eminent Painters, Sculptors, and Architects*, trans. Gaston DaC. De Vere, 10 vols. (London, 1912–14), 6:104–5.

58. *Selected Letters*, trans. George Bull (Harmondsworth, 1976), p. 156.

59. Lacroix, 5:326.

60. Raymond Rosenthal, trans., *Aretino's Dialogues* (New York, 1971), p. 17.

61. *Italian Literature*, Part 4 of *The Renaissance in Italy*, 2 vols. (1881, 2nd ed., London, 1898), 2:320.

62. *Ibid.*, 2:337.

63. *Ibid.*, 2:355.

64. *Ibid.*, 2:346.

65. *Ibid.*, 2:374n.

66. Rosenthal, p. 13.

67. *Ibid.*, pp. 285–86.

68. Quoted in H. Montgomery Hyde, *A History of Pornography* (New York, 1965), p. 104.

69. *Ibid.*, p. 76.

70. Quoted in Pisanus Fraxi (Henry Spencer Ashbee), *Catena Librorum Tacendorum* (1885; rpt. New York, 1962), p. 331.

71. Quoted in Greene, p. 109.

72. William Wycherley, *The Country Wife*, ed. Thomas H. Fujimura (Lincoln, NB, 1966), p. 10.

73. Robert Latham and William Matthews, eds., *The Diary of Samuel Pepys*, 11 vols. (Berkeley and Los Angeles, 1970–83), 9:21–22.

74. *Ibid.*, 9:58.

75. *Ibid.*, 9:59. Pepys kept his diary in code, which became particularly polyglot when, as here, sensitive matters were at issue. The code was deciphered in 1825, and new editions of the *Diary* appeared at regular intervals thereafter, but this passage was not put in the clear till 1976. The detailed story of Pepys's gradual de-bowdlerization is told in Perrin, pp. 229–38.

76. Ashbee, *Catena*, p. 301.

77. Foxon, p. 28.

78. *Unfit for Modest Ears: A Study of Pornographic, Obscene and Bawdy Works Written or Published in England in the Second Half of the Seventeenth Century* (Totowa, NJ, 1979), p. 187.

79. Foxon, p. ix.

CHAPTER THREE
ADVENTURES OF THE YOUNG PERSON

1. *The Bourgeois Experience: Victoria to Freud*, Vol. 1, *Education of the Senses* (New York, 1984), pp. 363–64.

2. *Gaslight and Daylight*, quoted in Gertrude Himmelfarb, *The Idea of Poverty: England in the Early Industrial Age* (New York, 1984), p. 378n.

3. *The Book of Household Management* (1861; rpt. New York, 1969), pp. 988–96.

4. An updated catalogue has recently been published, Patrick J. Kearney, *The Private Case: An Annotated Bibliography of the Private Case Erotica Collection in the British (Museum) Library* (London, 1981).

5. Introduction to *My Secret Life*, p. xxi.

6. *Ibid.*, p. xxii.

7. See *Ibid.*, *passim;* also the introduction to Kearney.

8. Especially Chapter Two.

9. *Index Librorum Prohibitorum* (1877; rpt. New York, 1962), pp. li–lii.

10. *Centuria Librorum Absconditorum* (1879; rpt. New York, 1962), pp. li–lii.

11. Marcus, p. 34. Though small even by the standards of the time, these quantities were not so infinitesimal as they appear from a modern perspective. "Serious" books were commonly printed in editions of 750 copies, while "ordinary" novels seldom exceeded 1,250. See Richard D. Altick, *The English Common Reader: A Social History of the Mass Reading Public, 1800–1900* (Chicago, 1957), pp. 263–64.

12. *Index*, pp. lxix–lxx.

13. *Catena*, p. lvi.

14. *Centuria*, p. lii.

15. *Index*, p. lvii.

16. *Catena*, p. 345.

17. *Catena*, p. lxvii.

18. *Ibid.*, p. xxxviii.

19. Marcus, p. 45.

20. *Ibid.*, pp. 268–71.

21. Marcus comments that *The 120 Days of Sodom* (1785, first published 1931–35) "represents one kind of perfection in this genre," thanks to its "psychotic rigidity and precision" (p. 270). As his own candidate for the almost-ideal, however, Marcus chooses *The Romance of Lust* (1873–76), which "comes as close as anything I know to being a pure pornotopia in the sense that almost every human consideration apart from sexuality is excluded from it" (p. 274). Ashbee might have agreed, if this terminology had been available to him; instead, however, he disapproved of the *Romance*. "The episodes," he wrote, "are frequently most improbable, sometimes impossible, and are as a rule too filthy and crapulous" (*Catena*, p. 185).

22. *Ibid.*, p. 260. In this murky district of publishing, we cannot be sure that these figures of quantity and price, given by Ashbee, are correct. Even if they were only false advertising, however, their purpose was clearly to make *Verbena House* seem choice and costly.

23. Leone Levi, *Wages and Earnings of the Working Classes* (London, 1885), p. 53; cited in Altick, p. 306.

24. Albert Ellery Berg, ed., *The Universal Self-Instructor and Manual of General Reference* (1883; facsimile rpt. New York, 1970), p. 627.

25. Sanger, pp. 521–22.

26. *Ibid.*, p. 522.

27. Montague Summer, *A Gothic Bibliography* (London, n.d.), p. 150.

28. Stanley J. Kunitz and Howard Haycraft, eds., *British Authors of the Nineteenth Century* (New York, 1936), p. 519.

29. See, for example, Himmelfarb, pp. 435–52; and Anne Humpherys, "The Geometry of the Modern City: G. W. M. Reynolds and *The Mysteries of London*," *Browning Institute Studies*, 11 (1983), 69–80.

30. The story of Mudie's is entertainingly told by Guinevere L. Griest in *Mudie's Circulating Library and the Victorian Novel* (Bloomington, 1970).

31. "Penny Novels," *Spectator*, 36 (March 28, 1863), 1808.

32. *"For Ever and Ever,"* *Saturday Review*, 22 (October 6, 1866), 432.

33. *The Times*, November 2, 1864, p. 9.

34. "The Work of Art in the Age of Mechanical Reproduction," in *Illuminations*, trans. Harry Zohn (New York, 1969), especially pp. 231–32 and 247–48.

35. "Fiction Fair and Foul," in *Works*, ed. E. T. Cook and Alexander Wedderburn, 39 vols. (London, 1903–12), 34:271.

36. *Joseph Andrews and Shamela*, ed. Martin C. Battestin (Boston, 1961), p. 7.

37. The pioneering study of the novel's early audience is Ian Watt's *The Rise of the Novel*, Chapter Two. Similar conclusions are reached in Altick, Chapter Two; Lennard J. Davis, *Factual Fictions: The Origins of the English Novel* (New York, 1983); and, with a sharp polemical edge, Terry Eagleton, *The Rape of Clarissa* (Minneapolis, 1983).

38. *Rambler*, 4 (March 31, 1750), in *The Rambler*, ed. W. J. Bate and Albrecht B. Strauss, 3 vols., Vols. 3–5 of *The Yale Edition of the Works of Samuel Johnson* (New Haven, 1969), 1:21–22.

39. Quoted in an anonymous review in *The Analytical Review*, 11 (December 1791), rpt. in Ioan Williams, ed., *Novel and Romance 1700–1800: A Documentary Record* (New York, 1970), p. 375.

40. Quoted in *Pernicious Literature* (1889), rpt. in George J. Becker, ed., *Documents of Modern Literary Realism* (Princeton, 1963), pp. 354–55.

41. Rpt. in Williams, p. 29.

42. Gay, p. 295.

43. *L'Onanisme*, 6th ed. (Lausanne, 1775), pp. 2–3.

44. *Ibid.*, p. 37.

45. *Ibid.*, p. 60. The obsolete French phrase *pertes blanches* (literally, "white losses") was analogous to *pertes séminales* ("spermatorrhea," or involuntary emission of semen).

46. It is tempting to view the old idiom "to spend" as a reflection of a close imaginative alignment of sex and money, especially when the phrase is contrasted with its apparently less anxious modern version, "to come." It seems likely, however, that "to spend" retained its primarily physiological sense well into the nineteenth century; blood and strength were "spent" like semen, and the fiscal sense was probably derived from that. One may doubt, too, that the demand for self-presentation implied by "to come" is significantly less anxiety-producing than the loss implied by "to spend."

47. She was, however, closely akin to Lesbians, whose *"clitoral* defilement" strongly resembled her "manual" habits. According to Tissot, the consequences of Lesbianism and masturbation followed the same route: "to exhaustion, languor, pain, death" (*L'Onanisme*, pp. 66–67).

48. Gay, p. 303.
49. *Ibid.*, p. 304.
50. *An Autobiography*, ed. Frederick Page (London, 1953), p. 188.
51. Mary S. Hartman, *Victorian Murderesses: A True History of Thirteen Respectable French and English Women Accused of Unspeakable Crimes* (New York, 1977), p. 63.
52. Trollope, pp. 189–90.

CHAPTER FOUR
TRIALS OF THE WORD

1. Emmanuel Le Roy Ladurie, *Montaillou, The Promised Land of Error*, trans. Barbara Bray (New York, 1978), p. viii.
2. Lucien Febvre and Henri-Jean Martin, *The Coming of the Book: The Impact of Printing 1450–1800*, trans. David Gerard, ed. Geoffrey Nowell-Smith and David Wootton (1976; rpt. London, 1984), p. 186.
3. *Ibid.*, p. 290.
4. Christiane Andersson, "Polemical Prints during the Reformation," in *Censorship: 500 Years of Conflict* (New York, 1984), p. 38.
5. *Italian Literature*, 2:245.
6. Adrian Hamilton, *The Infamous Essay on Woman, or John Wilkes Seated between Vice and Virtue* (London, 1972), p. 138.
7. *Ibid.*, p. 144.
8. *Ibid.*, p. 146.
9. Foxon, pp. 52–53.
10. On one occasion, he embarked on a seduction "taking a pair of garters, two small showy neckerchiefs, and *Fanny Hill* with me" (3:583); "this is the fourth or fifth time in my life," he added, "I have tried this manoeuvre with women." His success was due, however, less to Cleland's words than to the illustrations in his well-thumbed copy, especially the frontispiece: "a picture of a plump, leering, lecherous-looking woman squatting, and pissing on the floor, and holding a dark-red, black-haired, thick-lipped cunt open with her fingers. All sorts of little baudy sketches were round the margin of the picture. The early editions of *Fanny Hill* had that frontispiece" (586). Bibliographical imprecision indicates that the author of this passage cannot have been Henry Spencer Ashbee. Though Ashbee listed an edition of the *Memoirs of a Woman of Pleasure* containing a "Set of Elegant Engravings," this was an undated reprint (*Catena*, p. 60); the earliest editions had no illustrations, as Ashbee knew. Recent scholarship suggests that the first *Fanny Hill* with colored plates was produced no earlier than 1760 (Foxon, p. 63).
11. Quoted in Foxon, p. 54.

12. *Ibid.*, p. 63.

13. Quoted in Donald Thomas, *A Long Time Burning: The History of Literary Censorship in England* (New York, 1969), p. 113.

14. According, at least, to Lord Campbell, cited in *Ibid.*, p. 213.

15. L. W. Connolly, *The Censorship of English Drama 1737–1824* (San Marino, CA, 1976), p. 182.

16. *The Warden* (New York, 1964), Chapter 8.

17. D. G. Ellis, "Romans français dans la prude Angleterre (1830–1870)," *Revue de la littérature comparée*, 47 (1973), 315. The first Balzac novel to appear at full length in English was *Eugénie Grandet*, published in 1859, twenty-five year ifter French publication and nine years after Balzac's death. The first "complete" English Balzac was George Saintsbury's forty-volume edition of the *Comédie Humaine* (1895–99), but even it was pruned of the short stories "Sarrasine," "Une Passion dans le désert," and "La Fille aux yeux d'or," which contained, in Saintsbury's judgment, "inconvenient" matters—that is to say, sexual perversion. For a detailed discussion of Balzac's English fortunes, see my "Balzac and British Realism: Mid-Victorian Theories of the Novel," *Victorian Studies*, 20 (1976), 5–24.

18. Ronald Hayman, *De Sade: A Critical Biography* (New York, 1978), p. 124.

19. Austryn Wainhouse and Richard Seaver, trans., *The 120 Days of Sodom and Other Writings* (New York, 1966), pp. 185–86.

20. "Eugen Dühren" (Iwan Bloch) had published a limited edition in 1904 and a German translation in 1909, but Maurice Heine's 1931–35 edition, in three volumes, presented the first reliable text. It remains, however, a fragment. There were to have been six hundred stories, five per day, each involving a "passion"; these were divided into four types, arranged in order of increasing extravagance from "simple passions" in November to "murderous passions" in February. Perhaps on account of a shortage of paper, Sade fleshed out only the first 150 stories, the "simple" ones; the rest exist in outline form.

21. *Index*, p. 423.

22. Wainhouse and Seaver, pp. 791–92.

23. Irony upon irony: modern scholarship has established that Sade did not write *Zoloë*. As Simone de Beauvoir commonsensically points out, however, Napoleon and his ministers lacked the benefits of modern scholarship ("Must We Burn Sade?", trans. Annette Michelson, in Wainhouse and Seaver, p. 17).

24. *Ibid.*, p. 107.

25. The last phrase, *bonnes moeurs*, is often translated "morality."

26. F. W. J. Hemmings, *Culture and Society in France, 1848–1898: Dissidents and Philistines* (London, 1971), pp. 43–58.

27. Since the Middle Ages, "realism" in a philosophical sense had been distinguished from "nominalism"; the one school of thought attributed absolute

existence to universals, while the other regarded them as names or concepts only. In artistic usage, the English "realist" and "realism" made their first printed appearance in magazine articles of 1851 and 1853 respectively. Their cognates were treated as neologisms in French at the same period (Becker, *Documents*, p. 7).

28. Francis Steegmuller, ed. and trans., *The Letters of Gustave Flaubert*, 2 vols. (Cambridge and London, 1979–82), 1:219.

29. Quoted in Gustave Flaubert, *Oeuvres*, ed. Albert Thibaudet and René Dumesnil, 2 vols. (Paris, 1951), 1:643.

30. *Letters*, 1:221–22.

31. *Ibid.*, 1:222.

32. Quotations from the trial are translated from the text in Thibaudet and Dumesnil, 1:615–83.

33. Gustave Flaubert, *Madame Bovary*, "substantially new" trans. by Paul De Man (New York, 1965), p. 117.

34. *Ibid.*, p. 1.

35. Part of the confusion on both sides of the trial stemmed from Flaubert's employment of what would later be called *style indirect libre*. This technique consists, as Hans Robert Jauss has defined it, "in bringing forth a mostly inward discourse of the represented character without the signals of direct discourse . . . or indirect discourse . . . with the effect that the reader himself has to decide whether he should take the sentence for a true declaration or understand it as an opinion characteristic of this character" ("Literary History as a Challenge to Literary Theory," in *Toward an Aesthetic of Reception*, trans. Timothy Bahti [Minneapolis, 1982], p. 42). In 1857, the "free indirect style" was unfamiliar and unsettling; readers expected to be clearly informed who was speaking at any given moment, the character or the narrator. To complicate matters further, *Madame Bovary* can also be interpreted as an indictment of the very moral code that brought it into court. Dominick LaCapra has done this at length in Madame Bovary *on Trial* (Ithaca, 1982).

36. *Letters*, 1:226.

37. *Education of the Senses*, p. 359.

38. Quoted and translated in Alex de Jonge, *Baudelaire, Prince of Clouds* (New York, 1976), p. 154.

39. Quoted in Morris L. Ernst and William Seagle, *To the Pure . . . : A Study of Obscenity and the Censor* (New York, 1928), p. 116.

40. Quoted in Morris L. Ernst and Alan U. Schwartz, *Censorship: The Search for the Obscene* (New York, 1964), pp. 23–25.

41. Ernst and Seagle, p. 123.

42. *Ibid.*, p. 119.

43. Ernst and Schwartz, p. 25.

44. "Regina v. Hicklin," in David Copp and Susan Wendell, eds., *Pornography and Censorship* (Buffalo, 1983), pp. 325–26.

45. Letter to John Blackwood, April 1, 1858, in Gordon S. Haight, ed., *The George Eliot Letters*, 9 vols. (New Haven and London, 1954–78), 8:201.

46. Ashbee took notice of this and several earlier versions of the pamphlet, but he turned up his nose at its latest incarnation, because "some of the most disgusting enquiries and instructions by the Priest were omitted" from it (*Centuria*, p. 91).

47. Copp and Wendell, pp. 326–28.

CHAPTER FIVE
The American Obscene

1. Quoted in Ernst and Seagle, p. 127.

2. *Acts and Laws of Massachusetts Bay Colony* (1826), Acts of 1711–1712, c. 1, p. 218, quoted in Brennan, dissenting, *Paris Adult Theatre I et al. v. Lewis R. Slaton, District Attorney, Atlanta Judicial Circuit, et al.*, 413 U.S. 49 (1973), rpt. in Copp and Wendell, p. 378.

3. Rpt. in *Ibid.*, p. 13.

4. Quoted in *Ibid.*, p. 13. Seventeenth-century accounts of the Sedley affair are less reticent; he was accused of both blasphemy and "throwing down bottles (pissed in) *vi et armis* among the people" (quoted in Thomas, *A Long Time Burning*, p. 81). He was fined and imprisoned for a week.

5. Rpt. in Ernst and Schwartz, p. 12.

6. Quoted in *Ibid.*, p. 14.

7. The same problem came up six years later, in Massachusetts, at the trial of one Peter Holmes for publishing the first American edition of Cleland's *Memoirs of a Woman of Pleasure*. This volume contained a "lewd and obscene print," which might have been the gross frontispiece gloated over by the author of *My Secret Life*; both book and print were under indictment, yet neither was suitable to be shown. Chief Judge Parker countered Holmes's plausible claim that the jury was called upon to deliver a verdict without having inspected the evidence: "It can never be required that an obscene book and picture should be displayed upon the records of the court: which must be done, if the description in these charges is insufficient. This would be to require that the public itself should give permanency and notoriety to indecency, in order to punish it" (quoted in *Ibid.*, pp. 15–16).

8. Brennan in Copp and Wendell, p. 378.

9. *Index*, pp. xlix–l.

10. Heywood Broun and Margaret Leech, *Anthony Comstock: Roundsman of the Lord* (New York, 1927), p. 153.

11. Quoted in *Ibid.*, p. 84.

12. *Ibid.*, pp. 90–91.

13. Marshall Cushing, *The Story of Our Post Office: The Greatest Government Department in All Its Phases* (Boston, 1893), p. 615.

14. Quoted in Broun and Leech, p. 83.

15. *Ibid.*, p. 85.

16. Quoted in Anthony Comstock, *Traps for the Young*, ed. Robert Bremner (Cambridge, Mass., 1967), p. xiiin. The Act went on to specify punishments for those found implicated in such transactions; imprisonment at hard labor might range between one and ten years for each offense, at the judge's discretion.

17. Broun and Leech, p. 135.

18. Dauphin *v.* Key, 11 MacArthur 209–10, quoted by Comstock in *Traps*, p. 217.

19. Broun and Leech, p. 148.

20. Quoted in *Ibid.*, pp. 15–16.

21. D. M. Bennett, *Anthony Comstock: His Career of Cruelty and Crime, a Chapter from "The Champions of the Church"* (1878; rpt. New York, 1971), p. 1046. Unfortunately, our only detailed record of the Prosch episode, on which I have relied for this account, comes from an extremely biased source—De Robigné Mortimer Bennett, founder of Comstock's *bête noire*, the National Liberal League. In 1878, Bennett inserted into his vast anticlerical diatribe *The Champions of the Church* a chapter on Comstock's allegedly criminal career, which was later reprinted as a pamphlet. At the time *Champions* appeared, Comstock was endeavoring to suppress Bennett's newspaper *The Truth Seeker* because it advocated contraception and offered procedural advice. Bennett's hatred of Comstock is fiercely obvious, but the facts he cites ring true.

22. *Ibid.*, p. 1047.

23. *Ibid.*, p. 1049. Colgate's magnanimity may have been something less than disinterested. In the same year, 1878, Bennett's *Truth Seeker* gleefully informed its readers that the Colgate Company had been distributing a pamphlet proclaiming that Colgate's vaseline mixed with salicylic acid made an effective contraceptive. It does not, but that fact had little to do with the pamphlet's withdrawal from circulation "like greased lightning," as a modern historian phrases it (Peter Fryer, *The Birth Controllers* [New York, 1966], p. 194).

24. *Traps*, p. 2.

25. *Ibid.*, p. 9.

26. *Ibid.*, p. 154.

27. *Ibid.*, p. 52.

28. *Ibid.*, p. 41.

29. *Ibid.*, p. 132.

30. Quoted in Broun and Leech, pp. 226–27.

31. *Traps*, p. 198.

32. Quoted in *Ibid.*, p. 192.

33. Broun and Leech, p. 244.

34. *Ibid.*, p. 16. Of the fifteen titles Broun and Leech cite as typical, however, only two appear in Ashbee's bibliographies—the perennial *Fanny Hill* and *The Lustful Turk*, which Ashbee lists in several editions between 1828 and 1864 (*Catena*, pp. 134–36). It is impossible to tell how many of the others were native American products, though some titles, like *Kate Percival, The Belle of the Delaware*, certainly have that air.

35. *Traps*, pp. 168–72.

36. Broun and Leech, pp. 238–39.

37. *Ibid.*, pp. 250–51.

38. Letter to Robert W. Welch, ca. September 22–23, 1905, in Dan H. Laurence, ed., *Bernard Shaw: Collected Letters 1898–1910* (New York, 1972), pp. 559–61.

39. Quoted in Broun and Leech, p. 230.

40. *Ibid.*, pp. 231–32.

41. This opinion, from an unidentified source, is quoted in James D. McCabe, Jr., *Lights and Shadows of New York Life; or, The Sights and Sensations of the Great City* (1872; rpt. New York, 1970), p. 627. Madame Restell's unexceptionability did not extend, apparently, to her window shades, which were "of a most gaudy, though very vulgar, pattern. . . . No other house in Fifth Avenue or in New York possesses such shades, or, indeed, would any one else in the city want to" (p. 626).

42. Carl Sifakis, *The Encyclopedia of American Crime* (New York, 1982), p. 611.

43. Broun and Leech, p. 158.

44. McCabe, pp. 629–30. In his lower-key way, the hack McCabe also partook of Comstock's apocalyptic vision. "It is an appalling truth," he wrote, "that so many American wives are practicers of the horrible sin of 'prevention' that in certain sections of our country, the native population is either stationary or dying out" (p. 629).

45. Broun and Leech, pp. 159–60.

46. *Ibid.*, pp. 192–93.

47. *My Fight for Birth Control* (New York, 1931), pp. 54–55.

48. *An Autobiography* (1938; rpt. New York, 1971), p. 93.

49. *Ibid.*, pp. 75–77.

50. *My Fight*, p. 80.

51. *An Autobiography*, p. 111.

52. *Ibid.*, p. 114.

53. *My Fight*, p. 99.

54. Quoted in *Ibid.*, pp. 120–21.

55. *Ibid.*, p. 126.

CHAPTER SIX
GOOD INTENTIONS

1. Alec Craig, *The Banned Books of England and Other Countries: A Study in the Conception of Literary Obscenity* (London, 1962), p. 138.

2. Ernst and Schwartz, p. 30.

3. Roger Manvell, *The Trial of Annie Besant and Charles Bradlaugh* (New York, 1976), p. 44.

4. Quoted in *Ibid.*, p. 61.

5. Quoted in *Ibid.*, p. 114.

6. Quoted in *Ibid.*, p. 129.

7. *Ibid.*, p. 120.

8. The inevitable repetitiveness of obscenity trials is illustrated by the resemblance of Besant and Bradlaugh's self-defense to the tactics employed by Sénard in defending Flaubert twenty years earlier. Besant wished to quote in court a passage from *Tristram Shandy*, to demonstrate "how a worthy work could be condemned as obscene by the tone of a particular paragraph torn from its context" (quoted in *Ibid.*, p. 76). A point of law prevented her doing so, but she later published a pamphlet, *Is the Bible Indictable?*, listing more than a hundred passages from the Old and New Testaments that might come "within the ruling of the Lord Chief Justice as to obscene literature." Her list is reprinted in Ernst and Seagle, pp. 303–4.

9. Manvell, pp. 152–53.

10. Indictment in *Regina* v. *Bedborough*, rpt. in Ernst and Seagle, p. 289.

11. In *Havelock Ellis: A Biography* (New York, 1980), Phyllis Grosskurth suggests that the authorities' real motive in apprehending Bedborough was "as a way of striking terror into the hearts of the anarchists" with whom he was known to be involved (p. 194).

12. Quoted in *Ibid.*, pp. 195–97.

13. Quoted in *Ibid.*, p. 201.

14. Ernest A. Vizetelly, *Emile Zola, Novelist and Reformer: An Account of His Life and Work* (London, 1904), p. 243.

15. *Ibid.*, p. 262. Mr. Pecksniff, in Dickens's *Martin Chuzzlewit* (1844), had become the popular emblem of scheming hypocrisy, just as Mr. Podsnap, in *Our Mutual Friend* (1865), epitomized philistine squeamishness.

16. *Pernicious Literature* (1889), rpt. in Becker, *Documents*, p. 355.

17. *Ibid.*, p. 358.

18. *Ibid.*, p. 362.

19. Quoted in Vizetelly, p. 268.

20. *Ibid.*, p. 290.

21. Douglas Parmée, trans., *The Earth* (Harmondsworth, 1980), p. 29.

22. Vizetelly, p. 291.

23. *Ibid.*, pp. 255–56. While the prosecution was going on, French editions of Zola were openly on sale in England, and no move was made to confiscate them. As Ernest put it: "Thus all who knew French were privileged to read Zola *verbatim*, whereas those who did not know that language were not allowed to peruse expurgated renderings of his books" (p. 276).

24. Ernst and Seagle reprint the list, pp. 305–8.

25. Quoted in Vizetelly, p. 273.

26. Robert Buchanan in the *Athenaeum*, August 4, 1886, pp. 137–8; rpt. in Clyde K. Hyder, ed., *Swinburne: The Critical Heritage* (New York, 1970), p. 30.

27. John Morley in the *Saturday Review*, August 4, 1866, pp. 145–7; rpt. in *Ibid.*, p. 23.

28. *Index*, p. 345.

29. Clyde K. Hyder, ed., *Swinburne Replies* (Syracuse, 1966), p. 30.

30. "A Defence of Poetry," in Bruce R. McElderry, Jr., ed., *Shelley's Critical Prose* (Lincoln, NB, 1967), p. 36.

31. *Ibid.*, p. 11.

32. *Autobiography of John Stuart Mill* (New York, 1964), Chapter Five.

33. Herbert S. Gershman and Kernan B. Whitworth, Jr., eds., *Anthology of Critical Prefaces to the Nineteenth-Century French Novel* (Columbia, MO, 1962), p. 105.

34. *William Blake: A Critical Essay* (1868; rpt. New York, 1967), p. 91.

35. *Studies in the History of the Renaissance* (London, 1873), pp. 210–11.

36. "The Critic as Artist," in Vyvyan Holland, ed., *Complete Works of Oscar Wilde* (London and Glasgow, 1966), p. 1016.

37. *The Renaissance* (Chicago, 1977), p. 233n. No doubt deliberately, Pater echoed Lord Chief Justice Cockburn's already famous Hicklin test: "I think the test of obscenity is this, whether the tendency of the matter charged as obscenity is to deprave and corrupt those whose minds are open to such immoral influences, and into whose hands a publication of this sort may fall." The fact that the hands into which *The Renaissance* would most likely fall belonged to Oxford undergraduates (Pater was a fellow of Brasenose College from 1864 until his death in 1894) lent a perverse piquancy to this footnote. The most corruptive parts of the Conclusion, however, remained unchanged in its revised version.

38. *Studies*, p. 213.

39. *Works*, p. 17.

40. *Ibid.*, p. 985.

41. Quoted in H. Montgomery Hyde, *The Other Love: An Historical and Contemporary Survey of Homosexuality in Britain* (London, 1970), p. 134.

42. *Enemies of Promise*, rev. ed. (New York, 1948), p. 47.

43. It seems likely, however, that he played a significant role in the com-

position of *Teleny, or The Reverse of the Medal: A Physiological Romance*, first published, clandestinely, in 1893. In his introduction to the most recent reprint (San Francisco, 1984), Winston Leyland provides a detailed survey of the evidence supporting Wilde's partial authorship of this distinctly physiological novel.

44. *In re* Worthington Co., 30 N.Y.S. 361 (1894), quoted in Ernst and Schwartz, pp. 39–40.

45. Rosen v. United States, 161 U.S. 29 (1896), quoted in James Jackson Kilpatrick, *The Smut Peddlers* (Garden City, NY, 1960), pp. 44–45.

46. Swearingen v. United States, 161 U.S. 446 (1896), quoted in Ernst and Schwartz, p. 44. In these early cases, vulgarity did rather well for itself. In 1892, for example, an Indiana court made the same ruling—vulgar but not obscene—concerning a pungent Valentine's Day message: "You can keep this to wipe your dirty arse on" (United States v. Males, 51 Fed. 41 [D.C. Ind., 1892], quoted in Kilpatrick, p. 41).

47. United States v. Kennerley, 209 Fed. 119 (S.D.N.Y., 1913), quoted in *Ibid.*, pp. 118–19.

48. "Nana," *The Parisian* (February 26, 1880), rpt. in Leon Edel, ed., *The Future of the Novel: Essays on the Art of Fiction* (New York, 1956), p. 94.

49. Halsey v. New York Society for Suppression of Vice, 234 N.Y. 1, 136 N.E. 219, 220, quoted by Augustus N. Hand in United States v. One Book Called *Ulysses*, 5 Fed. Supp. 182 (S.D.N.Y., 1933), rpt. in Robert B. Downs, ed., *The First Freedom: Liberty and Justice in the World of Books and Reading* (Chicago, 1960), p. 87.

50. "Comstockery," in *Prejudices, Fifth Series* (1926), rpt. in Downs, p. 277.

51. The unrespectable classics, notably *Fanny Hill* and *My Secret Life*, would wait four more decades for rehabilitation, but it would come to even them eventually.

52. John Chandos, " 'My Brother's Keeper,' " in John Chandos, ed., *'To Deprave and Corrupt . . .': Original Studies in the Nature and Definition of 'Obscenity'* (New York, 1962), p. 34.

53. Prussic acid (hydrocyanic acid, an aqueous solution of hydrogen cyanide) is among the most toxic substances known; it was proverbial in the nineteenth century as the ultimate poison, because of its ready availability and nearly instantaneous effect. Before she resorted to the ax, Lizzie Borden is rumored to have considered it as a means of eliminating her father and stepmother. Early combatants of obscenity put prussic acid to wide use, particularly against metaphoric children. Preferences like Douglas's had often been expressed, with the confident expectation that the horror they aroused would choke off discussion. Chemistry, however, like literature, is subject to fashion. When Douglas invoked prussic acid, he received from Aldous Huxley a reply that had been waiting in the wings for decades. As Huxley gloated three years

later: "I offered to provide Mr. Douglas with a child, a bottle of prussic acid, a copy of *The Well of Loneliness*, and (if he kept his word and chose to administer the acid) a handsome memorial in marble to be erected wherever he might appoint, after his execution. The offer, I regret to say, was not accepted" ("To the Puritan All Things are Impure," in *Music at Night* [1931], rpt. in *Music at Night and Other Essays Including 'Vulgarity in Literature'* (London, 1949), pp. 184–85.

54. *The Diary of Virginia Woolf*, 3:207.

55. Quoted in St. John-Stevas, p. 101.

56. Quoted in *Ibid.*, p. 102. The judgment was upheld by Quarter Sessions, and *The Well of Loneliness* was not republished in England until 1949. When Covici-Friede brought out an American edition of Hall's novel early in 1929, the indefatigable Society for the Suppression of Vice took immediate action against it. At first, Biron's attitude won out: Judge Hyman Bushel of the City Magistrate's Court, New York City, ruled that the book was obscene on the grounds that, though it had "literary merit," it lacked "moral value," because it sought "to justify the right of a pervert to prey upon normal members of a community, and to uphold such relationships as noble and lofty." Citing the Hicklin test (then about to turn sixty-one), Bushel concluded that the novel's "antisocial and offensive" theme made it "strongly calculated to corrupt and debase those members of the community who would be susceptible to its immoral influence" (*People* v. *Friede*, 233 N.Y. Supp. 565 [Magis. Ct. 1929], rpt. in Ernst and Schwartz, pp. 75–76). In April, an appellate court overturned this antedeluvian decision, and *The Well of Loneliness* went on legal sale.

57. 2 Cir., 1948, 172 F. 2d 788, 790, rpt. in Downs, p. 119.

58. Foreword to *Ulysses* (New York, 1961), p. v.

59. *Ulysses*, p. 358.

60. *Ibid.*, p. 370.

61. Richard Ellmann, ed., *Letters of James Joyce, Volume III* (New York, 1966), p. 28n.

62. *Letters*, 2:231.

63. *Diary*, 2:69.

64. *The Outlook*, May 28, 1922; quoted in St. John-Stevas, p. 95.

65. Letter to Gerald Brenan, December 1, 1923, *Letters*, 3:380.

66. Quoted in Richard Ellmann, *James Joyce* (New York, 1959), p. 578n.

67. All quotations from Woolsey are found in the text reprinted in *Ulysses*, pp. vii–xii.

CHAPTER SEVEN
HARD AT THE CORE

1. Typically, Britain and the United States lagged far behind France and Germany in this regard, especially the latter. Richard von Krafft-Ebing's *Psychopathia Sexualis*, for example, first published in 1886 and continually expanded in eleven subsequent editions, contained far more outrageous material on "inversion" than Ellis's banned book, yet *Psychopathia Sexualis* was never prosecuted in its native land. When things got racy, however, Krafft-Ebing shifted from German to Latin, a time-honored strategy. The first English translation of *Psychopathia Sexualis* appeared about 1893, but the Latin was not decoded for English readers until 1965.

2. Ernst and Schwartz, p. 81.

3. *United States* v. *Dennett*, 39 F. 2d 564 (2d Cir. 1930), rpt. in Downs, pp. 78–80.

4. Like its predecessors since 1842, this new Act prohibited the importation of all "obscene" articles. It made, however, one provision: "the Secretary of the Treasury may, in his discretion, admit the so-called classics or books of recognized and established literary or scientific merit, but may, in his discretion, admit such classics or books only when imported for noncommercial purposes." The exception did not apply in the case of *Married Love*, since the importer's purposes were admittedly commercial.

5. *United States* v. *One Obscene Book Entitled* Married Love, 48 F. 2d 821 (S.D.N.Y. 1931), rpt. in Downs, pp. 82–83.

6. *United States* v. *Levine*, 83 F. 2d 156 (2d Cir. 1936), quoted in Ernst and Schwartz, pp. 109–10.

7. "Judicial Censorship of Obscene Literature," *Harvard Law Review*, 52 (1938), 40–76; rpt. in Downs, p. 65.

8. *People* v. *Larsen*, 5 N.Y.S. 2d 55 (Ct. Spec. Sess. 1938), rpt. in Ernst and Schwartz, p. 116.

9. Quoted in Kilpatrick, p. 162.

10. *People* v. *Viking Press, Inc.*, 147 Misc. 813, 264 N.Y. Supp. 534 (Magis. Ct. 1933), quoted by Curtis Bok in *Commonwealth* v. *Gordon*, 66 Pa. D. & C. 101 (Philadelphia County 1949), rpt. in Downs, p. 96.

11. "The 'Censorship' of Books," *The Nineteenth Century and After*, 626 (April 1929), 446–47.

12. *Jacobellis* v. *Ohio*, 378 U.S. 184, 197, quoted in Joel Feinberg, "Pornography and the Criminal Law," *University of Pittsburgh Law Review*, 40 (1979), rpt. in Copp and Wendell, p. 120.

13. Quoted in William B. Lockhart and Robert C. McClure, "Why Obscene?", in Chandos, p. 59.

14. Richard Ellmann, *James Joyce*, pp. 592, 598–99.

15. H. Montgomery Hyde, *A History of Pornography*, p. 185.

16. Felice Flanery Lewis, *Literature, Obscenity, and the Law* (Carbondale and Edwardsville, IL, 1976), p. 185.

17. Quoted in Downs, pp. 114–15.

18. *Roth* v. *Goldman*, 172 F. 2d 788, 790 (2d Cir. 1948), rpt. in Downs, pp. 116–19.

19. *Commonwealth* v. *Gordon*, rpt. in *Ibid.*, pp. 93–114. The phrase "clear and present danger" had occurred in *Schenck* v. *United States*, 249 U.S. 47 (1919), a Supreme Court case involving the conviction of Charles Schenck on a charge of having encouraged military insubordination during the recent war. The Court upheld the conviction.

20. *United States* v. *Roth*, 237 F. 2d 796 (2d Cir. 1956), rpt. in *Ibid.*, pp. 119–33. The survey by the Bureau of Hygiene apparently remained unique for decades. A full discussion of its findings is given in Ernst and Seagle, pp. 239–45.

21. Kilpatrick, p. 86.

22. For once, the Court had not been asked to judge the obscenity of any particular items; the constitutionality of the statutes was the only question at issue.

23. *Roth* v. *United States*, 354 U.S. 476 (1957), quoted in Ernst and Schwartz, pp. 204–7.

24. Like the proliferation of highly publicized obscenity trials, that of books about obscenity was principally an American phenomenon. Germany and France produced little on the subject, and Britain not much more, though the very best books of the kind were published in England. Among them should be mentioned Norman St. John-Stevas's *Obscenity and the Law* (1956), Alec Craig's *The Banned Books of England and Other Countries* (1962), H. Montgomery Hyde's *A History of Pornography* (1964), and Donald Thomas's *A Long Time Burning* (1969). The superiority of these books derives in part from their sociohistorical approach; American studies tended to get bogged down in court proceedings and to read like law textbooks.

25. Among other sidelights, Schroeder reported a sequel to the career of the earnest Dr. Sanger of Blackwell's Island. On November 15, 1907, R. M. Webster, acting Assistant Attorney General for the Post Office Department, banned from the mails an issue of the *American Journal of Eugenics*, because it contained an advertisement for Sanger's magnum opus. "On page 50," wrote Webster, "is advertised a book entitled 'The History of Prostitution,' which *from its very name* is clearly indecent and unfit for circulation through the mails . . ." (quoted in Schroeder, p. 68).

26. *To the Pure* may also be the major source of the appealing modern myth that "fuck" used to be a respectable word. Ernst and Seagle derive it from an old (unspecified) word meaning "to plant" and remark on its "former propriety

in English society" (p. 275); Ernst expanded upon this etymology at the *Ulysses* hearing, tracing "fuck" back to the Latin *facere* ("to make") and offering the example "the farmer fucked the seed into the soil" (quoted in Ernst and Schwartz, p. 94). In his influential decision in *Commonwealth* v. *Gordon* (1949), Curtis Bok perpetuated the idea: the four-letter word, he wrote (without naming it), "that is used to denote the sexual act is an old agricultural word meaning 'to plant,' and was at one time a wholly respectable member of the English vocabulary" (Downs, p. 98). The actual etymology of "fuck" is obscure—"owing," as the *American Heritage Dictionary* says, "to lack of early attestations"—but it seems always to have meant much what it does today. It was never even slightly respectable, though it may now be on its way to becoming so.

27. Ernst and Seagle, pp. 266–69.

28. *Ibid.*, p. 283.

29. According, that is, to the testimony of Herbert G. Muskett, "a literary critic without credentials," quoted in Harry T. Moore, *The Priest of Love: A Life of D. H. Lawrence*, rev. ed. (Harmondsworth, 1981), p. 310.

30. *Selected Literary Criticism*, ed. Anthony Beal (New York, 1966), p. 81.

31. Dorothy Brett, *Lawrence and Brett* (Philadelphia, 1933), p. 81, quoted in Ellmann, *James Joyce*, p. 628n.

32. "Literature and Censorship," *Books on Trial*, 14 (1956), 393–95; rpt. in Downs, p. 218.

33. "The Writer and the Frontiers of Tolerance," in Chandos, p. 144.

34. "Against Pornography," *Harper's*, 230 (1965), 51–60; rpt. in Grant S. McClellan, ed., *Censorship in the United States* (New York, 1967), pp. 33–34.

35. *Foolish Figleaves?: Pornography in—and out of—Court* (New York, 1967), p. 241.

36. *Obscenity and Public Morality: Censorship in a Liberal Society* (Chicago, 1969), p. 242.

37. *Pornography and the Law: The Psychology of Erotic Realism and Pornography*, rev. ed. (New York, n.d.), p. 18.

38. *The Other Victorians*, p. 274.

39. *Three Essays on the Theory of Sexuality*, trans. James Strachey (New York, 1975), p. 74.

40. Bowdlerized, however, to sometimes comical effect, as in this paragraph from *The Strange Cult*: " 'I know,' Felice interrupted. 'It's because they think I won't (vernacular for cunnilingus) a girl, but I will!' Here she slipped one hand between Inez' thighs and toyed with the moist [vernacular for the female genital] . . ." (quoted in *Pornography and the Law*, p. 209).

41. Quoted in Charles Rembar, *The End of Obscenity: The Trials of Lady Chatterley, Tropic of Cancer, and Fanny Hill* (New York, 1968), p. 479.

42. *Ibid.*, p. 473.

43. *Memoirs* v. *Massachusetts*, 383 U.S. 413 (1966), quoted in *Ibid.*, p. 480.

44. *Ibid.*, p. 493.

45. Another irony in the *Fanny Hill* case is that the text on trial, a paperback published jointly by G. P. Putnam's Sons and Dell, had been expurgated, though with scholarly intentions. Late in the novel, Fanny watches through a peephole as two young men engage in homosexual intercourse; the trial text omitted this passage on the grounds that it was a later addition, not written by Cleland. David Foxon, however, had already convincingly established that the "sodomitical passage" was Cleland's and had been included in the 1749 first edition (*Libertine Literature*, pp. 61–62).

46. *Catena*, p. 345.

47. *The End of Obscenity*, p. 467.

CHAPTER EIGHT

THE POST-PORNOGRAPHIC ERA

1. Quoted in *The Report of the Commission on Obscenity and Pornography* (New York, 1970), p. 1.

2. *Ibid.*, pp. 7–23.

3. Comprehensive figures are unavailable, but a 1983 "selected bibliography" lists nearly two hundred books and articles taking a "social scientific" approach to the subject, most published between 1965 and 1980 (Copp and Wendell, pp. 311–21).

4. *Report*, p. 32.

5. *Ibid.*, pp. 45–46.

6. *Ibid.*, p. 57.

7. *Ibid.*, pp. 456–57.

8. *Ibid.*, p. 62.

9. *Ibid.*, p. 458.

10. *Ibid.*, p. 578.

11. *New York Times*, October 25, 1970, p. 71.

12. *Understanding Media: The Extensions of Man* (New York, 1964), p. 9.

13. "The Pornographic Imagination," in *Styles of Radical Will* (New York, 1978), p. 35.

14. *Ibid.*, p. 41.

15. *On Photography* (New York, 1977), pp. 168, 174–75.

16. *Report*, p. 27.

17. *Against Our Will: Men, Women and Rape* (New York, 1975), p. 376.

18. *Ibid.*, p. 394.

19. *Report*, p. 23.

20. *The Interpretation of Dreams*, trans. James Strachey (New York, 1965), p. 155.

21. *Pornography: Men Possessing Women* (New York, 1980), pp. 29–30.

22. *Ibid.*, p. 223.

23. In 1985, the Indianapolis version was rejected by a federal court of appeals; the following year, with a no-comment "summary affirmance," the Supreme Court upheld the ruling, in effect declaring the ordinance unconstitutional.

24. Quoted in Mary Kay Blakely, "Is One Woman's Sexuality Another Woman's Pornography?", *Ms.*, April 1985, pp. 46ff.

25. Attorney General's Commission on Pornography, *Final Report*, 2 vols. (Washington, DC, 1986), 2:1709.

26. *Ibid.*, 1:383.

AFTERWORD

1. John Preston, "Introduction: My Life with Pornography," in John Preston, ed., *Flesh and the Word: An Anthology of Erotic Writing* (New York: Plume, 1992), p. 11. A revised version of this essay, "Flesh and the Word: My Life with Pornography," was included in Preston's *My Life as a Pornographer & Other Indecent Acts* (New York: Richard Kasak, 1993), pp. 27–36. *Flesh and the Word 2*, also edited by Preston, appeared in 1993.

2. In *The Other Victorians* (1964), Steven Marcus sniffed at such terms as "erotic books" and "Erotica," which, though "in general currency," were "little more than euphemisms." "Most of the writing which is classified as 'Erotica,'" Marcus added, anticipating Preston's bluntness, "seems to me in intention, in effect, and in fact pornographic, and I can find no sound reason for avoiding the term" (p. 36n).

3. John Leland, Maggie Malone, Marc Peyser, and Pat Wingery, "The Selling of Sex," *Newsweek* (Nov. 2, 1992), pp. 95–6.

4. *Congressional Record*, September 28, 1989. Quoted in Roberta Smith, "A Giant Artistic Gibe at Jesse Helms," *New York Times* (April 20, 1990), p. C28.

5. Peter Brooks, *Body Work: Objects of Desire in Modern Narrative* (Cambridge: Harvard UP, 1993), pp. 15–16.

6. I have discussed this subject in greater detail in "Here's Looking at You," *Salmagundi*, Nos. 101–102 (1994), pp. 124–41.

7. Gisele Freund, *Photography and Society* (Boston: David Godine, 1980), p. 85.

8. Early in 1995, an "educated guess" put the previous year's U.S. sales of "porn" CDs at approximately $260 million, or twenty percent of the consumer

market, according to Robert A. Jones, "Pssst! Want to Buy a Dirty CD?" *Los Angeles Times Magazine* (March 19, 1995), p. 28.

9. Charles Aaronson, ed., *The 1960 International Television Almanac* (New York: Quigley Publication, 1959), pp. 9A, 14A. Cited in Thomas Doherty, *Teenagers and Teenpics: The Juvenilization of American Movies in the 1950s* (Boston: Unwin Hyman, 1988), p. 24.

10. Nicholas Negroponte, *Being Digital* (New York: Knopf, 1995), pp. 5–6. Negroponte also estimated that between twenty and thirty million people used the Internet in 1994 and that a billion would be doing so by the year 2000 (pp. 181–82).

11. Harley Hahn and Rick Stout, *The Internet Complete Reference* (Berkeley, CA: Osborne McGraw-Hill, 1994), p. xix.

12. Marty Rimm, "Marketing Pornography on the Information Superhighway: A Survey of 917,410 Images, Descriptions, Short Stories, and Animations Downloaded 8.5 Million Times by Consumers in Over 2000 Cities in Forty Countries, Provinces, and Territories," *The Georgetown Law Journal*, 83 (1995), 1862, 1890.

13. Rimm, pp. 1895, 1879.

14. Ironically, this icon of computer-imperiled innocence was itself computer-generated (*Time*, July 3, 1995, p. 3).

15. Despite their twenty-inch color monitor, two of the three "judges" were "unable to perceive the ejaculate" (Rimm, pp. 1888–89).

16. Philip Elmer-DeWitt, "On a Screen Near You: Cyberporn," *Time*, July 3, 1995, p. 42.

17. Elmer-DeWitt, p. 40.

18. Rimm, p. 1890.

19. Elmer-DeWitt, p. 40.

20. Elmer-DeWitt, p. 40.

21. Jeffrey Rosen, "Cheap Speech: Will the Old First Amendment Battles Survive the New Technologies?" *The New Yorker*, August 7, 1995, p. 75.

22. Quoted in Peter H. Lewis, "Protest, Cyberspace-Style, for New Law: Dark Screens to Greet Signing of Telecommunications Bill," *The New York Times*, February 8, 1996, p. A16.

23. Quoted in Erik Ashok Meers, "New Technology, Old Rhetoric: Right-Wingers Use Familiar Arguments to Censor Computer Networks," *The Advocate*, March 19, 1996, p. 24.

24. Pamela Mendels, "Judges Visit Cyberspace Sites in Suit over an Indecency Law," *The New York Times*, May 12, 1996, p. 12.

25. Quoted in Calvin Reid, "Federal Judges Unanimous: CDA Is 'Unconstitutional,'" *Publishers Weekly*, June 17, 1996, p. 9.

26. *The Dunciad*, ed. James Sutherland, 3rd ed. (London: Methuen, 1963), p. 409.

27. See MacKinnon's *Only Words* (Cambridge: Harvard UP, 1993), where the entirety of human history is reduced to an endless series of rapes. Surveying Marty Rimm's subsequently discredited study, MacKinnon saw the same: "Pornography in cyberspace," she wrote, "is pornography in society—just broader, deeper, worse, and more of it. Pornography is a technologically sophisticated traffic in women; electronically communicated pornography trafficks [sic] women in a yet more sophisticated form." "Vindication and Resistance: A Response to the Carnegie Mellon Study of Pornography in Cyberspace," *The Georgetown Law Journal*, 83 (1995), 1959.

28. In Canada, however, Dworkin and MacKinnon's notions significantly influenced the Supreme Court case *Butler* v. *Regina* (1992). Upholding the conviction of Donald Victor Butler, a Winnipeg store owner, on obscenity charges, the unanimous decision commented that "if true equality between male and female persons is to be achieved, we cannot ignore the threat to equality resulting from exposure to audiences of certain types of violent and degrading material" (quoted in MacKinnon, *Only Words*, p. 101). The immediate result of the *Butler* decision was a rise in police raids on stores that specialized in feminist, gay, and lesbian publications, along with stepped-up seizure of such materials being imported from the U.S. Among the confiscated items were two of Dworkin's own books. For a full discussion of *Butler's* aftermath, see Nadine Strossen, *Defending Pornography: Free Speech, Sex, and the Fight for Women's Rights* (New York: Scribner, 1995), pp. 229–44.

29. I comment on it briefly in Chapter Five above and in "From Huck Finn to Calvin Klein's Billboard Nymphets." *New York Times Magazine*, October 8, 1995, pp. 84–87. For a crankily illuminating discussion of American pedophilia, see James R. Kincaid, *Child-Loving: The Erotic Child and Victorian Culture* (New York: Routledge, 1992).

30. William Wordsworth, *The Poems*. Ed. John O. Hayden. 2 vols. (New Haven: Yale UP, 1981), 1:525.

31. The "V-chip" (the V stands for "violence") would sense and block the reception of programs that had been coded as containing levels of violence or sex deemed inappropriate for the child. The 1996 Telecommunications Act contained a provision requiring V-chips in all new TV sets sold after 1998, and the television industry was handed the task of devising a rating code, so far without success. Since "violence" is no more easily defined than "pornography," absurdities cropped up at once. The National Television Violence Study, whose findings were released just before the Act became law, employed this plausible-sounding definition: "Any overt depiction of the use of physical force or the credible threat of such force intended to physically harm an animate being or group of beings." But as Barbara Wilson, a Study participant, admitted, some glitches remained: "If Wile E. Coyote is injured falling thousands of feet from a cliff in a Roadrunner cartoon, it probably would

count, she said, because there was intent to harm." Bill Carter, "A New Report Becomes a Weapon in Debate on Censoring TV Violence," *The New York Times*, February 7, 1996, pp. C11, C16.

32. Holographic or virtual-reality smut, perhaps. The only way that representations of any kind can get more vivid than they are is by moving out of the eyes and ears, across the entire body. If this occurs on any significant scale, pornography is bound to tag along.

33. Nigel Spivey, "Emma and the Great Toes," *TLS*, April 12, 1996, p. 12.

LIST OF WORKS CITED

Abrams, M. H., et al., eds. *The Norton Anthology of English Literature*, rev. ed., 2 vols. New York: Norton, 1968.

Acton, William. *Prostitution*. 2nd ed. 1870. Ed. Peter Fryer. New York: Praeger, 1969.

Altick, Richard D. *The English Common Reader: A Social History of the Mass Reading Public, 1800–1900*. Chicago: Univ. of Chicago Press, 1957.

Aretino, Pietro. *Selected Letters*. Trans. George Bull. Harmondsworth: Penguin, 1976.

Arnold, Matthew. *Complete Prose Works*. Ed. R. H. Super. 10 vols. Ann Arbor: Univ. of Michigan Press, 1971–74.

"A Strange World." *Saturday Review*, 39 (March 6, 1875), 320–21.

Athenaeus. *Deipnosophistai*. Trans. C. D. Yonge. 3 vols. London: Bohn, 1853.

Attorney General's Commission on Pornography, *Final Report*. Washington, DC: U.S. Government Printing Office, 1986.

Barker, Ernest, trans. *The Politics of Aristotle*. New York: Oxford Univ. Press, 1958.

Barré, M. L. *Herculanum et Pompéi, Recueil Général des Peintures, Bronzes, Mosaïques, etc. découverts jusqu'à ce jour et reproduits d'après Le Antichita di Ercolano, Il Museo Borbonico et tous les ouvrages analogues*. 8 vols. Paris, 1875–77.

Becker, George J., ed. *Documents of Modern Literary Realism*. Princeton: Princeton Univ. Press, 1963.

Beeton, Isabella. *The Book of Household Management*. 1861; rpt. New York: Farrar, Straus & Giroux, 1969.

Bell, Anne Olivier, ed. *The Diary of Virginia Woolf*. 5 vols. New York and San Diego: Harcourt Brace Jovanovich, 1977–84.

Benjamin, Walter. *Illuminations*. Trans. Harry Zohn. New York: Schocken, 1969.

Bennett, D. M. *Anthony Comstock: His Career of Cruelty and Crime. A Chapter from "The Champions of the Church."* 1878; rpt. New York: Da Capo, 1971.

Berg, Albert Ellery, ed. *The Universal Self-Instructor and Manual of General Reference*. 1883; rpt. New York: Winter House, 1970.

Berns, Walter. *Freedom, Virtue and the First Amendment*. Baton Rouge: Louisiana State Univ. Press, 1957.

Blakely, Mary Kay. "Is One Woman's Sexuality Another Woman's Pornography?" *Ms.*, April 1985.

Blanshard, Paul. *The Right to Read: The Battle against Censorship*. Boston: Beacon, 1955.

Bonucci, Charles. *Pompéi décrite*. Naples, 1830.

Boswell, James. *Life of Johnson*. Ed. R. W. Chapman. London: Oxford Univ. Press, 1953.

Boswell, John. *Christianity, Social Tolerance, and Homosexuality: Gay People in Western Europe from the Beginning of the Christian Era to the Fourteenth Century*. Chicago: Univ. of Chicago Press, 1980.

Breton, Ernest. *Pompéia décrite et dessinée*. 3rd ed. Paris: L. Guérin, 1870.

Broun, Heywood, and Margaret Leech. *Anthony Comstock: Roundsman of the Lord*. New York: Albert and Charles Boni, 1927.

Brownmiller, Susan. *Against Our Will: Men, Women and Rape*. New York: Simon and Schuster, 1975.

Bulwer-Lytton, Edward. *The Last Days of Pompeii*. 1834; rpt. Boston: Little, Brown, 1893.

Butcher, S. H. *Aristotle's Theory of Poetry and Fine Art with a Critical Text and Translation of the Poetics*. 4th ed. 1911; rpt. New York: Dover, 1951.

Byron, George Gordon, Lord. *Poetical Works*. London: Oxford Univ. Press, 1945.

Caldwell, Mark, and Walter Kendrick, eds. *The Treasury of English Poetry: A Collection of Poems from the Sixth Century to the Present*. Garden City, NY: Doubleday, 1984.

Censorship: 500 Years of Conflict. Ed. William Zeisel. New York: New York Public Library, 1984.

Chandos, John, ed. *'To Deprave and Corrupt . . .': Original Studies in the Nature and Definition of 'Obscenity.'* New York: Association Press, 1962.

Childs, J. Rives. *Restif de la Bretonne: Témoignages et Jugements. Bibliographie.* Paris, 1949.

Clor, Harry M. *Obscenity and Public Morality: Censorship in a Liberal Society*. Chicago: Univ. of Chicago Press, 1969.

Coleridge, Samuel Taylor. *Poetical Works*. Ed. Ernest Hartley Coleridge. London: Oxford Univ. Press, 1967.

Comstock, Anthony. *Traps for the Young*. Ed. Robert Bremner. 1883; rpt. Cambridge: Harvard Univ. Press, 1967.

Connolly, Cyril. *Enemies of Promise*, rev. ed. New York: Macmillan, 1948.

Conolly, L. W. *The Censorship of English Drama 1737–1824*. San Marino, CA: The Huntington Library, 1976.

Copp, David, and Susan Wendell, eds. *Pornography and Censorship*. Buffalo, NY: Prometheus Books, 1983.

Cornford, Francis MacDonald, trans. *The Republic of Plato*. New York: Oxford Univ. Press, 1945.

Corte, Egon Caesar, Conte. *The Destruction and Resurrection of Pompeii and Herculaneum*. London: Routledge & Kegan Paul, 1951.

Craig, Alec. *The Banned Books of England and Other Countries: A Study in the Conception of Literary Obscenity*. London: George Allen & Unwin, 1962.

Cushing, Marshall. *The Story of Our Post Office: The Greatest Government Department in All its Phases*. Boston: A. M. Thayer, 1893.

Davis, Lennard J. *Factual Fictions: The Origins of the English Novel*. New York: Columbia Univ. Press, 1983.

De Jonghe, Alex. *Baudelaire, Prince of Clouds*. New York: Paddington Press, 1976.

Dickens, Charles. *Our Mutual Friend*. 1865; rpt. Harmondsworth: Penguin, 1971.

Downs, Robert B., ed. *The First Freedom: Liberty and Justice in the World of Books and Reading*. Chicago: American Library Association, 1960.

Dryden, John. *Of Dramatic Poesy and Other Critical Essays*. Ed. George Watson. 2 vols. New York: Everyman, 1962.

Dufour, Pierre (Paul Lacroix). *Histoire de la Prostitution chez tous les peuples du monde depuis l'antiquité la plus reculée jusqu'à nos jours*. 6 vols. Paris, 1851–53.

Dworkin, Andrea. *Pornography: Men Possessing Women*. New York: Putnam's, 1980.

Dyer, Thomas H. *Pompeii*. 2 vols. 4th ed. London: Charles Knight, 1836.

Dyer, Thomas H. *Pompeii: Its History, Buildings, and Antiquities*, rev. ed. London: George Bell, 1883.

Eagleton, Terry. *Literary Theory: An Introduction*. Minneapolis: Univ. of Minnesota Press, 1983.

Eagleton, Terry. *The Rape of Clarissa*. Minneapolis: Univ. of Minnesota Press, 1983.

Ellis, D. G. "Romans français dans la prude Angleterre (1830–1870)." *Revue de la littérature comparée*, 47 (1973), 315.

Ellmann, Richard. *James Joyce*. New York: Oxford Univ. Press, 1959.

Ernst, Morris L., and Alan U. Schwartz. *Censorship: The Search for the Obscene*. New York: Macmillan, 1964.

Ernst, Morris L., and William Seagle. *To the Pure . . . : A Study of Obscenity and the Censor*. New York: Viking, 1928.

Farley-Hills, David, ed. *Rochester: The Critical Heritage*. New York: Barnes and Noble, 1972.

Febvre, Lucien, and Henri-Jean Martin. *The Coming of the Book: The Impact of*

Printing 1450–1800. Trans. David Gerard. Ed. Geoffrey Nowell-Smith and David Wootton. 1976; rpt. London: Verso, 1984.

Fielding, Henry. *Joseph Andrews and Shamela*. Ed. Martin C. Battestin. Boston: Houghton Mifflin, 1961.

Flaubert, Gustave. *Madame Bovary*. Trans. Eleanor Marx Aveling. "Substantially new" trans. Paul De Man. New York: Norton, 1965.

Flaubert, Gustave. *Oeuvres*. Ed. Albert Thibaudet and René Dumesnil. 2 vols. Paris: Gallimard, 1951.

"*For Ever and Ever*." *Saturday Review*, 22 (October 6, 1866), 432–33.

Foucault, Michel. *The History of Sexuality*. vol. 1. *An Introduction*. Trans. Robert Hurley. New York: Pantheon, 1978.

Foxon, David. *Libertine Literature in England 1660–1745*. New Hyde Park, NY: University Books, 1965.

Freud, Sigmund. *The Interpretation of Dreams*. Trans. James Strachey. New York: Avon, 1965.

Freud, Sigmund. *Three Essays on the Theory of Sexuality*. Trans. James Strachey. New York: Basic, 1962.

Fryer, Peter. *The Birth Controllers*. New York: Stein and Day, 1966.

Fryer, Peter, ed. *Forbidden Books of the Victorians: Henry Spencer Ashbee's Bibliographies of Erotica*. London: Odyssey, 1970.

Gay, Peter. *The Bourgeois Experience: Victoria to Freud*. vol. 1, *Education of the Senses*. New York: Oxford Univ. Press, 1984.

Gell, Sir William, and John P. Gandy. *Pompeiana: The Topography, Edifices, and Ornaments of Pompeii*. 2 vols. London, 1824.

Gershman, Herbert S., and Kernan B. Whitworth, Jr., eds. *Anthology of Critical Prefaces to the Nineteenth-Century French Novel*. Columbia: Univ. of Missouri Press, 1962.

Gilbert, Stuart, and Richard Ellmann, eds. *Letters of James Joyce*. 3 vols. New York: Viking, 1966.

Grant, Michael, Antonia Mulas, Antonio De Simone, and Maria Teresa Merella. *Eros in Pompeii: The Secret Rooms of the National Museum of Naples*. New York: Bonanza, 1982.

Greene, Graham. *Lord Rochester's Monkey, Being the Life of John Wilmot, Second Earl of Rochester*. New York: Viking, 1974.

Griest, Guinevere L. *Mudie's Circulating Library and the Victorian Novel*. Bloomington and London: Indiana Univ. Press, 1970.

Grosskurth, Phyllis. *Havelock Ellis: A Biography*. New York: Knopf, 1980.

Grosskurth, Phyllis. *The Woeful Victorian: A Biography of John Addington Symonds*. New York: Holt, Rinehart and Winston, 1964.

Haight, Gordon S., ed. *The George Eliot Letters*. 9 vols. New Haven: Yale Univ. Press, 1954–78.

Hamilton, Adrian. *The Infamous Essay on Woman, or John Wilkes Seated between Vice and Virtue*. London: André Deutsch, 1972.

Hartman, Mary S. *Victorian Murderesses: A True History of Thirteen Respectable French and English Women Accused of Unspeakable Crimes.* New York: Schocken, 1977.

Hayman, Ronald. *De Sade: A Critical Biography.* New York: Crowell, 1978.

Hayward, John, ed. *Collected Works of John Wilmot, Earl of Rochester.* London: Nonesuch, 1926.

Hemmings, F. W. J. *Culture and Society in France 1848–1898: Dissidents and Philistines.* London: B. T. Batsford, 1971.

Henderson, Jeffrey. *The Maculate Muse: Obscene Language in Attic Comedy.* New Haven: Yale Univ. Press, 1975.

Highet, Gilbert. *The Classical Tradition: Greek and Roman Influences on Western Literature.* London: Oxford Univ. Press, 1949.

Himmelfarb, Gertrude. *The Idea of Poverty: England in the Early Industrial Age.* New York: Knopf, 1984.

Horace. *The Satires and Epistles.* Trans. Smith Palmer Bovie. Chicago: Univ. of Chicago Press, 1959.

Humpherys, Anne. "The Geometry of the Modern City: G. W. M. Reynolds and *The Mysteries of London.*" *Browning Institute Studies,* 11 (1983), 69–80.

Huxley, Aldous. *Music at Night and Other Essays Including "Vulgarity in Literature."* London: Chatto and Windus, 1949.

Huxley, Thomas Henry. *Science and Education.* London: Macmillan, 1899.

Hyde, H. Montgomery. *A History of Pornography.* New York: Farrar, Straus & Giroux, 1965.

Hyde, H. Montgomery. *The Other Love: An Historical and Contemporary Survey of Homosexuality in Britain.* London: Heinemann, 1970.

Hyder, Clyde K., ed. *Swinburne Replies: Notes on Poems and Reviews, Under the Microscope, Dedicatory Epistle.* Syracuse, NY: Syracuse Univ. Press, 1966.

Hyder, Clyde K., ed. *Swinburne: The Critical Heritage.* New York: Barnes and Noble, 1970.

James, Henry. *The Future of the Novel: Essays on the Art of Fiction.* Ed. Leon Edel. New York: Vintage, 1956.

Jauss, Hans Robert. *Toward an Aesthetic of Reception.* Trans. Timothy Bahti. Minneapolis: Univ. of Minnesota Press, 1982.

Johns, Catherine. *Sex or Symbol: Erotic Images of Greece and Rome.* Austin: Univ. of Texas Press, 1982.

Johnson, Samuel. *The Rambler.* Ed. Walter Jackson Bate and Albrecht B. Strauss. 3 vols. New Haven: Yale Univ. Press, 1969.

Joyce, James. *Ulysses.* New York: Random House, 1961.

Kearney, Patrick J. *The Private Case: An Annotated Bibliography of the Private Case Erotica Collection in the British (Museum) Library.* Introduction by G. Legman. London: Jay Landesman, 1981.

Keats, John. *Poetical Works.* Ed. H. W. Garrod. London: Oxford Univ. Press, 1956.

Kendrick, Walter M. "Balzac and British Realism: Mid-Victorian Theories of the Novel." *Victorian Studies*, 20 (1976), 5–24.

Kilpatrick, James Jackson. *The Smut Peddlers*. Garden City, NY: Doubleday, 1960.

Kronenberger, Louis. *The Extraordinary Mr. Wilkes*. London: New English Library, 1974.

Kronhausen, Eberhard, and Phyllis Kronhausen. *Pornography and the Law: The Psychology of Erotic Realism and Pornography*. 1959; rev. ed. New York: Bell, n.d.

Kuh, Richard H. *Foolish Figleaves?: Pornography in—and out of—Court*. New York: Macmillan, 1967.

Kunitz, Stanley J., and Howard Haycraft, eds. *British Authors of the Nineteenth Century*. New York: H. W. Wilson, 1936.

Kyle-Keith, Richard. *The High Price of Pornography*. Washington, DC: Public Affairs Press, 1961.

LaCapra, Dominick. Madame Bovary *on Trial*. Ithaca: Cornell Univ. Press, 1982.

Lang, Cecil Y., ed. *The Swinburne Letters*. 6 vols. New Haven: Yale Univ. Press, 1959–62.

Laurence, Dan H., ed. *Bernard Shaw: Collected Letters 1898–1910*. New York: Dodd, Mead, 1972.

Lawrence, D. H. *Selected Literary Criticism*. Ed. Anthony Beal. New York: Viking, 1966.

Le Roy Ladurie, Emmanuel. *Montaillou: The Promised Land of Error*. Trans. Barbara Bray. New York: Braziller, 1978.

Lewis, Felice Flanery. *Literature, Obscenity, and the Law*. Carbondale and Edwardsville: Southern Illinois Univ. Press, 1976.

Macaulay, Thomas Babington. *Critical and Miscellaneous Essays and Poems*. New York: 1860.

Macaulay, Thomas Babington. *Selected Writings*. Ed. John Clive and Thomas Pinney. Chicago: Univ. of Chicago Press, 1972.

Mansel, Henry Longueville. "Sensation Novels." *Quarterly Review*, 113 (April 1863), 482–514.

Manvell, Roger. *The Trial of Annie Besant and Charles Bradlaugh*. New York: Horizon, 1976.

Marcus, Steven. *The Other Victorians: A Study of Sexuality and Pornography in Mid-Nineteenth-Century England*. 2nd ed. New York: New American Library, 1974.

Maréchal, Pierre Sylvain. *Les Antiquités d'Herculanum, ou les plus belles Peintures antiques, et les Marbres, Bronzes, Meubles, etc. etc. trouvés dans les excavations d'Herculanum, Stabia et Pompeïa, avec leurs explications en françois*. 9 vols. Paris, 1780.

McCabe, James D., Jr. *Lights and Shadows of New York Life; or, The Sights and Sensations of the Great City.* 1872; rpt. New York: Farrar, Straus & Giroux, 1970.

McClellan, Grant S., ed. *Censorship in the United States.* New York: H. W. Wilson, 1967.

McElderry, Bruce R., Jr., ed. *Shelley's Critical Prose.* Lincoln: Univ. of Nebraska Press, 1967.

McHugh, Paul. *Prostitution and Victorian Social Reform.* New York: St. Martin's, 1980.

McLuhan, Marshall. *The Gutenberg Galaxy: The Making of Typographic Man.* 1962; rpt. New York: New American Library, 1969.

McLuhan, Marshall. *Understanding Media: The Extensions of Man.* New York: McGraw-Hill, 1964.

Mill, John Stuart. *The Autobiography of John Stuart Mill.* New York: New American Library, 1964.

Moore, Harry T. *The Priest of Love: A Life of D. H. Lawrence.* rev. ed. Harmondsworth: Penguin, 1981.

Müller, C. O. *Ancient Art and Its Remains; or a Manual of the Archaeology of Art.* 2nd ed. Trans. John Leitch. London, 1850.

Myers, Reney, and Robert J. Ormsby, trans. *Catullus: The Complete Poems for American Readers.* New York: Dutton, 1970.

My Secret Life. 1966; rpt. Secaucus, NJ: Castle Books, n.d.

Nicolson, Nigel, and Joanne Trautmann, eds. *The Letters of Virginia Woolf.* 6 vols. New York and San Diego: Harcourt Brace Jovanovich, 1976–80.

Parent-Duchâtelet, Alexandre-Jean-Baptiste. *De la Prostitution dans la ville de Paris, considérée sous le rapport de l'hygiène publique, de la morale et de l'administration.* 2 vols. 3rd ed. Paris: J.-B. Ballière et Fils, 1857.

Pater, Walter. *The Renaissance.* 1922; rpt. Chicago: Academy Chicago, 1977.

Pater, Walter. *Studies in the History of the Renaissance.* London: Macmillan, 1873.

Paul, James C. N., and Murray L. Schwartz. *Federal Censorship: Obscenity in the Mail.* New York: Free Press of Glencoe, 1961.

Payne Knight, Richard. *A Discourse on the Worship of Priapus and Its Connection with the Mystic Theology of the Ancients.* 1786; rpt. in *Sexual Symbolism: A History of Phallic Worship.* New York: Bell, 1957.

"Penny Novels." *Spectator*, 36 (March 28, 1863), 1806–8.

Pepys, Samuel. *The Diary of Samuel Pepys.* Ed. Robert Latham and William Matthews. 11 vols. Berkeley and Los Angeles: Univ. of California Press, 1970–83.

Perrin, Noel. *Dr. Bowdler's Legacy: A History of Expurgated Books in England and America.* New York: Athenaeum, 1969.

Pisanus Fraxi (Henry Spencer Ashbee). *Bibliography of Prohibited Books.* 3 vols. New York: Jack Brussel, 1962.

Pistolesi, Erasmo. *Antiquities of Herculaneum and Pompeii: Being a Selection of All the Most Interesting Ornaments and Relics Which Have Been Excavated from the Earliest Period to the Present Time; Forming a Complete History of the Eruptions of Vesuvius. To Which Is Added, A Selection of Remarkable Paintings by the Old Masters. Comprising the Principal Objects Preserved in the Museo Borbonico, at Naples.* 2 vols. Naples, 1842.

Pistolesi, Erasmo. *Real Museo Borbonico descritto ed illustrato.* 3 vols. Rome, 1838–39.

Rembar, Charles. *The End of Obscenity: The Trials of Lady Chatterley, Tropic of Cancer and Fanny Hill.* New York: Random House, 1968.

Report of the Commission on Obscenity and Pornography. Toronto, New York, and London: Bantam, 1970.

Restif de la Bretonne, Nicholas Edme. *L'Oeuvre de Restif de la Bretonne.* 9 vols. Paris, 1930–32.

Richlin, Amy. *The Garden of Priapus: Sexuality and Aggression in Roman Humor.* New Haven: Yale Univ. Press, 1983.

Robinson, F. N., ed. *The Works of Geoffrey Chaucer.* Boston: Houghton Mifflin, 1957.

Rosenthal, Raymond, trans. *Aretino's Dialogues.* New York: Stein and Day, 1971.

Ruskin, John. *Works.* Ed. E. T. Cook and Alexander Wedderburn. 39 vols. London: George Allen, 1903–12.

Sade, Donatien-Alphonse-François de. *The 120 Days of Sodom and Other Writings.* Trans. Austryn Wainhouse and Richard Seaver. New York: Grove, 1967.

Sanger, Margaret. *An Autobiography.* 1938; rpt. New York: Dover, 1971.

Sanger, Margaret. *My Fight for Birth Control.* New York: Farrar and Rinehart, 1931.

Sanger, William W. *History of Prostitution.* 1858; rev. ed. New York, 1895.

Schroeder, Theodore, *"Obscene" Literature and Constitutional Law.* New York: Privately Printed for Forensic Uses, 1911.

Schueller, Herbert M., and Robert L. Peters, eds. *The Letters of John Addington Symonds.* 3 vols. Detroit: Wayne State University Press, 1967–69.

Sherbo, Arthur, ed. *Johnson on Shakespeare.* 2 vols. New Haven: Yale Univ. Press, 1968.

Sifakis, Carl. *The Encyclopedia of American Crime.* New York: Facts on File, 1982.

Smith, G. Gregory, ed. *The Spectator.* 4 vols. London: Dent, 1907.

Sontag, Susan. *On Photography.* New York: Farrar, Straus & Giroux, 1977.

Sontag, Susan. *Styles of Radical Will* (969; rpt. New York: Delta, 1978)

Spenser, Edmund. *Poetical Works.* Ed. J. C. Smith. 3 vols. Oxford: Clarendon Press, 1909.

Steegmuller, Francis, ed. *The Letters of Gustave Flaubert*. 2 vols. Cambridge: Harvard Univ. Press, 1979–82.

St. John-Stevas, Norman. *Obscenity and the Law*. London: Secker and Warburg, 1956.

Summers, Montague. *A Gothic Bibliography*. London: Fortune Press, n.d.

Swift, Jonathan, *Gulliver's Travels*. Ed. Peter Dixon and J. Chalker. 1726; rpt. Harmondsworth: Penguin, 1967.

Swinburne, Algernon Charles. *William Blake: A Critical Study*. 1868; rpt. New York: Benjamin Blom, 1967.

Symonds, John Addington. *Italian Literature*. 2 vols. 1881; 2nd ed. London: Smith, Elder, 1898.

Ternite, Wilhelm. *Wandgemälde aus Pompeji und Herculanum nach den Zeichnungen und Nachbildungen in Farben von W. Ternite mit einem erläuternden Text von F. G. Welcker*. Berlin, 1839–58.

Thomas, Donald. *A Long Time Burning: The History of Literary Censorship in England*. New York: Praeger, 1969.

Thompson, Roger. *Unfit for Modest Ears: A Study of Pornographic, Obscene and Bawdy Works Written or Published in England in the Second Half of the Seventeenth Century*. Totowa, NJ: Rowman and Littlefield, 1979.

Tissot, Samuel-Auguste-André-David. *L'Onanisme, Dissertation sur les maladies produites par la masturbation*. 1758; 6th ed. Lausanne: François Grasset, 1775.

Trollope, Anthony. *An Autobiography*. Ed. Frederick Page. London: Oxford Univ. Press, 1953.

Trollope, Anthony. *The Warden*. 1855; rpt. New York: New American Library, 1964.

Vasari, Giorgio. *Lives of the Most Eminent Painters, Sculptors, and Architects*. Trans. Gaston DaC. De Vere. 10 vols. London: Medici Society, 1912–14.

Vieth, David M., ed. *The Complete Poems of John Wilmot, Earl of Rochester*. New Haven: Yale Univ. Press, 1968.

Vizetelly, Ernest A. *Emile Zola, Novelist and Reformer: An Account of His Life and Work*. London: John Lane, 1904.

Walkowitz, Judith R. *Prostitution and Victorian Society: Women, Class, and the State*. Cambridge: Cambridge Univ. Press, 1980.

Ward-Perkins, John, and Amanda Claridge. *Pompeii A.D. 79*. New York: Knopf, 1978.

Watt, Ian. *The Rise of the Novel: Studies in Defoe, Richardson and Fielding*. Berkeley and Los Angeles: Univ. of California Press, 1957.

Wilde, Oscar. *Complete Works*. Ed. Vyvyan Holland. London: Collins, 1966.

Wilde, Oscar (attributed author). *Teleny, or The Reverse of the Medal: A Physiological Romance.* Ed. Winston Leyland. San Francisco: Gay Sunshine Press, 1984.

Williams, Ioan, ed. *Novel and Romance 1700–1800: A Documentary Record.* New York: Barnes and Noble, 1970.

Wimsatt, W. K., and Cleanth Brooks. *Literary Criticism: A Short History.* New York: Knopf, 1957.

Winter, Thomas Nelson. "Catullus Purified: A Brief History of Carmen 16." *Arethusa,* 6 (1973), 257–65.

Woolf, Virginia. "The 'Censorship' of Books." *The Nineteenth Century and After,* 626 (April 1929), 446–47.

Wordsworth, William. *Poetical Works.* Ed. Thomas Hutchinson, rev. ed. Ernest de Selincourt. London: Oxford Univ. Press, 1936.

Wrench, Frederick. *Recollections of Naples, Being a Selection from the Plates contained in Il Real Museo Borbonico, of the Statues, Vases, Candelabra, &c. discovered at Herculaneum and Pompeii.* London, 1839.

Wycherley, William. *The Country Wife.* Ed. Thomas H. Fujimura. Lincoln: Univ. of Nebraska Press, 1966.

Zola, Emile. *The Earth (La Terre).* Trans. Douglas Parmée. Harmondsworth: Penguin, 1980.

INDEX